10.95 II

D1257587

DISCARDED

DISCARDED

Date Due

DISCARDED

BRODART, INC.   Cat. No. 23 233   Printed in U.S.A.

OAKTON COMMUNITY COLLEGE LIBRARY
E183
CH... WATCH BALTIMORE

3

China-Watch

58596

China-Watch
Toward Sino-American Reconciliation

Robert G. Sutter

with a foreword by Allen S. Whiting

OAKTON COMMUNITY COLLEGE
DES PLAINES CAMPUS
1600 EAST GOLF ROAD
DES PLAINES, IL 60016

THE JOHNS HOPKINS UNIVERSITY PRESS • Baltimore and London

This book has been brought to publication with the generous assistance of the Andrew W. Mellon Foundation.

Copyright © 1978 by The Johns Hopkins University Press

All rights reserved. No part of this book may be reproduced or transmitted in any form or by any means, electronic or mechanical, including photocopying, recording, xerography, or any information storage and retrieval system, without permission in writing from the publisher.

Manufactured in the United States of America
The Johns Hopkins University Press, Baltimore, Maryland 21218
The Johns Hopkins Press Ltd., London

Library of Congress Catalog Number 77–21486
ISBN 0–8018–2007–3

Library of Congress Cataloging in Publication data will be found on the last printed page of this book.

To my beloved Valerie

Contents

Foreword   ix
Acknowledgments   xiii

CHAPTER ONE
    The Asian Balance and Sino-American Rapprochement   1

CHAPTER TWO
    CCP-U.S. Relations during World War II   10

CHAPTER THREE
    Peking's Response to U.S. Containment in Asia   31

CHAPTER FOUR
    The Ambassadorial Talks in Geneva, 1955–57   47

CHAPTER FIVE
    China's First Overture to the Nixon Administration   63

CHAPTER SIX
    China's Response to the Sino-Soviet Border Clashes   83

CHAPTER SEVEN
    Sino-American Rapprochement in the 1970s   103

CHAPTER EIGHT
    Conclusion   118

Notes   123
Bibliography   137
Index   151

Foreword

Robert Sutter's book fills an important gap in the understanding of Sino-American relations since World War II. Not only is it an exceptionally readable and reliable survey of developments prior to 1976, but it also combines new evidence with perspectives gained since the dramatic visit of President Nixon to Peking in February 1972. For more than twenty years, the People's Republic of China appeared to most Americans as a demonic, aggressive force. Cold war assumptions of a monolithic Sino-Soviet expansionist bloc were gradually relinquished as the dispute between Moscow and Peking moved from ideological polemics to military confrontation and border clashes. But Moscow was thought moderate when compared with Peking and Mao Tse-tung's militant support of "people's wars." To stop this ostensible threat the United States sent 500,000 troops and spent billions of dollars fighting in Indochina.

Détente with Moscow, first tried at the 1955 Geneva Conference, succeeded briefly when President Eisenhower met with Premier Khrushchev at Camp David in 1959. However, détente with Peking would not occur for another thirteen years. The memory of Senator Joseph McCarthy and the China Lobby influenced public opinion on "the China question" and threatened Democratic electoral prospects. Eisenhower personally warned the newly elected President Kennedy that any move to bring "Red China" into the United Nations would provoke the general's open opposition, and Kennedy stonewalled on changing China policy, deferring it to a second term that was not meant to be.

The Nixon visit to Peking and the end of the Indochina war opened up new perspectives on China. But more than a changed perspective justifies this reexamination of the past; new evidence from long-locked government archives requires it. Until 1969, the Department of State suppressed documents revealing early efforts of the

Chinese Communist leadership to probe American attitudes, in contemplation of a possible alternative to total dependence on the Soviet Union. The import of these documents is debatable, but their significance is not.

Even more valuable is the dispassionate, disciplined analysis by skilled government specialists of the Chinese Communist press and radio, heretofore unavailable to the general public. This analysis implicitly contradicted official American rhetoric at the time but was only released a few years ago under the new declassification procedures. The work was produced by the Foreign Broadcast Information Service (FBIS), a unique assemblage of eminently qualified personnel and detailed files. This rare combination of human and material resources is responsible for subtle, sophisticated, and rigorous research in the massive volume of communications that have emanated from the Chinese mainland over the past three decades. Dr. Sutter benefited from his long association with FBIS, as acknowledged in his preface and as is manifest from his footnotes.

Given his background, it is natural that Sutter's presentation should focus primarily on official statements and public media. Such evidence might appear to be of doubtful reliability or simply propaganda. However, this material fully deserves the attention that the author accords it. No regular, direct diplomatic relations existed to facilitate communications between Washington and Peking from 1949 to 1972. Only in 1973 were liaison offices established in both capitals, replacing the intermittent ambassadorial exchanges that began in 1955, first in Geneva and later in Warsaw. Under these circumstances, both sides carefully studied public statements and media output for implicit intent. This was particularly true of Washington, which had virtually no other evidence than the official Chinese media, whereas Peking could draw on the wider range of material emanating from the pluralistic United States.

This account, therefore, is especially relevant to understanding how perception and misperception have affected Sino-American relations. The most tragic case of misperception is undoubtedly the Korean War. Both sides misread "signals" and unwittingly sent messages that resulted in the first major conflict between the Chinese and Americans. Other, less dramatic, instances have proved equally important in retrospect. Thus, when Peking probed for détente from 1955 to 1957, Washington failed to respond in kind. A handful of analysts in the government and academia saw Sino-Soviet relations as strained from the start, the evidence of which emerged through careful comparison of the public media in both communist countries. These inferences were subsequently borne out by revelations of Mao's secret speeches, clandestinely circulated during the Cultural Revolution and officially released after his death.*

Despite these early clues to Sino-Soviet friction, official policy and public opinion still held the image of monolithic communism and a China implacably hostile to the United States. Robert Sutter's analysis of Peking's abortive effort at compromise throws fresh light on the first effort to untangle the Taiwan problem. His account suggests both deviousness and blindness on the part of American negotiators and Secretary of State John Foster Dulles, who were determined to avoid any sign of being "soft on Red China."

Domestic politics have plagued policymakers in Peking; this study shows how the Chinese differed over U.S. policy on more than one occasion. In particular, it traces the tortuous path of Mao and Chou in testing the prospects for détente in 1968–71 against considerable doubt, if not outright opposition. The U.S. conception of a monolithic China was as misplaced as the earlier image of monolithic communism. The evidence proves that contention over foreign policy can result from internal differences as well as from interpretations of external developments.

It must be remembered that Sino-American relations do not develop in a vacuum. They are intricately related to the East Asian region, where Japan and Korea influence the interests of the two larger Pacific powers. In the period under examination Sino-American relations are uniquely related to the global system, where the Soviet-American contest for hegemony has shaped the basic course of events since World War II. Sutter repeatedly widens his focus to encompass these two considerations, skillfully and succinctly introducing the larger context within which the Sino-American relationship evolved and the reactions of both parties to it.

The more recent ebb and flow of euphoric expectation and disgruntled disappointment on both sides of the Sino-American relationship since 1971 is briefly chronicled by the author. Although he necessarily closes his study with the deaths of Mao and Chou, his analysis

---

*For a remarkable instance of prescient "Pekinology," see Philip Bridgham, Arthur Cohen, and Leonard Jaffe, "Mao's Road and Sino-Soviet Relations: A View from Washington, 1953," *China Quarterly*, no. 52 (October/December 1972). Writing for the Central Intelligence Agency, the authors declared in September 1953: "Differences in viewpoint . . . may represent latent, but nonetheless vital, tensions in the relations between Soviet and Chinese Communist leaders. In fact, a deterioration in Sino-Soviet relations, for whatever cause, may quite probably be signalized first in divergent assertions regarding theoretical matters." For a parallel analysis, see my "Communist China and 'Big Brother,'" *Far Eastern Survey* (October 1955), and "Contradictions in the Moscow-Peking Axis," *Journal of Politics* (February 1958). Official confirmation emerged in *Selected Works of Mao Tse-tung*, vol. 5 (Peking: Foreign Language Press, 1977).

remains pertinent to the impasse that confronted the new administrations in Peking and Washington during 1977.

The cultural gulf separating China and America has been widened by the ideological gulf between communism and capitalism. Yet the two societies can have a mutually fruitful interaction even while their systems remain in antithesis. For this relationship to develop, however, it is essential that each nation understand the other and communicate its own intent clearly as well as credibly. That effort can be facilitated by a more sensitive "tuning in" to the official media, so as to cut through the repetitious rhetoric to the inner images and purposes that both contribute to, and flow from, policy. Sutter's work is exemplary in this regard and should encourage others to follow suit. Perhaps with sufficient effort Kipling's pessimistic adage, warning of East and West that "ne'er the twain shall meet," may eventually be proven wrong.

Allen S. Whiting
Professor of Political Science
Associate, Center for Chinese Studies
University of Michigan

Acknowledgments

The signing of the Sino-U.S. communiqué in Shanghai during President Nixon's 1972 visit to China marked the end of twenty years of U.S. efforts to block the spread of Chinese communist influence in Asia and signaled the beginning of U.S. normalization with the People's Republic of China (PRC). The new Sino-American relationship has not developed smoothly over the past five years, and many American observers now see it as based on unsteady ground. It is hoped that this history of Chinese communist interaction with the United States will provide U.S. officials and the general public with a useful perspective on Sino-American relations as they attempt to comprehend and grapple with the numerous issues facing Washington and Peking.

In writing this book, I have benefited from the advice and encouragement of many friends and colleagues. Early versions of the manuscript were read and commented on extensively by John K. Fairbank and Roy Hofheinz of Harvard University. Akira Iriye of the University of Chicago and Henry Tom of the Johns Hopkins University Press encouraged me to publish the manuscript. Allen Whiting of the University of Michigan offered many helpful and encouraging comments and kindly agreed to write the foreword for the book. I also benefited greatly from insights offered by foreign affairs analysts in the U.S. Government, especially Richard Wich, Avis Boutell, Gwen Baptist, Arthur Berger, Lyman Miller, Gary Bietz, and Joyce Forrest. In addition, Karen Lamis thoroughly edited the manuscript.

I am deeply indebted to all those mentioned above. However, I owe an immeasurable debt to my close friend and talented colleague, Thomas Bjorkman. Dr. Bjorkman read the entire manuscript several times and offered detailed comments and numerous editorial suggestions. It is safe to say that without his help this book never would have been published.

China-Watch

CHAPTER ONE

The Asian Balance and Sino-American Rapprochement

The rapprochement in Sino-American relations achieved during President Richard M. Nixon's February 1972 visit to China marks the most important breakthrough in modern Chinese foreign policy. Peking's normalization of relations with Washington has been especially useful in fostering China's vital interests in the East Asian balance of power. In the late 1960s, the Chinese leadership* became increasingly aware of China's vulnerable strategic position. That vulnerability stemmed in part from disruptions of China's military preparedness during the Cultural Revolution, and it was enhanced by significantly greater Soviet military power deployed along the Chinese frontier. But at its heart lay Peking's strident opposition to both superpowers.

The August 1968 Soviet incursion into Czechoslovakia and Moscow's concurrent formulation of the so-called Brezhnev Doctrine of limited sovereignty demonstrated to the Chinese that Moscow might be prepared to use overwhelming military superiority in order to pressure, and even to invade, the People's Republic of China (PRC). The Sino-Soviet border clashes of 1969 increased Peking's concern over the Soviet threat. In response, Chinese officials—under the leadership of Mao Tse-tung and Chou En-lai—began a major effort in 1969 to broaden Peking's leverage against the Soviet Union by ending China's

---

*I wish to alert the reader at the outset that terms like "the Chinese leadership" are used in this book solely for the sake of convenience. Such terms are not meant to imply that all Chinese leaders held the same views on policy toward the United States. Indeed, evidence of Chinese leaders disagreeing over policy toward the United States over the past ten years is discussed in chapters 5, 6, and 7.

1

international isolation. In this pursuit they utilized conventional diplomacy, devoid of the ideological shrillness characteristic of Chinese foreign policy during the Cultural Revolution.

Because of Moscow's massive power, Peking realized that improving diplomatic relations with most foreign nations would be of relatively minor significance in helping China with its pressing need to offset the USSR. In East Asia, only the other superpower, the United States, seemed to have sufficient strength to serve as an effective deterrent to Soviet pressure. Moscow in the past had shown uneasiness over signs of possible reconciliation between China and the United States. Thus, the Chinese leaders were aware that they held an important option: they could move closer to the United States in order to readjust Sino-Soviet relations and form a new balance of power in East Asia favorable to Chinese interests.

While the Chinese faced increasingly heavy Soviet pressure in 1969, the newly installed Nixon administration was beginning policy initiatives designed to pull back American military forces from Asia and to reduce U.S. commitments along the periphery of China. It was soon apparent that the so-called Nixon doctrine of gradual troop withdrawal was perceived favorably by Peking. The Chinese leaders saw the American pullback as solid evidence of the Nixon administration's avowed interest in improved relations with China. They also viewed it as a major opportunity for China to free itself from the burdensome task of maintaining an extensive defense network along China's southern and eastern borders against possible U.S.-backed armed incursions. Peking now saw greater opportunity for China to spread its own influence in neighboring East Asian areas as the United States gradually retreated.

Primarily on the basis of these two factors—a need to use Sino-American rapprochement to offset Soviet pressure on China and a desire to take advantage of prospects opening for the PRC under terms of the Nixon doctrine in Asia—Peking agreed to receive President Nixon and to begin the process of normalizing Sino-American relations. Though the joint communiqué signed by Nixon and Chou En-lai in Shanghai in February 1972 acknowledged major differences between the two sides over ideology, Taiwan, and several foreign policy issues, it showed that they had reached an important agreement on what principles should govern the future international order in East Asia. In particular, both sides agreed that they would not seek hegemony in the Asia-Pacific region and would oppose efforts by any other country to establish hegemony there.

This accord served China's interests well. For the previous two decades, Peking had existed within a generally hostile East Asian environment and had periodically faced threats to its national security. The Sino-American rapprochement presented Peking with an opportunity for a more relaxed stance on its eastern and southern flanks. It also provided major support for China against Soviet pressure. Support from the United States for the so-called anti-hegemony clause in the Shanghai communiqué represented for China an important strategic guarantee. It put Washington on record as opposing any effort by Moscow to dominate China and made it possible for Peking to relax its vigilance on the eastern and southern flanks and concentrate on the north.

Chinese-American agreement on the anti-hegemony clause also conformed with U.S. strategic interests in East Asia. By the late 1960s, the cost and futility of massive U.S. military involvement in Vietnam had vividly demonstrated the limitations of the American use of force to counter what Washington had previously viewed as the strategic menace of international communism. The experience forced Washington to reassess the prevailing international order in light of its newly perceived weakness. Over the previous decade, while the United States had become increasingly involved in Vietnam, the Soviet Union had drawn abreast of the United States in strategic weapons. During the previous twenty years the United States had enjoyed strategic superiority and relative world dominance, allowing it to pursue an ideological campaign against international communism and to support the free world. Washington now realized that it could no longer afford such a policy. In particular, it saw that the United States could no longer, on its own, sustain the balance of forces on continental Asia.

Thus, the United States, under the Nixon administration, began to put aside past, undifferentiated prejudice against communist regimes in general and to actively capitalize on nationalist divergencies in Asia, hoping thereby to achieve a more favorable strategic balance. The major divergence Washington chose to exploit was that between Moscow and Peking. The United States realized that by withdrawing from forward military positions along China's periphery—a move that would conserve American resources for use in support of more important interests against Moscow—it could reach agreement with Peking and establish a more favorable equilibrium in the area. In a broad sense, therefore, indigenous developments affecting the balance of power in East Asia—culminating in the U.S. withdrawal from the area —brought about a convergence of Chinese and American interests and prompted the two sides to work together in monitoring future events in the region.

The new Sino-American accord—symbolized in the Shanghai communiqué's anti-hegemony clause—is particularly striking against the background of over thirty years of mutual hostility that preceded the Nixon visit. It casts into sharp relief two previous attempts by the Chinese communist leaders to reach accommodation with the United States.

The rise of the Chinese Communist Party (CCP) at the head of a growing political and military organization in China during World War II had coincided with Washington's emergence as one of the dominant powers in East Asia. The early postwar years found them on opposite sides during the Chinese civil war and the Korean conflict. Subsequently, the two sides maintained an armed confrontation along China's periphery over the next two decades. Despite such longstanding hostility, however, the Mao-Chou leadership did seek accommodation with the United States during World War II, when CCP leaders encouraged the United States to establish a military mission at the communists' headquarters in northwestern China and offered close cooperation with the United States during negotiations with American envoy Patrick Hurley. The Mao-Chou leadership again sought closer cooperation with the United States during the 1955–57 Sino-American negotiations in Geneva.

As in Peking's more recent move toward the United States, the prime factors motivating the CCP leaders to seek a modus vivendi with the United States on these earlier occasions centered on the evolving balance of power in China and in East Asia. They failed because American policy refused to recognize that the vital interests of the United States and the Chinese communists in East Asia could be compatible, choosing instead to emphasize American ideological differences with the communists.

Even before World War II, Mao, Chou, and their colleagues in the CCP had long proven themselves to be adroit practitioners of balance-of-power politics. Their experiences as leaders of a hunted minority group in China since the 1920s had taught them to be keenly aware of the balance of power around them. The CCP leaders had to consider first of all their ability to survive and expand in a hostile environment. They had to understand how to manipulate the power balance in China in order to offset the superior strategic power of their chief enemy, Chiang Kai-shek. The communists, of course, had ideological plans and programs with which to remake the ancient Chinese society into one that would stand as a unique model in the modern world. But they realized that all these plans would come to naught if they failed to survive and develop vis-à-vis their adversaries in China.

Thus, the communists usually viewed the establishment and maintenance of a favorable balance of power as critically important in pro-

4

tecting the vital interests of their movement. The most important CCP interest was to ensure its own survival and security so that other goals could be attained. A major communist concern was to complete the revolution begun in the 1920s, which would entail the dismantling of the rival Chiang government and the assertion of CCP authority over all Chinese territory. The communists were anxious to develop China into a strong, modern state, free from intimidation and pressure from adjacent powers.

Soon after the founding of the communist party in the early 1920s, the communists realized how slim were their chances of survival alone in warlord-ruled China, and they agreed to compromise ideological principles and join forces with the more powerful Kuomintang (KMT) under Sun Yat-sen. Following the Sian incident of 1936, the communists agreed to join in a united front with Chiang Kai-shek in order to end the nationalists' extermination campaigns, which were threatening to snuff out the communist resistance. The American entrance into the war against Japan on the side of Chiang Kai-shek in December 1941 resulted in another major shift in the balance of power against CCP interests, which in turn prompted the CCP's first major effort at accommodation with the United States.

The United States rapidly became the predominant power in East Asia, and in China it brought its power, influence, and aid to bear solely on the side of Chiang Kai-shek's nationalists. For the CCP leaders, there was a serious likelihood that the United States, because of growing association with Chiang Kai-shek, might use its enormous power against the CCP during an anticipated Chinese civil war following Japan's defeat. To counter this prospect, the communists had the option of looking to their Soviet ally for support. But Moscow at that time was showing little interest in defending CCP interests against a challenge by U.S.-backed, nationalist forces.

The communists saw that only at great risk could they ignore the change that had taken place. Hoping that the United States would not become closely associated with Chiang Kai-shek against CCP interests, the communists decided to take steps on their own to ensure that Washington would adopt a more even-handed position. They strove to put aside historical difficulties with the United States and soft-pedaled ideological positions that might alienate Washington, in order to arrive at a power arrangement that would better serve CCP interests in China.

The United States chose to rebuff the communist initiatives, an action which resulted in a period of about six months during which the communists faced the likelihood of a CCP confrontation against a strong, U.S.-backed KMT army at the end of the Pacific war. Fortun-

5

ately for the CCP, Moscow gradually built its strength in East Asia during the final months of the war and the period following Japan's defeat, and the United States rapidly withdrew its forces from East Asia at the war's end, shifting the balance of power in a direction less unfavorable to the communists. Later in the 1940s, the communists obtained more support from Moscow, finally solidifying bilateral ties in the February 1950 Sino-Soviet alliance. On this basis, the Chinese leaders judged that their national security in the face of U.S.-backed power in Asia was fundamentally secure. Peking was accordingly sure of its continued national survival when it chose to confront rather than appease the American forces that were threatening Chinese frontiers in the first months of the Korean War.

After the Korean armistice, the Chinese were still prepared to confront the United States, not only to protect PRC frontiers but also to obtain other CCP interests concerning Taiwan. Since China's security was guaranteed by the Sino-Soviet alliance, Peking now strove to attain such goals as the dismantling of the Chiang Kai-shek regime, the reunification of all Chinese territory under the PRC, and the establishment of an independent Chinese international position free from outside pressure. While Peking seemed prepared to keep pushing against U.S.-backed positions in East Asia that blocked its objectives, Moscow, in the wake of Stalin's death, showed decidedly less interest in supporting such Chinese moves.

This reduced Soviet support, combined with increased American military-political containment efforts against Chinese interests following the Korean War, marked another major shift in the power balance against PRC interests, prompting the communists' second effort to achieve a modus vivendi with the United States. Though China's security did not appear threatened, and the Sino-Soviet alliance remained in force, Peking realized that any progress toward completing the Chinese civil war and establishing an independent foreign policy would be seriously impeded by the developing East Asian balance in the mid 1950s. Moscow's unwillingness to back PRC confrontation with the United States ruled out Chinese use of force to achieve the objectives. Peking instead tried to establish a more favorable balance by compromising with the United States during the ambassadorial talks of 1955–57 held in Geneva. Peking hoped that accommodation with the United States in the talks would lead to a relaxation of American containment in East Asia and a loosening of Washington's stance on Taiwan. Despite the attractiveness of the communist initiatives, however, the United States chose to rebuff Peking once again.

As in the case of the Chinese leadership, American policy makers also have long been affected by the shifting correlation of forces in

East Asia. Ever since the release of the Open Door notes at the turn of the century, and perhaps earlier, the United States has endeavored to respond to shifts in the East Asian balance in a way that would maintain an equilibrium favorable to American interests. In particular, Washington has historically followed policies designed to prevent any individual state from dominating the area. In China, Washington supported British efforts in the nineteenth and early twentieth centuries to ensure that no power gained the dominant position. It refrained from recognizing Japan's territorial acquisitions in China in the 1930s, and it determined to resist Tokyo in the Pacific war, in part because it judged that Japan's hegemony over East Asia ultimately would seriously threaten American national interests.

Since the United States became actively involved in Pacific affairs in the late nineteenth century, Washington has seen some basic U.S. security interests tied in with the East Asian power balance. In particular, the United States has judged that any power that is able to dominate East Asia would soon pose a serious security threat to American territorial interests in the Pacific islands, including Hawaii. It has also held that such a power would gravely endanger longstanding U.S. trade, business, missionary, and other activities in the region. Washington has thus striven to ensure that a balance of power favorable to these interests is maintained.

However, over the past thirty years, the United States, unlike the Chinese communists, has generally not responded realistically to changes in the East Asian power equation affecting vital American interests. Rather, its dedication to ideology has frequently led the United States into policies that, on balance, have been detrimental to its own national interests.

Toward the end of World War II, for instance, the United States realized that the correlation of forces in East Asia would change drastically following Japan's defeat. Washington was especially concerned over future Soviet dominance on the Asian mainland. At first, the United States hoped to foster a strong, Chiang Kai-shek–led China that would block Soviet expansion, but Chiang's weakness and poor administration scuttled the plan. Washington then settled on a policy designed to achieve a favorable balance through direct political arrangements with the USSR, culminating in the understanding on East Asia reached at the Yalta conference of February 1945. Washington naïvely judged that such accords would guarantee a stable power equation in which China would maintain its independence without the need for continued U.S. military presence in the area.

In view of a traditional American ideological concern that the use of U.S. military power had to be justified on grounds higher than

7

national interest, American planners judged that they could not support a continued U.S. military presence in Asia after Japan's defeat. American strategists—though they themselves were not necessarily moralists convinced of the ethical mission of U.S. foreign policy— were well aware that a pervasive moralism among the American people and their representatives in Congress regarding the conduct of U.S. foreign policy blocked Washington's use of military force to maintain the postwar East Asian balance of power. Use of such power in a time of peace was still seen as anathema to the American way. Because of such ideological considerations, Washington became wedded to an unrealistic policy, in effect relying on Soviet good will to secure a favorable East Asian balance.

This policy was directly responsible for the American rejection of the CCP leaders' offers at this time to cooperate closely with the United States. Because of its reliance on Moscow, the United States was intent on maintaining a stable internal situation in China that would not complicate the Yalta arrangements worked out with the USSR. Rather than risk disrupting the Chinese situation by aligning with the CCP, the United States continued to back Chiang Kai-shek. It judged that undermining Chiang's leadership would have led to a civil war in which the American-Soviet agreements on the postwar situation might have become unraveled. As a result of its focus on Chiang, the United States rebuffed the communists, who were demanding a greater role in Chinese internal affairs.

Although the emerging bipolar confrontation of the Cold War in the late 1940s prompted a briefly more realistic U.S. approach to East Asia, subsequent Chinese involvement in the Korean War served to solidify an ideological prejudice that was to dominate American China policy until the 1960s. Peking's unexpected entry on the side of Pyongyang caused U.S. planners to consider the Sino-Soviet bloc as a monolith and to scrap earlier hopes that Peking would eventually come into conflict with Moscow. The United States now judged that it would have to expand its containment policy to secure not only against Moscow but against Peking as well.

This ideological world view caused Washington to fail to perceive the significance of CCP overtures in the mid-1950s. It was inconceivable to chief American strategists that China would follow a policy that was basically more in the interests of the United States than of the Soviet Union. Washington had lost sight of the fact that the interests of the Chinese state might lead Peking to an independent posture vis-à-vis Moscow, which in turn might be compatible with American national interests in Asia. Washington did not completely put aside its ideological view until the late 1960s, when fundamental shifts in the international and East Asian balance of forces constrained the U.S. leadership to reassess its policy in China, resulting in the Nixon administration's initiatives toward the Peoples Republic of China.

The experience of the past thirty years demonstrates clearly that the evolving balance of power in East Asia has played the crucial role in leading to the Sino-American rapprochement of the 1970s. Although the ideologies, historical experiences, and different cultures of the two sides have tended to keep them apart, the developing East Asian balance has forced them to put aside such negative factors and has prompted both sides to see that their vital national interests in the area are compatible and provide the basis for mutual understanding.

CHAPTER TWO

CCP-U.S. Relations during World War II

Prior to the Second World War, a wide gap in understanding, fostered by the political situation in China as well as by the ideological biases and historical experiences of each side, divided the Chinese communists and the United States. In general, the communist view of the United States was conditioned by a lack of interest in international affairs, a strongly doctrinaire opposition to such "imperialist-capitalist" nations, an allegiance to the foreign policy of the USSR and international communist movement, and a history of affronts received as a result of American policy in China. The U.S. view of the Chinese communists was colored by general American ignorance of the CCP following the nationalist-communist split of 1927, which resulted in indifference toward the communists in the formulation of American China policy.

The Chinese communist leaders in this period were chiefly concerned with the survival of their movement against Chiang Kai-shek's nationalist government, and they accordingly devoted little attention to events outside China. Reflecting their isolation and apparent lack of information concerning foreign affairs, the CCP leaders showed little evidence of a sophisticated view of world events. In particular, they relied heavily on guidelines set by the Soviet-dominated international communist movement (Comintern) in assessing the policies of capitalist states such as the United States.[1] Thus, when the USSR opposed the foreign policies of the United States and other Western powers in the early 1930s, Chinese party spokesmen carefully followed suit.[2] A few years later, the CCP promptly echoed the Comintern's "united front" line, which drew a distinction between the "principal" enemy of the fascist states, as opposed to the capitalist democracies, calling for alliance with the latter against the former.[3] This line, of course, conformed nicely with CCP interests inside China, allowing the communists to exploit an anti-Japanese approach in order to broaden their appeal within the country.

The CCP also followed the Comintern line in foreign affairs even when it proved damaging to the communists' position in China, as during the period of erratic shifts in Soviet foreign policy in 1939–41. Mao Tse-tung personally supported the Comintern position on the most notorious example of expedient Soviet policy in this period—the German-Soviet pact of August 1939—even though this step seriously tarnished the CCP image in China.[4] The Soviet move notably disappointed a prevailing Chinese hope that the USSR would unite with the capitalist democracies against the Axis powers and accordingly would assist China, which was bearing the brunt of Japan's military might.

The significance of the Chinese communists' subservience to Moscow's line in foreign affairs remains unclear. It may be, as some have asserted, that the CCP was in fact demonstrating an intense desire to win favor with Moscow as well as a genuine, ideologically based determination to follow the Soviet lead.[5] On the other hand, the CCP may have been demonstrating little more than *pro forma* backing for the Comintern line, in the relatively unimportant sphere of foreign affairs, in order to keep on good terms with the international communist movement—the only real source of foreign support that the Chinese communists had at this time.

At the same time, the Chinese communists judged the United States negatively on the basis of their ideological training in Marxism-Leninism and their particular belief in Lenin's theory of imperialism. Prior to World War II, the communists generally assessed the policies of the "imperialist" powers in China, such as the United States, as motivated chiefly by economic gain; this desire for financial return allegedly caused the powers to intervene actively in China's internal affairs, militarily dominate the treaty ports, patrol rivers and coastal waterways, and supply warlords and other nonprogressive power holders in China with arms and loans to suppress the CCP-supported, anti-imperialist movement.[6]

The communists' negative assessment was reinforced by a number of U.S. military and political actions in China, which appeared from the CCP vantage point to be hostile to the communist movement in China. In particular, American involvement in the suppression of the CCP-backed insurrections in Canton in 1927, and in Yochow and Changsha in 1930, as well as increased U.S. economic and military aid to Chiang Kai-shek during the height of the anticommunist extermination campaigns against the CCP's Kiangsi Soviet in the early

1930s, were repeatedly cited by the communists as vivid examples of American hostility.[7]

Communist Initiatives toward the United States

The termination of the nationalist blockade and military campaigns against the communists following the start of the CCP-KMT united front in late 1936 prompted the communist leaders to try to break out of their isolated position. Overlooking past disputes with the United States, they tried to woo American newsmen and other Westerners who visited their base in northwestern China, hoping thereby to improve the CCP image and gain greater leverage within China and abroad.[8] This opening to the West was short-lived and had little lasting significance, however. It ended before a meaningful channel of communication could be established linking the communists with the rest of China or the United States. The nationalists soon reimposed a tight blockade around the communist base, while American interest was diverted to concern over the expanding power of Japan in East Asia in the late 1930s.

Following America's entrance into the Pacific war, the Chinese communist leadership initiated a more serious effort to win U.S. favor. In Chungking—the major point of contact between the two sides—CCP spokesmen began a concerted effort during private conversations with U.S. officers to enhance the CCP image at the expense of Chiang's nationalists.[9] They also encouraged the Americans to send official representatives to the communist-held areas in north China for liaison work with the CCP leadership in the war against Japan. Communist rationale for a U.S. liaison mission usually centered on the need for a more effective Allied war effort against Japan. By sending officers to north China, the spokesmen argued, the United States would be better able to assess the strength and potential military utility of communist forces, survey the strength of Japanese forces in the area, and determine areas for possible Allied operations and installations. In this connection, the communists emphasized their allegedly far-flung intelligence network throughout north China, which they claimed would be invaluable in future Allied war planning.

The communists at the same time denounced repeatedly the nationalists' military blockade of the communist base areas as the cause of the CCP forces' continued inability to participate actively in the anti-Japanese effort. The issue of the blockade was also central to communist arguments that the nationalists were unwilling to fight the Japanese and were more concerned with hoarding U.S.-supplied weapons and ammunition in order to strengthen their military forces against the communists. CCP spokesmen argued that the nationalists had left Japanese forces in peace and had been collaborating closely with Tokyo-aligned Chinese "puppet" forces in order to devote primary military attention to blockading the communists. Noting the implications for the United States, the spokesmen pointed out that the brunt of Japanese power was being felt by U.S. forces in the Pacific as a result of nationalist inactivity on the Asian mainland. In contrast, they often stated, communist forces were ready to fight with the United States against Japan at any time, provided the United States pressured Chiang Kai-shek into lowering the blockade and allowing the supply of the communist forces.

The communists also took advantage of the interaction with U.S. representatives to build on the image they had already established through their brief contacts with American and other Western newsmen in north China in the late 1930s. Consistent with their approach to Edgar Snow and other American visitors in that period, the communists emphasized their relatively democratic and honest political administration, the popular support received by the Yenan leadership, and the CCP's relatively positive attitude toward the free enterprise economic system. In this way, they attempted to appeal to American ideals. At the same time, the spokesmen tried to drive a wedge between the Americans and Chinese nationalists by criticizing the allegedly corrupt, oppressive, and totalitarian rule of the nationalist government. Consistent with their approach toward Snow and other visitors in the 1930s, the spokesmen did not disavow the CCP's ultimate Marxist-Leninist intentions regarding the future of China but indicated that such goals were to be achieved at the end of a long "democratic" period. They thus revealed to American officials the image of a Chinese party worthy of U.S. support, willing to compromise with Washington, and deserving of a share of power in China. In this context, heavy stress was placed on the nationalists' unwillingness to share power as the prime cause for continuing communist-nationalist confrontation in China.

The central role in CCP policy toward the United States at this time was played by Chou En-lai, the chief communist representative in Chungking during World War II. In his contacts with Americans, Chou demonstrated repeatedly a preference for realistic diplomatic interaction—unencumbered by ideological constraints or bitterness over the past—in order to enhance the practical power interests of the Chinese Communist Party. Chou set the stage for stepped-up CCP efforts to win American support during private conversations with U.S. Second Secretary John P. Davies in mid-1942.[10] Chou's approach

13

emphasized the crucial role the United States was playing in Chinese internal affairs. He initiated a CCP proposal for the establishment of an American liaison mission in Yenan, cast doubt on nationalist willingness to pursue the war against Japan, and attacked Chungking's legitimacy as the regime best serving the interests of the Chinese people.

Lin Piao, who had arrived in Chungking in late 1942 for negotiations with the nationalists over ending the blockade of communist areas, complained in talks with American representatives that the lack of supplies in the CCP base areas and the communists' general suspicion of Chungking stemmed largely from the continuing nationalist military blockade of the CCP bases.[11] In a 19 January 1943 conversation with another second secretary of the American embassy, Chou En-lai charged that alleged inaction in nationalist economic and military policy was condemnable and implied that Chungking's lack of dynamism might be a cause of foreign dissatisfaction with China's contribution in the struggle against Japan. Chou continued with his attempts to influence the officer, who was scheduled to go to Sian within a few months, by assuring him that he would be welcome to visit the communist headquarters near that city.[12]

At a 29 January 1943 luncheon given by Chou En-lai for American military attachés and lower-level diplomats in Chungking, Lin Piao described the CCP troops' dearth of ammunition and other supplies, and he affirmed that the CCP army would go on the offensive against Japan if it were provided by the United States with needed war materiel.[13] On 16 March, Second Secretary Davies asked Chou En-lai if the communists would supply intelligence about their base areas directly to American officials in Chungking for use in the war against Japan—a step that would have reduced the need for an American observer presence in the CCP area. Scotching this half measure, which would not have met the communists' desire for more formal and visible contacts with Washington, Chou rejoined that really effective liaison could be brought about only with the stationing of a group of American officers in the communist areas, and he reiterated his invitation of the previous summer for a small group from the United States.[14]

Communist Motivation

The communists' accommodating approach toward the United States came in spite of their past ill feeling toward Washington and their ideologically based antagonism toward the capitalist American government. It no doubt was in part prompted by the general line of

14

the Communist International at this time, which emphasized the need for world communists to unite with the capitalist democracies in order to defeat the fascist powers.[15] However, the intensity of Yenan's effort to woo American favor also appeared to be closely tied to the situation in China and to the CCP's competition for power with the Kuomintang.

The top priority of the Chinese Communist Party during the previous two decades had been to attain unchallenged power in China and to defeat the major "reactionary" Chinese power centers, notably the Kuomintang government of Chiang Kai-shek. Major changes in the Chinese political-military balance affecting the communists' vital interests during this period had triggered CCP efforts to adjust strategy. Thus, the CCP had altered its policy to take into account the Japanese invasion of China in the early 1930s,[16] the Sian incident of 1936, and the commencement of the Sino-Japanese war in 1937.[17]

The American entrance into the Pacific war was a similar occasion, calling for CCP reassessment and adjustment. After Pearl Harbor, it was clear to observers in China that the defeat of Japan at the hands of the United States was only a matter of time and that the United States would soon become the predominant international influence in China.[18] The Yenan leadership realized that to ensure its progress toward power in China, it would have to adjust to the new influence of the United States. The approach it chose was to court American sympathies in order to guarantee that Washington would not become too closely aligned with Chungking. It tried at the same time to obtain some American support for the communist cause.

The most pressing CCP objective in the period following the American entrance into the war was to ensure the party's survival as a viable political and military force in China. At this time, annihilation campaigns of the Japanese army together with the Kuomintang blockade had severely pressured the communists, according to official CCP histories.[19] The size of the CCP military forces and the population under the party's control were reduced. Cadre rolls were unusually short and economic conditions were desperate in some places. Indications of communist weakness were apparent in reports from U.S. officials,[20] who disclosed that, since CCP forces were unable to break out of the Kuomintang blockade, even basic military supplies such as copper were lacking in the northern bases. Apart from their military weakness, the Yenan leaders were concerned that the nationalist government, now relieved of Japanese pressure as a result of the American entrance into the war, would attempt to exploit its clear military advantage in order to launch a full-scale attack against the communists. American officials in China were informed that CCP worry over such an attack remained high through 1943.[21] Further adding to their concern, the communists recognized the obvious inability of the USSR to provide any substantial assistance while engaged in heavy fighting with Germany along the western front. The Soviets in fact were trying to keep their relations with the nationalists cordial, and they were even acquiescing to Chungking's gradual reassertion of control over Sinkiang at the expense of USSR interests in the province.[22] Meanwhile, in May 1943 the Communist International was formally disbanded, further adding to CCP isolation and vulnerability.

In this context, it was clear to the Yenan leaders that their continued survival depended on a closer relationship with the United States. Only in this way could they best ensure against a nationalist attack and block nationalist efforts to have Washington align with the Kuomintang in the civil dispute in China. In its *démarche* toward the United States, therefore, the CCP leadership stressed the need for a formal American liaison office in the CCP-held areas. The CCP leaders were well aware of the nationalists' acute dependence on American support as well as of Washington's aversion to any civil conflict in China that might disrupt the war effort against Japan.[23] The presence of an American observer mission in the communist areas would mean that any nationalist attack against the communists would run the risk of being detected by the United States. This could result in U.S. irritation with Chungking, that might in turn be translated into a reduction of American support. Such considerations would have had an obvious negative effect on any nationalist offensive plans.

Over the longer term, Yenan's motivations centered on what the CCP leaders saw as the critical role the United States would play in China as the war with Japan moved toward a climax and the question of a postwar settlement in China became increasingly important.[24] The communists realized that unimpaired American support and assistance for the nationalists would have the effect of freezing U.S. interests behind Chiang Kai-shek. This could lead to the possible elimination of the CCP in the face of U.S.-backed KMT power. Indeed, the acute danger of CCP-KMT conflict during 1942 had done nothing to limit continued one-sided American military support for the nationalist government. The communists accordingly moved to neutralize this potentially disastrous intrusion of American power in China. Using a moderate, solicitous approach in contacts with U.S. representatives, the CCP leaders attempted to persuade Washington to reassess its policy concerning the internal conflict in China. They attempted to block close U.S. association with Chiang Kai-shek and to encourage American policy makers to take a more even-handed approach toward the Chinese Communist Party.

16

In view of their previous experience in dealing with the United States, the Yenan leaders entertained little immediate hope of undermining the American-nationalist relationship. But by opening contacts with Washington, the communists would at least have the opportunity to move the Americans away from Chungking over the critical issue of the Chinese civil dispute. In particular, a formal American mission in Yenan would allow the CCP leaders to present their case to the highest levels in Washington; it would enable Mao and his group to scotch many ill-founded nationalist allegations concerning the communist leaders and communist policies, which had heretofore enjoyed credibility with U.S. policy makers. Moreover, the communist leaders were confident and proud of the economic, political, and military situation in their base areas, and they felt assured that if their administrative achievements could be shown to the United States, they would compare favorably with the deteriorating situation in the nationalist-held areas.

More formal ties with Washington would also enhance the communists' ability to solicit U.S. military supplies. Though well aware that the nationalist leaders, representing the legitimate government, would continue to receive the bulk of American assistance, Yenan seemed to judge that the communists' emphasis on their desire to fight Japan, provided they received needed equipment, might result in some U.S. aid for the CCP forces. Such supplies would of course substantially alter the major CCP weakness in military fire power vis-à-vis Chungking. Further, a link with Washington would significantly improve the tarnished communist image in China and abroad. Communist contacts with Western journalists during the united front period of the 1930s had helped break the prevailing view of the CCP leaders as unprincipled "bandits." And reports from American military and diplomatic officers, depicting the communists as an attractive and efficient group, would considerably enhance CCP respectability. The Yenan leadership would desperately need the image of a responsible and respectable party during the anticipated political-military confrontation with Chungking at the end of the Pacific war.

In a broad sense then, the Chinese communists were responding pragmatically to the abrupt intrusion of American support in China on the side of Chiang Kai-shek. They realized that if the U.S. power were not properly handled by the CCP leaders, it would move in a direction contrary to vital CCP interests, endangering the party's very survival. They recognized at the same time that there was little countervailing force within China that could be used to block American power, and they judged that if the CCP was to survive and prosper now and in the postwar period, it would have to ensure that Wash-

17

ington adopted a more neutral stance concerning the Chinese civil dispute.

The communists realized that they would have to deal pragmatically with American officials and accommodate U.S. interests in order to move Washington's overriding power to a more neutral position. Because of its strength, the United States held the key to the balance of power in China and had to be courted by the CCP. The communists were on the defensive, but they also knew that they had several cards to play in order to win favor with the United States. They had considerable armed strength and held strategic locations that could be of use to Washington in the war against Japan. By playing up what it had to offer the United States, and by soft-pedaling CCP ideological and historical disagreements with Washington, the CCP hoped to win the United States over to a more impartial position in China, thereby reestablishing a power balance agreeable to its vital concerns.

The U.S. Response

The conciliatory approach of the Chinese communists began to have an effect on the thinking of some U.S. officials. Most notably, a third secretary in the American embassy, John S. Service, suggested in a memo—written for policy consideration on 23 January 1943 while Service was on assignment in Washington—that the United States should consider sending American observers to the communist-held areas of China in order to gather information for use in the war against Japan and to assess at close range the CCP leaders and their possible future role in China.[25] Subsequently, Service's suggestion was actively considered at the State Department but was soon put aside. An embassy report from Chungking, as well as deliberations within the department, concluded that the unprecedented step involved in establishing a U.S. observer mission in the CCP areas would not be worth the disruption and possible damage it would cause in American relations with Chiang Kai-shek.[26] An 11 February memo prepared by the Division of Far Eastern Affairs concluded that while an observer mission was worthy of continued consideration, "the Chinese government authorities would resent our sending representatives to the communist areas without obtaining prior approval of the government. Under present circumstances, it is doubtful whether the Chinese government would welcome a request for such support."[27]

Second Secretary John P. Davies raised the issue of American liaison with the communists in a memo written in Washington on 24 June 1943, and he received a more favorable response. Davies not only advocated sending officers to Yenan, but pointedly questioned the utility of the traditional "hands-off" policy in dealing with Chinese internal affairs. Davies's memo gained the approval of high-level U.S. authorities, marking a turning point in American thinking on Chinese affairs.[28]

Unlike Service, who had cited various aspects of American policy interest in China in attempting to justify the stationing of observers in CCP areas, Davies focused specifically on American concern over possible Soviet entrance into the Pacific war and the resulting implications for China and for Washington's goals in East Asia. (Stalin's confirmation to the United States in fall 1943 that the USSR in fact did intend to participate in the war against Japan gave additional potency to this line of reasoning.)[29] Though claiming that an outbreak of civil war in China was not likely until after the defeat of Japan, Davies raised the specter of Soviet cooperation with the CCP forces in such a civil conflict. He held that this development on one hand might result in a "Russo-Chinese bloc, with China the subservient member of the partnership"—a development that "would not be welcomed by us" and would have an undesirable effect on Asian and world stability.[30] On the other hand, in the event of Soviet support for the CCP, he argued, Chiang-Kai-shek could be expected to exert every effort to get the United States involved on his side. Thus, Washington would in this case find itself fighting in a civil war in China in opposition to the Soviet Union.[31] After painting the alternatives of a Soviet-Chinese bloc or a Soviet-American confrontation in China, Davies pushed for an end to Washington's hands-off policy. In particular, he insisted that the United States should have a better grasp of the nature and capabilities of the CCP leaders, organization, and resources. Specifically citing proposals put forth earlier by Chou-En-lai, Davies argued that if a U.S. military delegation were to be sent to Yenan, ostensibly for the purpose of pursuing the war against Japan, Chiang Kai-shek could hardly refuse it.[32] Echoing Chou, Davies suggested that the proposal for the mission should come from the highest levels in Washington. He indicated that General Joseph Stilwell, the chief U.S. military representative in China, should be consulted but judged that his approval would be forthcoming.[33]

The favorable response that greeted Davies's memo is significant not only as a signal of change in the American attitude over the observer mission and over internal Chinese affairs, but also as a reflection of a growing U.S. concern to block suspected Soviet expansion in postwar East Asia. American planners realized that once Japan was defeated there would be a power vacuum in East Asia and an accompanying danger of Russian expansion, especially in such areas as Manchuria, Inner Mongolia, and north China.[34] Washington's strategy to block such undesired Soviet moves centered on efforts to keep China strong and united. However, the nationalist-communist split endangered needed unity in China. As Davies vividly pointed out, a divided China, or the outbreak of civil war in China, might well invite Soviet intervention, with dire consequences for American interests.

Davies's report thus heralded a fast approaching time when the United States would be constrained to put aside its past refusal to deal directly with the Chinese Communist Party. American strategists were gradually coming to the judgment that they were compelled to run the risk of alienating Chiang and of weakening his leading position in China by establishing American links with the Chinese communists. The combination of the growing specter of Soviet entrance into the war against Japan with continuing nationalist-communist division in China appeared to make imperative U.S. mediation of the Chinese civil dispute. The United States accordingly had to obtain more solid intelligence concerning the nature of the CCP in order to decide how to unite this movement with that of the nationalists, and thereby consolidate a solid Chinese front against the USSR in the postwar period in East Asia.

The importance of closer U.S. contacts with the communists was underlined by subsequent events in China. In June 1943 the intermittent negotiations between nationalists and communists again reached an impasse. Lin Piao and Chou-En-lai traveled to Yenan for consultations in late June.[35] No high-level CCP negotiator returned to Chungking for over a year. The American embassy reported that the nationalists now felt strong enough to pressure the communists to accept their terms. It judged that some members of the nationalist leadership viewed the dissolution of the Comintern and the quiet withdrawal of Soviet forces from Sinkiang as a demonstration of Moscow's intention to maintain good relations with the nationalists, even at the expense of the interests of the communist forces in China.[36] In particular, the embassy reported that during the recent round of CCP-KMT negotiations in Chungking, Chiang Kai-shek had presented harsh demands to the communist side and had requested a positive response by the end of August. In the absence of CCP acceptance by that time, Chiang reportedly asserted that he would be forced to take "appropriate steps."[37] The embassy predicted that the communists would reject Chiang's conditions, and it warned of the possible outbreak of armed CCP-KMT clashes.[38]

Concern in the United States was heightened by a report from an aide of Chou En-lai on 7 July that the nationalists had recently transferred seven divisions of central government troops, including an armored unit, to the border of communist areas in Shensi. According to the aide, there were already fourteen nationalist divisions in the area as well as troops under the command of anticommunist warlord Yen Hsi-shan. While passing along this news, the embassy discounted the possibility of an outright clash between the two sides but pointed to the danger of the development of a situation similar to the New Fourth Army incident of January 1941, when local nationalist commanders attacked communist forces allegedly without explicit orders from Chungking.[39]

Meanwhile, the Soviet Union for the first time began voicing open concern over internal tension in China, both through diplomatic channels and in the press. Soviet officials in China used conversations with American envoys to accuse the nationalist government of seeking to impose its terms for settlement on the communists by threat of force. They additionally attempted to discover what the United States would do in the event of an outbreak of civil war and showed special concern over American assistance to the nationalists. There also appeared in the Soviet press a number of articles openly championing the CCP cause and criticizing the nationalist government, though refraining from open attack on Chiang Kai-shek.[40]

Against this backdrop, American officials in the summer of 1943 for the first time began serious efforts to guard against the outbreak of civil war in China and to encourage a settlement of the internal Chinese dispute. As part of this approach, the United States initiated moves designed to gain a better understanding of the Chinese communists, leading by early 1944 to a formal presidential request to Chiang for the establishment of an American military observer mission in the communist-held areas. The proposal was finally approved by Chiang during the visit to China of American Vice-President Henry A. Wallace in June 1944. The observer mission departed for Yenan in July.

Liaison Mission Begins

During the early months of the U.S. liaison mission in the CCP areas, the initiative in communist-American relations shifted back to the communists, who fully exploited the observer group in order to communicate to ruling circles in Washington. As predicted by Chou En-lai two years earlier, the Americans were warmly welcomed at the communist headquarters in Yenan and were given a full measure of cooperation. Like the Western journalists who had visited the communist base following Edgar Snow's initial trip in the mid-1930s, the American observers found the communist leaders and the area under

21

their control decidedly more attractive than the nationalists and their domain.[41] The appeal of the communists to the Americans derived from the simplicity and directness of the CCP leaders and their concern for the welfare of the people under their control. In comparison with the chaotic, inequitable, and oppressive atmosphere prevailing in nationalist-held areas, Yenan appeared to the American visitors to be refreshingly serene. They responded by adopting a generally favorable view of the communists and their policies.

The CCP leaders clearly worked hard to ensure that the visitors from the United States would receive a favorable impression of the communist areas.[42] The communists had experienced the positive effects of good publicity stemming from Edgar Snow's visit in the 1930s, and they welcomed the consequences—including the establishment of the U.S. liaison mission—which had derived from the pleased response Chou En-lai and others had invoked in Americans in Chungking. Yenan clearly wished to sustain the positive momentum in order to win greater American good will. Thus, the Yenan leaders, including Mao Tse-tung, made themselves available for long discussions with the Americans. They were particularly careful to talk with John Service— the sole political officer in the initial observer group—whom they rightly saw as their most important link with policy makers in Washington.

The highlight of Yenan's early approach was a six-hour talk Mao had with Service on 23 August, covering the full range of communist views on the situation in China and the triangular U.S.-KMT-CCP relationship.[43] The meeting was held at Mao's initiative, and he directed the conversation. Following a pattern similar to that used by the CCP spokesmen in Chungking, Mao spoke of the CCP in a way agreeable to American interests. He portrayed the party's policies as moderate and democratic, and he affirmed a CCP desire to work actively for the defeat of Japan. Thus, Mao contrasted his party's favorable behavior with the alleged maintenance of a monopoly of "oppressive" political power by the nationalists, who were portrayed in stock terms as concerned largely with the elimination of the communists and other dissidents, by military force if necessary. Demonstrating CCP awareness of American sensitivity and suspicion of the Soviet Union and the international communist movement, Mao minimized the importance of the role that the Soviet Union might play in the defeat of Japan and in the postwar situation in China; he emphasized instead that the United States was and would remain the most important power in China and would have a profound impact on the people and political parties of China. In this connection, Mao made a strong pitch for a more even-handed American policy on the Chinese civil dispute and for the possible provision of some American political and military aid for the CCP.

CCP Position at the Close of World War II

By late 1944, therefore, the Chinese communists had reason to believe that their adroit efforts to woo the United States and to preclude continued one-sided American association with the nationalist government had achieved some success. In part because of communist prodding, the United States had pressured Chiang Kai-shek to lower the nationalist blockade against the CCP bases and to allow American military observers to travel to Yenan. The CCP leadership was using this new channel to win American good will and to ask for support. Expecting a civil war to break out following Japan's defeat and realizing that Chiang Kai-shek would do his utmost to involve the United States on the side of the nationalists, the CCP chiefs saw America as a potentially dangerous adversary blocking the communists' route to power in China. To limit U.S. backing for Chiang and thereby reduce the danger of CCP-American confrontation in the event of civil war in China, the communists showed themselves to be quite flexible in accommodating American interests. They submerged the longstanding CCP ideological distaste for compromising interaction with agents of U.S. "imperialism," and they were even willing to put aside memories of past bad treatment they had received as a result of American military support for the nationalists over the previous fifteen years.

Against this backdrop, the communists approached their first official negotiations with the United States in November 1944 under the auspices of U.S. envoy Patrick Hurley. Hurley had been sent to China two months earlier as an American presidential envoy whose mission was to smooth the deteriorating relations between Chiang Kai-shek and the chief U.S. military officer in China, General Stilwell, and to encourage a unification of Chinese forces—nationalist and communist —in the war effort against Japan. In spring 1944 the Japanese forces in China launched their last major offensive, and by the summer they had rapidly advanced against a number of Allied air bases and installations in southwestern China.[44] It was judged to be only a matter of time before the American bomber base at Kweilin would fall, while Kunming, the critical logistics hub for supplies flown in from India, and even Chungking appeared vulnerable. The newly critical military situation, combined with a concurrent record of poor nationalist cooperation in the stalled Allied effort to open a land supply route to China over the old Burma road, impelled Washington to push for the appointment of Stilwell as commander in chief of nationalist forces.[45] Chiang resisted Stilwell's appointment, triggering the crisis which prompted Hurley's dispatch. Because the United States also remained highly concerned over the continuing Chinese civil dispute, the presidential envoy was additionally charged with using American influence to bring about a solution to the CCP-KMT conflict that would result in a unified Chinese military effort against Japan and in the establishment of a stable Chinese state in the aftermath of the war.

To fully understand the communist approach and intentions toward Hurley and the United States during these critically important CCP-U.S. negotiations, one must have a good assessment of the role the CCP leadership expected American influence to play in the communists' future development in China. Unfortunately, such an assessment has been difficult to make with complete assurance, especially since the political and military balance was rapidly changing in China at that time.

As a result, some American observers in China tended to see the communists as quite sure of their strategic position by November 1944 and as sanguine regarding their future control of China.[46] These individuals tended to disregard CCP concern over the possibility of serious reverses in the communist position as a result of American actions in China or other factors. In some instances, they contended that the communists were moving toward the United States at this time largely to prevent a long civil war in China and thus to quicken what the communists already saw as their inevitable rise to power in China.[47] If the United States could have been persuaded not to give strong unilateral support to the nationalists, this argument holds, then the nationalists would have been more quickly defeated by the CCP forces. Other observers contended that the CCP leaders were anxious to cultivate the United States chiefly because they feared that they would otherwise fall under heavy Soviet influence at the end of the Pacific war. The CCP wanted to establish good relations with America, according to this thesis, in order to balance more effectively what it feared would be a growing Soviet influence in the Far East.[48]

These arguments obviously have a great deal of merit. It was evident by late 1944 that the communist leaders were more confident that their military forces would now survive and expand, as a result of the shifting military and political situation in China. They were aware that nationalist forces had behaved poorly in the defense of south-central China against the Japanese offensive. Moreover, following the start of the Japanese advance in April 1944, the communists had managed to extend their underground control network into south-central China.[49] The communists also frequently voiced the belief that there

24

was growing governmental and economic deterioration in the areas under Chiang Kai-shek's administration.[50] Furthermore, the Soviet Union had begun to signal openly an intention to enter the anti-Japanese war at a future date—a development that presumably also strengthened the communists' confidence.[51]

In spite of these arguments, however, the communist planners could not afford to be entirely sanguine regarding CCP prospects. The United States clearly posed the greatest problem in this respect. Mao and other CCP spokesmen had openly stated that they expected Chiang to involve the Americans as actively as possible on the side of the nationalists in a Chinese civil conflict.[52] The likelihood of close American military cooperation with Chiang, including even the use of American forces in a future Chinese civil war, was a contingency that Yenan—in late 1944—could not dismiss lightly.[53] Past CCP experience with the United States had shown that there was a clear American bias against the communists and an identification of American interests with Chiang Kai-shek. Although the CCP had recently won some favor with American officials, it had yet to receive a solid commitment from the United States that assured the communists of America's future course in China.

Moreover, while Chiang appeared militarily weak in late 1944, the communists were well aware that the nationalists still held many military advantages. Chiang's forces blockading the communists, generally considered the best under his command, were still solidly intact. The American training effort for nationalist forces in Yunnan was also beginning to pick up steam. With an expected reopening of a land supply route through Burma, the American training and supply of nationalist forces would increase considerably.[54] The defeat of Germany was also expected to allow the United States to place a higher priority on the training and supplying of the nationalist armies. American observers in late 1944 judged that the war with Japan would continue for at least one more year following the victory in Europe in 1945, thereby allowing the Americans considerable time to build up Chiang's armies.[55] Another major advantage the nationalists held was the fact that the several hundred thousand puppet troops which controlled the industrial heartland and vital agricultural areas of China were expected to side with Chiang against the communists in the event of civil war.[56] Thus, with the cooperation of the puppet forces and the continuation through one more year of increasingly heavy materiel and training support from the United States, it appeared likely that Chiang Kai-shek would be able to reassert control over most vital areas of China south of the Yellow River.[57]

These circumstances certainly did not put the CCP leaders in a

25

favorable position. Although there are no precise estimates of communist military strength at this time, it is generally clear from the reports of American observers that the communist armed forces were still lacking a broad range of basic military supplies, including even small-arms ammunition.[58] In such circumstances, the communists were unable to take the offensive and would have been vulnerable to blockade and offensive action taken by nationalist forces. The communists may well have hoped that the Russians would come to their aid with military supplies, once Moscow entered the war against Japan. But such assistance was not at all certain, since Moscow continued to cooperate with Chiang and the United States, avoiding significant contact with the CCP. There almost certainly remained some serious doubt among CCP planners whether Moscow might see it more in Russian interests to continue to cooperate with the nationalists and the United States at the expense of communist concerns in China.

At bottom, however, Chiang's greatest asset in a civil war with the CCP—and the communists' greatest concern—was the close Kuomintang relationship with the United States. As the CCP leaders repeatedly stated, the United States was clearly the predominant power in Asia, and if it brought its might to bear on the internal situation in China, the action would be decisive. While there remained the possibility that the USSR, the other great power in the area, might forcefully challenge an American military action in China, this possibility was far from definite in late 1944. The Russians had suffered great damage in the war against Germany, and they might have seen it in their interests to accommodate U.S. military expansion in China rather than confront American power directly in the area. In sum, it seems fair to say that the Chinese communists were aware of the continued vulnerability of their strategic position in late 1944. They were actively wooing the United States and were accommodating American interests and sensitivities across a broad front because of their need to assure CCP survival and future development in China.

The U.S. Approach in the Hurley Mission

This situation presented the United States with an important opportunity during the initial stages of the Hurley negotiations with the communists in late 1944. By adroitly exploiting the concerns and circumstances of the CCP leaders and by responding forthrightly to their various initiatives, the United States might have overcome the ill will and distrust that had characterized CCP-American relations in the past and thus have aligned itself with what would turn out to be the ascending ruling group of China. This opportunity was clearly seen by some American observers, notably those serving in Yenan with the military mission.[59] These officials gradually adopted the view that there was no basic contradiction between the interests of the CCP and the United States in China. John Service claimed that the CCP was a decidedly more benevolent administration than that of Chiang's Kuomintang;[60] both Service and Davies alleged that, man for man, the communists would better serve American interests in the war against Japan than would the nationalists.[61] Davies stressed the importance of the independent spirit of the communist leadership, observing that China under Mao and the communists would provide a stronger bulwark against suspected expansion of Soviet influence in East Asia than a weak and dependent regime under the nationalists.[62]

Unfortunately for the later course of U.S.-CCP relations, these perceptive assessments of American interests in China were not followed in the formulation of a China policy under the dominant influence of presidential envoy Hurley. During this critical juncture,[63] Washington was preoccupied with redefining China's role in the war against Japan and was also attempting to decide how best to secure American interests in the postwar period. For one thing, because of continued success of the Allied "island hopping" campaign in the western Pacific, American planners were now looking with more interest at a military strategy in which the Americans would bypass the large Japanese armies on the Asian mainland. As a result, the need to employ massive, U.S.-backed Chinese armies in a united effort against Japanese forces in China appeared less pressing than it had in the past. In this new situation, it was assumed that the brunt of whatever fighting took place against Japanese forces in China and Manchuria would be borne by Russian armies, once Moscow entered the war.

At the same time, the Americans were becoming increasingly exasperated over their inability to encourage Chiang Kai-shek to undertake what Washington deemed as the political and military reforms necessary to strengthen the unity of China and to shore up China's power as a bulwark against the USSR in the Far East. Chiang's armies had failed miserably against the Japanese military offensive in mid-1944. The United States judged that if the nationalists were to be a postwar power, they would need to undergo radical reform—a judgment that led Washington to push for the appointment of General Stilwell as the commander in chief of nationalist forces. Yet, when Chiang resisted strongly, Washington backed down, removing Stilwell from China.

The American general's recall in October 1944 marked a milestone in American China policy. It signaled the collapse of Washington's efforts to pressure Chiang to revitalize his government in order to provide a greater war effort and to prepare for a postwar role as a regional power.[64] The United States realized that it no longer could look to Chungking as the bulwark of its balance-of-power strategy.

Instead, Washington gradually shifted to a policy which called for American-Soviet agreements to provide the foundation for the postwar balance. By granting concessions to Moscow, as it did at the Yalta conference of February 1945, the United States hoped to establish bilateral American-Soviet agreement concerning postwar East Asia.[65] Washington attempted to use the Yalta agreements to set boundaries to Soviet influence, to ensure a future role for an independent China, and to secure thereby that a balance of power in East Asia would be sustained. Thus, the Americans realized that the relatively weak China under Chiang was not a solid safeguard for American interests in the face of growing Russian influence. By accommodating the USSR with gains along the Soviet-Asian periphery, Washington hoped to preclude further Soviet encroachment at the expense of the Asian balance.

Clearly, the revised American strategy was still concerned with pursuing the establishment of a stable balance of power in East Asia, but its methods reflected with equal clarity the lack of realism and the naïveté of traditional U.S. foreign policy. Specifically, the United States judged that a balance of power could be maintained on the basis of paper agreements and American-Soviet good will and that sustained U.S. power politics would not be required. Washington had no intention of maintaining a large military presence in China after Japan's defeat. Indeed, the American people expected that Washington would rapidly "bring the boys home." After the "evil" of the Axis had been destroyed, there would be no moral rationale for further wide-ranging American military activity abroad. Any overt use of power by the United States government would be seen at home as an abuse of authority, a deviation from the idealistic and moral American way—something that would not long be tolerated by concerned voters.

What the United States expected from China, then, was the maintenance of a stable situation that would not complicate the postwar arrangements then being worked out with Moscow. Under Hurley's dominant influence, U.S. strategy stressed that Chiang Kai-shek should be retained in power as the best alternative for American interests. American planners predictably did not want to risk the dangers of becoming directly involved in running Chinese internal affairs. Though they were increasingly disenchanted with Chiang's performance during the war and were well aware of the steady deterioration of his military and political position in China, they still judged that the process of changing the regime would lead to such chaos that it would be contrary to American interests. Washington particularly felt that any further undermining of Chiang's ruling position might trigger a civil war in China, with an accompanying danger that the United States would become actively involved.[66] Such a conflict might seriously jeopardize concurrent American efforts to reach agreement with Moscow over China and might possibly trigger a Soviet response that would set the stage for Soviet-American confrontation.

There were reports from American observers in Yenan at this time that maintained that the CCP leaders, and not Chiang Kai-shek, were the most dynamic and capable leaders in China—the ones who should be supported by the United States.[67] But such reports were not incorporated into general American strategy. Although for several years there had been an interest in the CCP movement at high levels in Washington—exemplified by President Franklin D. Roosevelt's efforts to initiate the military observer mission—the United States had never formally committed itself to the communists. Since American policy toward China was strongly focused on sustaining a stable internal Chinese situation that would not complicate U.S. negotiations with the USSR over East Asia, Washington was reluctant to begin support for a Chinese dissident group. It judged that such a step might bring about the collapse of the existing nationalist government and result in civil war. Washington planners instead supported the views of General Hurley, who voiced concern over alleged CCP ties with the USSR[68] and judged that the CCP at any rate was too weak and ineffective to become the dominant ruling group in China.[69] Implicit in Hurley's position was the view that the CCP was of little consequence and the judgment that the party's actions could be easily controlled by means of U.S. negotiations with the Chinese communists' mentors in Moscow. Chiang Kai-shek on the other hand was well known, had long identified himself with U.S. interests in China, and had been a close ally during the war. Though he was weakened and frequently uncooperative, he was viewed as a more reliable and better alternative than the CCP leaders.

Thus, after initial interest, Washington failed to respond to CCP initiatives. In a broad sense, it was American ideology that precluded a successful U.S.-CCP understanding on the basis of their mutual interests in the power equation in East Asia. Washington's distaste for and refusal to engage in power politics had resulted in an American policy based both on agreements and understanding with Moscow and on an endorsement of Chiang Kai-shek as the leader to bring stability to China.

Washington's concern over unrest in China had led the United

States to support the fundamental tenet in the policy of American envoy Hurley during his 1944–45 stint in China—thus placing full U.S. support behind Chiang and using American influence to coerce the communists to unite under Chiang's lead. This stance, of course, was diametrically opposed to primary Chinese communist interests and, indeed, posed a serious threat to the survival of the communist movement in China. Though Yenan was willing to accommodate the United States in order to help ensure basic CCP goals in China, Hurley demanded in effect that the communists sacrifice their fundamental goals for the sake of American amity.

Hurley's one-sided policy was not at first clearly evident to the communists, however. The CCP leaders initially attempted—in a pattern similar to that used with other American officials—to win him over to their point of view, hoping to persuade Hurley to urge the United States to assume a more balanced position vis-à-vis the CCP-KMT rift. In this endeavor they judged at first that they had made considerable progress. Most notably, Hurley verbally endorsed the basic communist political demands for a settlement of the nationalist-communist dispute during his initial formal negotiating session with the CCP leaders in early November 1944. He promised the communists that he would persuade Chiang Kai-shek to accept the communist stance.[70] Hurley—ignorant of the impact of his decision or of the significance of the communist terms—subsequently discovered to his dismay that Chiang totally rejected them.[71] Hurley soon moved to a position strongly supporting the nationalists and maintained this posture over the next year.[72] Because of Hurley's sharp turnabout, CCP leaders became more and more distrustful of him, perceiving that he was increasingly aligning with the interests of Chiang Kai-shek.[73] Hurley was subsequently appointed ambassador in late 1944 and was given dominant power by Washington in the conduct and formulation of American policy in China. His critics within the State Department, who advocated a more conciliatory approach to the communists, were soon transferred at Hurley's instigation.[74] By early 1945, the communists began to see that American policy in China was opposed to their interests. America had firmly sided with Chiang Kai-shek for the foreseeable future.[75] The United States was no longer seen as a potential source of assistance for the communists, but was viewed increasingly as a menace to CCP survival. Thus, this initial encounter in CCP-U.S. relations ended with an opportunity lost and with old feelings of animosity and suspicion once again rising to the surface.

CHAPTER THREE

Peking's Response to U.S. Containment in Asia

At the end of World War II the Chinese communists endeavored to win the United States over to their side in the Chinese civil dispute, but Washington chose to remain tied to Chiang Kai-shek. The United States supported Chiang during the civil war by providing substantial material and training assistance to nationalist forces. Such support caused the communists to view Washington as a dangerous potential adversary. Even after defeating Chiang on the mainland and taking power in Peking in 1949, the communists were unsure of American intentions and predictably sought security for their young state by moving closer to their ideological allies in Moscow. The Soviet Union provided protection and acted as a safeguard for China against American intimidation and possible attack.

At about the same time, the United States began to realize the failings of its earlier strategy in China. The Cold War in Europe in the late 1940s demonstrated vividly to American planners that their goal of establishing a favorable balance of power in the postwar world could not be met by mere paper agreements and international amity. If Washington were to secure its interests against what it viewed as the alarming expansion of Soviet power in Europe, it would have to engage in protracted power politics and shore up a strategic balance satisfactory to American interests. This judgment was at the root of the March 1947 Truman Doctrine—a policy of active U.S. military preparedness and economic and military assistance supporting pro-American positions on the periphery of the Soviet orbit. U.S. goals were to be achieved through a policy of power politics designed to "contain" Soviet influence.

The Cold War similarly caused Washington to assess the situation in East Asia more realistically. By late 1948, communist victories in the Chinese civil war signaled that there was no hope of sustaining a pro-American Chinese government under Chiang Kai-shek. Cold War conflicts with Moscow also gave evidence of the futility of relying on Soviet good will to bolster East Asian stability. Washington thus had to find a new way to achieve a balance on continental Asia—a task complicated by the reduction in U.S. leverage as a result of rapid American military demobilization after Japan's defeat.

Washington, at this time, perceived no great need for active containment of Soviet influence in East Asia. The United States saw as yet little sign of the kind of Soviet expansion there that seemed so apparent in Europe. To be sure, the Soviet-supported Chinese communists had decisively defeated Chiang's forces by 1948 and were on their way to total control of the China mainland, but this was deemed more a result of Chiang's ineptitude and of the dynamism of the Chinese Communist Party than due to Soviet expansion.

The revised American China policy that ensued was exemplified by the famous White Paper on China released by the U.S. State Department in 1949. Washington now judged optimistically that there were ample grounds for expecting sharp Sino-Soviet disagreement to emerge in East Asia in the not-too-distant future. American strategists hoped that simply by withdrawing from the continent, the United States would then be able to watch for such conflicts and exploit them in such a way as to reestablish an Asian power balance favorable to American interests. In particular, Washington believed that CCP leaders could be won over eventually to a position friendly to the United States and opposed to the Soviet Union.

Unfortunately, there was no corresponding concern in the People's Republic of China over improving relations with the United States at this time. The CCP leaders were well on their way to obtaining full control of the China mainland, and they had gained a strategic guarantee against outside pressure by aligning with the Soviet Union. They viewed the United States with great suspicion and saw no great need to strive for better relations with the Americans.

American policy toward China changed again with Peking's unexpected entry into the Korean War in 1950 and the concurrent surge of domestic frustration in the United States over foreign policy failures. Peking's war action was considered in the United States as an indication that hopes for Sino-Soviet conflict were unrealistic and that a solid Sino-Soviet alliance would face the West for some time to come. Further, Washington interpreted the North Korean attack in 1950 as proof that the Sino-Soviet alliance supported expansion in Asia and that the United States would, therefore, have to extend its containment policy from Europe to include the entire periphery of the Sino-Soviet bloc. Washington now judged Peking to be solidly allied with Moscow in a campaign to erode American positions in Asia, and it concluded that this Sino-Soviet bloc would have to be continuously held in check by free-world forces led by the United States.

American strategists now dismissed the possibility of Sino-Soviet disagreement and placed great stress on communist ideology as a source of continuing unity in Sino-Soviet relations. They inferred that, even though nationalistic and historical differences might exist between Peking and Moscow, their common devotion to communism would keep them tightly united and firmly opposed to the West. Washington's revised assessment precluded exploitation by the United States of potential or existing Sino-Soviet differences for the next twenty years.

In a broad sense, American policy changed from a pragmatic balancing of national interests within the international state system in the late 1940s to an ideologically based drive against international communism in the early 1950s. Washington continued to seek a balance of power and was willing to employ power politics to achieve it; but, by overreacting to the early communist advances, it had lost sight of the continuing importance of the state system and of nationalism. As a result of their misconceptions, American planners decided that they had little choice but to extend a ring of containment around China as well as the USSR, establishing defense alliances and U.S. bases along Peking's eastern and southern flanks.

Peking's foreign policy in the years following the end of the Korean War was dominated by an effort to come to grips with the growing American-backed power in Asia. In the wake of the war and the death of Stalin, China's Soviet mentors adopted a more accommodating stance vis-à-vis the United States, especially in Asia. Moscow, hoping to capitalize on increasing international pressure for East-West relaxation, pursued a generally nonprovocative stance designed to accentuate Soviet reasonableness. Since China had been dependent upon the Soviet bloc for international support since 1949, it came as no surprise when Peking followed Moscow's lead.

However, American efforts in the latter half of 1954 to incorporate Taiwan into the East Asian containment ring against China complicated the emerging moderate stance of Peking toward the United States. The Chinese communists feared that Washington's actions would permanently separate the island from the mainland, resulting in a "two Chinas" situation fundamentally antagonistic to PRC goals. In response, Peking launched a major propaganda campaign in 1954 along with armed probes against American-supported forces in the area. The Chinese also tried to elicit more militant support from their Soviet allies.

The communist efforts were unsuccessful, however. Their campaign in Taiwan failed to reduce U.S. commitment to Taipei or to weaken Washington's containment policy. In addition, the Soviet Union did not increase its support for PRC objectives in East Asia, not even for the campaign on Taiwan. As a result, Peking by early 1955 saw the East Asian power balance moving in a direction increasingly unfavorable to its vital interests, and it again moved to change strategy. The Chinese leaders, viewing the United States as the key element in the East Asian balance, now attempted to establish a new working relationship with the Americans during Sino-American ambassadorial talks in Geneva.

Sino-Soviet Divergence over Asia

Although the Chinese strove to follow Moscow's newly moderate policy in foreign affairs in the wake of the Korean War, Peking began to register some dissatisfaction with the Soviet approach by 1954. At bottom, Peking feared that it had little to gain by pursuing a moderate approach like that of Moscow, and it began to emphasize Chinese dissatisfaction by offering its own assessments of the situation in East Asia and of the American role there. These Sino-Soviet differences of opinion were expressed by both sides throughout the next year.[1]

In September 1953, Soviet comment started to redefine China's international position in a formula that implicitly signaled reduced Soviet concern for PRC interests in Asia. Previously, both Peking and Moscow had called the Sino-Soviet alliance and friendship the "mighty factor" in the defense of peace in the Far East. This sentiment had been evident in Chinese and Soviet 1953 May-day slogans, and, as late as 3 September 1953, V-J Day messages exchanged between Soviet Party leader Georgi M. Malenkov and Mao Tse-tung reaffirmed the harmony between the two nations. Malenkov promised that Sino-Soviet friendship would "continue to serve as a reliable basis for winning peace and security *in the Far East* and the strengthening of peace throughout the world."[2]

But on 19 September 1953, Malenkov told a Korean delegation in Moscow that objective conditions now enabled social forces in the East, in particular those of the PRC, to turn Asia into a fortress of peace. He maintained that a new epoch had begun, characterized by the emergence of China as the "mighty stabilizing factor" in Asia and the world and symbolized by the entry of the Chinese People's Volunteers (CPV) into the Korean War.[3] He did not cite the Sino-Soviet friendship and alliance as the reliable foundation for peace in Asia, nor did he refer at all to the joint role of the two countries in dispelling Asian unrest. Thus, China's strength alone was portrayed as having supplanted the Sino-Soviet friendship as the Asian stabilizer; future Soviet statements about the international effort of the Sino-Soviet pact would no longer be concerned with the Far East specifically.

On the February 1954 anniversary of the 1950 Sino-Soviet treaty, disagreement on the applicability of the alliance to Asia was voiced by Mao and Malenkov and was evident in other authoritative comment. Concerning the role of the agreement in the defense of peace, Mao remarked, "The events of the past four years have shown more clearly than ever before that the great alliance between China and the Soviet Union is the reliable foundation for safeguarding of peace and security *in the Far East* and the whole world."[4] Malenkov declared that "the unbreakable friendship of this alliance between the Chinese People's Republic and the USSR, which is growing stronger day by day, will continue in the future as a powerful factor for the preservation of peace and the defense of the security *of all the peoples.*"[5] *People's Daily*, in its editorial commemorating the pact anniversary, made a point of juxtaposing Mao's and Malenkov's descriptions of what the pact was a "reliable foundation" or "solid basis" for, thereby implying that the Soviets supported the PRC position. The editorial stated:

> Comrade Mao Tse-tung declares in his message that: "The events of the past four years have shown more clearly than before that the great alliance between China and the Soviet Union is the reliable foundation for safeguarding of peace and security in the Far East and the world." Comrade G. M. Malenkov's message says that "This treaty is the solid basis for the all-round political, economic and cultural cooperation between the peoples of the Chinese People's Republic and the USSR."[6]

Sino-Soviet divergence over the alliance and the PRC role in Asia was again visible on May Day in 1954. Soviet slogans coincided with the position maintained by Malenkov in September 1953 and excluded altogether the previous May Day's reference to the role of Sino-Soviet friendship in securing peace in the Far East. Meanwhile, the Chinese slogans still clung to the older formulation, committing the USSR to this joint task.[7]

Because of this lack of Soviet support in the face of increasingly strong American containment efforts in East Asia, Peking judged that it had little alternative but to follow a foreign policy that was carefully tailored to accord with Moscow's peaceful coexistence line and to avoid potentially dangerous military confrontation with Washington. The Chinese communists attempted to make the best of this poor situation by using the Soviet-fostered approach of peaceful coexistence to project a more attractive Chinese image abroad and thereby enhance Peking's heretofore weak leverage in world affairs. The new Chinese efforts reached high points during the 1954 Geneva peace conference attended by Chou En-lai and during Chou's official visits to India and Burma in mid-1954.

Crisis over Taiwan, July–August 1954

It was plain by mid-1954 that Peking was prepared to soft-pedal the earlier stress on confrontation and conflict with adversaries such as the United States in favor of a moderate line emphasizing the peaceful settlement of disputes and the employment of the five principles of peaceful coexistence. The Chinese thus hoped to slowly build their international image and support, especially in Asia. As a result of this new effort, the Chinese had already scored notable breakthroughs in relations with various states such as Great Britain, Indonesia, Japan, and the Netherlands.[8] Peking, by mid-1954, had moved to reciprocate London's earlier appointment of a chargé d'affaires to its embassy, had sent trade delegations to London and Djakarta, had signed a trade agreement with Finland, and had begun negotiations with the recently arrived Norwegain envoy on establishing formal diplomatic relations.[9]

The continuation of this conciliatory approach was hampered, however, by a rise in Chinese concern over American policy toward the Chiang government in Taiwan. Throughout the next ten months, Peking demonstrated acute uneasiness over growing American involvement in Taiwan. The communists were especially disturbed when an American presidential envoy visited Taiwan in the summer of 1954 to discuss the establishment of a formal defense treaty with the Republic of China (ROC). Peking was no less upset when the treaty was formally signed that December. The communists launched an unprecedented, hard-line propaganda campaign emphasizing their determination to "liberate" Taiwan. This harsh approach concerning Taiwan seriously damaged their chances of projecting a moderate image abroad and of winning broad international support.

Chinese comment indicated that Peking feared that the United States planned to bring Taiwan into the American system of anti-PRC defense alliances in Asia by means of a mutual security pact similar to those already signed with South Korea and Japan. Such a treaty would virtually rule out PRC attainment of control of Taiwan in the foreseeable future. It would thereby preclude the attainment of basic Chinese goals, such as gaining control of all Chinese territory and completing the Chinese civil war. Chinese comment reflected the judgment that to continue a moderate PRC foreign approach in the face of the U.S.-ROC treaty—which the communists viewed as a massive American affront to Chinese sovereignty—might be erroneously interpreted as a sign of Chinese weakness. It might be seen as an indication that Peking was, in fact, willing to accept the existing power balance in Asia and to give up claims to Taiwan, for the sake of avoiding confrontation with the more powerful United States and salvaging China's new accommodating image abroad. Demonstrating the high priority Peking placed on the Taiwan issue, the Chinese leaders instead chose to risk conflict with Washington and the loss of China's peaceful image by launching a strong Taiwan liberation campaign.

Chinese propaganda on the Taiwan issue was eventually accompanied by military probes against some ROC-controlled offshore islands. The military actions were carefully calibrated to avoid head-on conflict with Washington, but they were also designed to probe U.S.-ROC defenses in the area and to forcefully emphasize Peking's determination not to give up the struggle for Taiwan.[10] Though Peking tried to characterize this strong military-propaganda campaign as being compatible with its overall peaceful international approach, it failed. Many nations that had become sympathetic toward Chinese concern over the United States' presence in Asia came to see communist actions over Taiwan as willfully provocative and diametrically opposed to the development of Asian peace. Moreover, the United States continued to solidify its relations with the Republic of China without prompting significant international criticism. Peking, in turn, became increasingly impatient with nations that had adopted an equivocal stance on the Taiwan issue. It began to criticize some countries by name, even those deemed important to the development of China's international influence. Thus, whereas the communists had spent a great deal of effort to win Britain over to a pro-PRC position, they did not now hesitate to attack British rulers by name over London's tentative support for the American position on Taiwan.[11]

Peking media had often broached the Taiwan issue by criticizing U.S. containment efforts in Asia, but, in March 1954, they began talking of Taiwan as only one part of an American-fostered "military crescent" being formed around the PRC.[12] The communists complained about American aid in support of Chinese nationalists occupying numerous offshore islands during early 1954 and also noted the extensive modernization of nationalist forces then being supported by the United States.[13]

The major turning point in Chinese coverage of Taiwan came in July, when it appeared likely that the United States would formally align with the ROC and thereby legitimize U.S. defense of Taiwan against Peking. Peking's first assessment of this possibility came in a harshly worded 7 July attack by the PRC's official news agency, the New China News Agency (NCNA) on the visit of American presidential envoy Gen. James A. Van Fleet to Taipei. The visit occurred against the background of disclosures in the Western press that Van Fleet's mission was to lead to the establishment of a U.S.-ROC security pact. NCNA asserted: "As a representative of the U.S. ruling bloc hostile to the Chinese people, [Van Fleet] is arranging with the Chiang Kai-shek gang a so-called bilaterial mutual security agreement. It was reported that while in Taiwan he had told the press that there should be a bilateral mutual security pact between the Kuomintang remnants and the United States. This is a naked expression of the American war policy toward this part of the world."[14]

A more authoritative comment in a 9 July *People's Daily* editorial set forth Peking's strenuous objection to any U.S.-ROC alliance.[15] It signaled the beginning of what was to become a massive propaganda campaign on the Taiwan issue.[16] By late July, the editorial had been followed by more than a dozen commentaries of mounting belligerency —including four more editorials in *People's Daily* on 16, 23, 24, and 26 July.[17] Each piece explicitly denounced American support for Chiang Kai-shek as aggression against China and revived the previously dormant theme of Taiwan's liberation and return to China. The 23 July *People's Daily* editorial entitled "Taiwan Must Be Liberated" characteristically stressed that the liberation of Taiwan was a "sacred duty" that must be carried out "for the complete victory of China's revolution." And the 24 July *People's Daily* editorial explicitly stated that the Chinese military was committed to liberating the island.

Conspicuously absent in Peking's extensive criticism of the United States over the issue of Taiwan was any indication of Soviet support for China's position. Rather, Sino-Soviet comment continued to reflect the two sides' previous disagreements over East Asian issues. Thus, 1 August PRC Army Day greetings from the Soviet bloc capitals praised the Chinese People's Liberation Army (PLA) for its defense of peace in the Far East and the world, but Peking's spokesmen limited China's commitment to the joint defense of Asian and world peace, assumed together with the Soviet Union and the people's democracies. Chang Tsung-hsien, a leader of the Chinese Revolutionary Military Council's General Staff, claimed that it was the PLA's task to "defend peace in Asia and the rest of the world, alongside the powerful armies of the Soviet Union and the people's democracies."[18] Deputy Chief of Staff Su

Yu elaborated on this point in a *People's Daily* article calling upon the PLA to work "shoulder to shoulder with the Soviet army and those of the other people's democracies to share the glorious responsibility of safeguarding peace in Asia and throughout the world."[19] By contrast, the Soviet congratulatory messages on the PLA anniversary committed neither China nor the Soviet Union to the task of defending peace in Asia.[20] Moscow's lone comment on that occasion noted that China's armed forces constituted a "mighty bulwark of peace and security, not only of their country, but of the whole Far East."[21]

Sino-Soviet divergence was reflected even more vividly in commentary marking 2 September 1954, V-J Day, an occasion that had traditionally had strong implications regarding the applicability of the Sino-Soviet alliance in the Far East. In comparison with past years, there were a number of substantial changes: specific reference to the Sino-Soviet pact, previously the cornerstone of comment by both sides on V-J Day, was contained only in the Chinese greetings message to the USSR;[22] contrary to previous years, Moscow failed to publicize the exchange of messages between the Soviet and Chinese leaders,[23] thereby sidestepping the necessity of replaying Peking's claim to the applicability of the alliance to Asia; only Peking noted the fact of Soviet participation in the defeat of Japan; and Chinese comment represented the Japanese problem as being one of immediate concern, while Soviet media presented a more long-range view of Japan's hostility to U.S. domination.[24]

Sino-Soviet comment on the anniversary was typified by the messages exchanged between the Soviet and Chinese leaders. The Chinese concern over Asian problems was reflected in the joint message dispatched by Mao and Chou on 2 September but was not paralleled in the answering note from Malenkov and Molotov. The Chinese cable declared that the restoration of normal relations with Japan was needed "to check the revival of Japanese militarism" and that it was the "urgent task of all peace-loving nations" to implement this strategy. China, the message asserted, would devote herself to this task. The American revival of Japanese militarism was linked by the Chinese to the U.S. organization of a Pacific war bloc and to the U.S. abetment of Chiang Kai-shek's "continued harassing and attacking of the Chinese mainland and the islands along the coast."[25] In contrast, the reply of the Soviet leaders blandly hailed the anniversary of the defeat of Japanese militarism and expressed the hope that "the Japanese people will never allow themselves to be drawn into new military adventures."[26] No mention was made of the threat of American aggression in the Pacific or the role of Chiang Kai-shek.

The Chinese leaders followed their references to the revival of Japanese militarism with an invocation of the "friendship and alliance" between the Soviet Union and China, which assured the consolidation of "peace and security in the Far East and the world." The Soviet reply depicted Sino-Soviet friendship as a "fortress of peace and security in the Far East," but it omitted all reference to the Sino-Soviet alliance and its possible application in both Asia and the world. Another departure from the usual propaganda exploitation of the V-J anniversary was the failure of the Russian leaders to credit the Soviet war effort as a major cause of the defeat of Japan. Consistent with Moscow's desire to portray China as the defender of peace in Asia, the Soviet note gave sole credit to the Chinese, stating that "the heroic Chinese people have made outstanding contributions to the defeat of imperialist Japan."

Khrushchev's Visit to China, September–October 1954

Celebrations marking the fifth anniversary of the founding of the People's Republic of China on 1 October provided a unique opportunity for Sino-Soviet leaders to discuss and resolve differences over their attitudes concerning the defense of peace in the Far East and the Taiwan issue. A high-level Soviet delegation, led by Khrushchev and presidium chief Nikolai A. Bulganin, traveled to Peking for the occasion and stayed in China for almost two weeks of discussions with Chinese leaders.[27] Though Khrushchev's rally speech at the start of the visit on 30 September was relatively supportive of China's efforts to liberate Taiwan, his later comments and other authoritative Soviet pronouncements emphasized that Moscow's reluctance to become involved in support of Chinese goals in the Far East remained basically unchanged. Peking, by contrast, persisted in its prodding commentaries, stressing that Moscow's commitment in the Sino-Soviet alliance directly involved the USSR in the preservation of peace in the Far East.

Khrushchev's lengthy rally address in Peking focused on the rising international stature of the PRC, particularly its position and influence among countries engaged in "national liberation struggle." Khrushchev lauded China's leading role in Asia, essentially bestowing upon the PRC the role of defender of peace in Asia. In this connection, he characterized the founding of the PRC as marking a "new epoch" in the history of the "national liberation struggle of the peoples in colonial and dependent countries." He claimed that the PRC had "already become an international force preventing the imperialists from continuing their enslavement of Asian peoples and turning Asia into a hotbed of a new world war." Khrushchev cited the role of the Chinese People's Volunteers in the Korean War as a hallmark of the strong ties binding the Asian people and of the Asian peoples' determination to fight for their national freedom. In addition, he declared that the PLA had "grown into a formidable force confronting the enemy" and was a "sure safeguard against imperialism and for the defense of the Chinese motherland."[28]

Peking spokesmen carefully avoided concurring with this line of thought. Chou En-lai, in the course of three separate speeches given on Chinese National Day, made no mention of the "new era" in Asia or of China's individual role as the defender of Asian peace. Chou, in fact, reasserted the familiar Chinese claim that the Sino-Soviet alliance was "demonstrating its growing influence on the safeguarding of peace in the Far East and the world."[29] Moscow's observations, typified by Khrushchev's address, avoided any explicit linkage of the joint Sino-Soviet ties to Asia with the same care shown by Chou in avoiding any assumption for China of the role of Asia's defender. Additionally, Khrushchev's purely historical references to Japanese aggression—the principal object of the Sino-Soviet alliance—and his failure to cite the imminent threat of U.S.-fostered Japanese militarization contrasted with the allusion by Chou to the threat posed by a remilitarized Japan.[30]

On the Taiwan issue, Khrushchev pledged in his rally address that the "Soviet people deeply sympathize" with the Chinese people's "noble cause" of Taiwan liberation and "support the Chinese people in their determination" to liberate the island. This speech marked the first pronouncement on the subject by the Soviet elite since before the start of the Chinese campaign in July. Earlier in his address, Khrushchev declared that the Chinese desire "to liberate Taiwan . . . is dear and entirely understandable to the Soviet Union"—a pronouncement more consistent with Moscow's past circumspect treatment of the issue. Although Khrushchev agreed that "Taiwan can certainly be liberated," his affirmation of support was all the more stark since there was no reference to Taiwan in the official National Day greetings transmitted by Khrushchev from the central committee of the Communist Party of the Soviet Union (CPSU) and from the Soviet Presidium.[31] Khrushchev's use of the terms *sympathy* and *support* also left open the question of degree. Similar Soviet propaganda pronouncements had been made in the past on such highly diverse subjects as the Japanese people's efforts to achieve an independent foreign policy and the North Korean war effort.[32]

Subsequent Chinese media commentary on the Soviet leaders' visit stressed the great unity and cooperation of the Sino-Soviet alliance. Chou En-lai, speaking at a 12 October banquet given by Soviet Ambassador Yudin in honor of the Soviet delegation, significantly singled out Sino-Soviet cooperation in Asia as his key theme. Chou declared that bilateral agreement reached during the visit "epitomizes the genuine cooperation and joint efforts to preserve peace in the Far East and the world." He saw the joint role extended to "safeguarding the national independence and rights of the Asian people"—a formula with pointed implications concerning Peking's campaign for Taiwan. Speaking of the Soviet assistance program, Chou expressed gratitude to Soviet technicians and praised the Russian people as China's "most trustworthy and most faithful friends."[33] By contrast, Khrushchev, speaking on 13 October at the Peking airport prior to his departure, avoided mentioning Soviet responsibility in the Far East. He declared that the Sino-Soviet agreements helped to "develop and consolidate the impregnable friendship between us and strengthen world peace," and that Sino-Soviet unity was a "powerful factor in world peace."[34] Khrushchev's remarks at the Yudin banquet at which Chou spoke were publicized neither by Moscow nor by Peking.

At the same time, Khrushchev's National Day protestations of Soviet sympathy and support for the Chinese communists' determination to liberate Taiwan were echoed neither in Chinese nor Soviet comment. The issue was avoided entirely in the *Pravda* and *People's Daily* editorials marking the conclusion of the Soviet delegation's visit as well as in speeches made prior to the group's departure. Chou's 12 October speech at the Soviet embassy banquet in Peking was typical in that it emphasized Sino-Soviet cooperation in broad terms and voiced gratitude for Soviet aid without reference to Taiwan. Discussion of Taiwan in the 11 October Sino-Soviet joint declaration on Asian affairs was limited to denunciation of U.S. "occupation" of the island as "incompatible with . . . peace in the Far East," with no mention of liberation. The 13 October *People's Daily* editorial on the declaration did not refer to Taiwan, and *Pravda*'s editorial of the same date merely reiterated the declaration as given.[35]

PRC Reaction to the U.S.-ROC Treaty

Several weeks after Khrushchev's departure from China, a major resurgence in Peking's Taiwan liberation propaganda campaign was precipitated by the formal signing of the U.S.-ROC defense treaty on 2 December 1954.[36] The liberation campaign reached an unusually high intensity in the last week of December. The Peking session of the Second National Committee of the Chinese People's Political Consultative Conference (CPPCC) in late December prompted many speeches on the issue and raised the level of attention given to Taiwan to the unprecedented peak of 24 percent of all items in Peking radio's domestic service coverage. The December resurgence of the campaign even surpassed the intense propaganda efforts of the previous summer. In broadcasts beamed abroad, mention of Taiwan rose promptly and appreciably with the signing of the U.S.-Chiang treaty. The peak in late December coincided with the CPPCC resolutions and denunciations of the pact.

Peking criticism of the pact was bellicose from the outset, reminiscent of propaganda concerning the Chinese volunteers' entry into the Korean War. The treaty was categorized as a new manifestation of U.S. aggression and a challenge to PRC sovereignty.[37] The signing was assailed as a predatory act flouting international law, violating the Cairo and Potsdam decisions, contravening the United Nations charter, and openly proclaiming American intent to wage war to prevent China from liberating her own territory. Demonstrating Chinese willingness to allow the Taiwan issue to disrupt Peking's concurrent efforts to win friends abroad, Peking repeatedly attacked Britain for complicity with the American "warmongers."[38] Chou En-lai, in his first reference to the treaty in an address on 8 December, was critical of the broad sector of international opinion that wished to see a peaceful settlement of the Taiwan issue, even at the expense of Peking's claims. He asserted that "some people wish that the Chinese people would forget the lessons of history and accept the status quo of the U.S. occupation of Taiwan."[39] Editorials in the leading papers echoed Chou's 8 December refusal to accept neutralization, trusteeship, or any solution short of Taiwan's reunion with the mainland. Chou restated this refusal in his 21 December speech before the CPPCC, and Peking publicists seconded the CPPCC resolution's denunciation of the U.S.-Chiang treaty as part of a "war plan" that must be opposed by "all nationals and peoples who are for peace."[40]

Peking observers decried the pact as a manifestation of an American, Asian, and global policy of war preparation and provocation. Ridiculing the treaty's allegedly defensive motivation, NCNA on 10 January 1955 cited a "secret note" from Secretary of State John Foster Dulles to the nationalist government assuring Taipei that the United States would not prevent a nationalist attack on the mainland. NCNA maintained that this communication proved that the pact was not intended as a brake on Chiang.[41] Concurrenly, the Chinese communists claimed that the United States planned to form a "Northeast Asia Treaty Organization" along the lines of SEATO. They averred that a primary mission of the American envoy then visiting the Far

East, Adm. Arthur William Radford, was to bring together "traitor Chiang Kai-shek's group, Japan, and the Syngman Rhee clique in a Northeast Asian aggressive alliance."[42]

By early 1955, the prolonged Taiwan campaign had made clear to the United States, the world at large, and the domestic Chinese audience that the PRC leaders would not accept a permanent alienation of Taiwan from mainland control. Concurrent PRC-ROC air and sea battles, artillery duels, and other military action had shown Washington that Peking was not unwilling to confront U.S.-backed forces in this vital area, if necessary, and would even directly challenge American-supported ROC troops with armed attack. Thus, Washington realized that its continued support for a forward ROC military presence in the area could run the risk of invoking a sharp PRC response.

However, the campaign clearly had not weakened American resolve to maintain a solid front in defense of the Republic of China. U.S.-ROC ties were solidified with the mutual defense treaty of December and the passage of the Formosa resolution by the U.S. Congress in January 1955. Also, continued hostile Chinese comment and military action had alienated China from broad sectors of world opinion, which were calling for a negotiated settlement of the issue. By continuing the campaign, the communists also ran the risk of triggering an outbreak of Sino-American armed hostilities. This prospect was of particular concern to the PRC leaders at this time because of persisting Soviet unwillingness to back China's drive for goals in Asia.

Thus, Peking, by early 1955, was faced with an increasingly counterproductive campaign over Taiwan, a potentially dangerous confrontation with Washington, no active public support from its primary international ally, and increased alienation from world sympathy. In this context, the Chinese clearly had reason to shift to a more moderate stance when they were presented with the opportunity by the American offer in mid-January 1955 of a cease-fire on Taiwan. Peking responded to the U.S. proposal with criticism but indirectly signaled interest in the offer by gradually reducing PRC demands concerning Taiwan.

The 18 January American cease-fire proposal prompted a formal statement by Chou En-lai on 24 January. He took issue with U.S. plans for engineering "a conspiracy for a so-called cease-fire through the United Nations," restated that no foreign body or nation had the right to interfere in Chinese internal affairs, and added that the PRC could not possibly agree to a cease-fire with the "traitorous Chiang Kai-shek clique."[43] However, Chou's statement signaled a reduction in Peking's heretofore uncompromising demands over the Taiwan issue. Specifically, Peking had emphasized throughout the campaign of 1954 that

44

there could be no reduction of tension in the Taiwan area until the United States left the area and the island was liberated and returned to the mainland. Indeed, the last part of Chou's statement on 24 January reaffirmed this line, stating, "To safeguard China's sovereignty and territorial integrity, to safeguard the security of China and peace in the Far East, the Chinese people must liberate Taiwan and the United States must stop interfering in China's internal affairs and withdraw all its armed forces from Taiwan Straits."[44] But, earlier in the message, Chou significantly separated the discussion of Taiwan's liberation from the issue of U.S. withdrawal, and he stressed only the latter factor as a precondition for easing tension in the area. He affirmed; "It is very obvious that the source of this tension [in the Far East] is the United States and not China. This tension will be eliminated as a matter of course, if the United States stops its intervention in China's internal affairs and withdraws all its armed forces from Taiwan and the Taiwan Straits."[45]

This line of thought was also evident in a *People's Daily* editorial of 2 February. Asserting that the Chinese "will certainly liberate Taiwan," the editorial focused on "the United States' occupation of China's Taiwan" as "the root of tension in the Far East." It affirmed that "an easing of the situation in the Taiwan area and the Far East can be brought about only by halting American intervention in China's internal affairs, stopping American military operations which are creating tension in the Taiwan area, and withdrawing all American armed forces from the Taiwan area."[46]

By mid-March the volume of comment on Taiwan dropped to the low level sustained prior to the signing of the U.S.-ROC treaty—5½ percent of news programs broadcast to China's domestic audience.[47] Moreover, a 7 March *People's Daily* editorial on the Taiwan situation —the first released in over two weeks—took a position of notable restraint, in sharp contrast to the previous bellicosity characteristic of Peking's observations on the issue. For example, the liberation cause was described in unusually restrained terms: "For China to liberate Taiwan is an act of simple justice to safeguard her national independence, sovereignty and territorial integrity."[48] On the other hand, a 12 February editorial had stated: "The 600 million people of China are firmly resolved to liberate Taiwan, Penghu, and other offshore islands. This is their sacred struggle in defending China's territorial sovereignty and independence. This solemn resolve is unshakeable and unalterable. All U.S. armed forces must be withdrawn from Taiwan and the Taiwan Straits. The liberation of Taiwan is China's internal affair and no foreign interference is permissible."[49]

The 7 March editorial also noted Chinese support for a negotiated settlement, particularly an 18 February Soviet proposal that an international conference of twelve nations be convened to settle the Taiwan problem. It also affirmed for the first time Peking's support for Soviet Foreign Minister Molotov's contention that withdrawal of American forces would bring peace to the Taiwan area. Speaking on 8 February before the Supreme Soviet, Molotov had averred that "the United States must withdraw from Formosa and the Formosa Strait all its armed forces, including its air forces. Then military actions will cease in the Far East and peace will prevail."[50] *People's Daily* on 7 March declared, "As the Chinese government has repeatedly pointed out, the Taiwan situation *can be eased at once* if only the United States withdraws its armed forces from the Taiwan area."[51] Previous Peking statements had not been so explicit in avowing that U.S. withdrawal from Taiwan would, in itself, ease the tension.

As soon as the United States and China had signaled—by late January 1955—their willingness to settle their confrontation over Taiwan without resort to force and had thereby eased the crisis situation in the area, the Soviet Union began to show more support for PRC interests in Asia. Specifically, Peking's consistent contention that the Sino-Soviet alliance represented the reliable "bulwark of peace in the Far East and throughout the world" was finally endorsed by Moscow comment on the 14 February anniversary of the alliance.[52] The Chinese communists were also able to speak more freely regarding Soviet support for the Chinese goal of liberating Taiwan. *People's Daily* of 14 February carried an article that pointed out that "the righteous support given us by the Soviet government and people in our struggle to liberate Taiwan and safeguard Asian peace gives us great encouragement and confidence in victory."[53] Kuo Mo-jo cited a promise of support made by Nikolai A. Bulganin, presidium chief, on 9 February as a definite official commitment of the Soviet government.[54] At the same time, Peking's stress on broad support in the USSR for the PRC position on Taiwan was typified by NCNA's citation of the Soviet Chargé d'Affaires in Peking who observed on 13 February that "the Soviet people warmly desire the great Chinese people to exercise their sovereign rights and liberate Taiwan."[55]

CHAPTER FOUR

The Ambassadorial Talks in Geneva, 1955–57

Chou En-lai's call for Sino-American talks over the Taiwan problem—voiced at the April 1955 conference of nonaligned nations
in Bandung—prompted immediate American diplomatic maneuvering,
which resulted in the commencement of formal ambassadorial talks in
Geneva on 1 August 1955. In view of the international circumstances
and pressures that encouraged the Chinese leaders to resume direct
communication with Washington, it was not surprising that Peking
strove diligently to use the talks to achieve forward movement in Sino-
American relations. As in Yenan during the mid-1940s, the Chinese
leaders were confronted with the bleak prospect of continued heavy
U.S.-backed pressure opposing them, with only weak international
backing from the USSR, their major ally. They adopted a policy similar to that pursued in the 1940s, having decided that, once again, it
would be to their advantage to establish a cordial relationship with
the United States. Peking again compromised previously rigid CCP
ideological opposition to an accommodation with "U.S. imperialism"
and put aside memories of past bitter experiences received at the hands
of the Americans. The initiative signaled a willingness to adopt a flexible position over fundamental Chinese national interests, including
the recovery of Taiwan.

The Chinese had been careful to separate the question of U.S.
"occupation" of Taiwan from that of the "liberation" of the island, in
order to smooth the way for the opening of talks with Washington.
During the early months of the ambassadorial sessions, the communists endeavored to encourage forward movement by offering several
draft proposals on Taiwan that would have accommodated American
demands at the expense of Chinese sovereign claims there. A number
of Chinese proposals either explicitly or implicitly acceded to the

47

American demand in the sessions that Peking sign an accord renouncing the use of force in the Taiwan area. This concession came despite past Chinese statements that had insisted that the American demand was a severe infringement on PRC sovereignty over the island.

Washington's more limited intentions were made amply clear by the U.S. treatment of two issues discussed at Geneva. First, the United States exploited the only announced agreement reached in the talks—an accord on the mutual return of citizens, which was made public on 10 September 1955—in a way designed to embarrass the Chinese and to pressure Peking to accede to American demands that all detained Americans should be allowed to leave China immediately. Second, the Americans repeatedly demanded that Peking agree to renounce the use of force in the Taiwan area, a rigid proposal already known to be unacceptable to the People's Republic of China. In short, there was a major contradiction between the two countries' approach to the ambassadorial talks.

U.S., PRC Objectives

American policy pronouncements and actions in East Asia as well as the memoirs of U.S. officials active at the time demonstrate that American intentions in the talks with the Chinese were carefully limited. The two sides had earlier engaged in low-level talks in Geneva at the time of the 1954 foreign ministers' conference there and had attempted to resolve the problem of repatriation of detained citizens. But the talks had made little progress. Thus, one of the primary American objectives in the new round of talks was to ensure the speedy release of the detained Americans, including those who had been convicted of crimes and were serving sentences in Chinese jails.

Moreover, the United States viewed participation in low-level bilateral talks with Peking as less distasteful than being forced to accept Chinese participation in a planned big-power summit in Geneva in July 1955. Secretary Dulles reportedly feared that the big-power summit would mark a repeat of the successful Chinese participation in the 1954 foreign ministers' conference, which he judged as having been unfavorable to American interests.[1] It was Dulles's hope that American agreement to formal ambassadorial talks with China could be used to counter demands that Peking be represented at the 1955 summit.[2] He was also aware of the international apprehension and the uneasiness among some American political leaders at this time concerning the possibility of serious Sino-American confrontation in the Taiwan area. The commencement of the ambassadorial talks served to ease tension and thus reduce this concern.

Another U.S. objective centered on achieving a PRC renunciation of the use of force in the Taiwan area.[3] By this time, the United States judged that there was little likelihood that the Chinese communist government would fall or that nationalist forces under Chiang Kai-shek would regain control of significant areas on the mainland. Thus, Washington now wanted the situation in East Asia to stabilize. It wanted to halt what the United States saw as Chinese communist expansion, in a way that would not place a financial burden on the American taxpayers. A PRC pledge to forgo forceful tactics in the Taiwan area would have gone far toward helping achieve these ends.[4]

PRC initiatives during the talks showed that Peking's goals in Geneva were much more wide-ranging than those of Washington. The communists' aspirations involved problems stemming from China's extreme isolation. Having no strong foreign backing and facing continued pressure from the world's greatest power, Peking felt compelled to take the bull by the horns and deal directly with Washington. Since Moscow had shown that it would not help Peking out of its predicament by actively supporting PRC interests in Asia, the Chinese attempted to persuade the United States to withdraw its pressure of its own accord. Having dealt with the United States and John Foster Dulles in the past, the Chinese communists were well aware that this new approach could be a frustrating and slow process, but they also judged that they had little better alternative at this time. At the very least, China's amicable participation in the ambassadorial talks assured the continuation of the sessions. The PRC thus attained de facto recognition by the United States and a new level of international prestige. The Chinese communists' stance also demonstrated to a world-wide audience that they were now willing to deal peacefully with all nations, even former enemies, thus helping to alter China's prevailing image as an aggressive power.

The Chinese almost certainly realized that to bring about forward movement in the talks they might have to de-emphasize past concerns over Taiwan. In fact, they had already compromised their position on Taiwan in preparation for the talks. Peking still retained hope that improved relations with the United States might cause Washington to reduce its commitment to Chiang Kai-shek and thereby improve prospects for the reunification of Taiwan with the mainland. Indeed, the talks did serve to unnerve Taipei and to inject a degree of mistrust and suspicion in the ROC-U.S. relationship.

Peking's conciliatory policy was anticipated by Chou En-lai's discussion of Sino-American relations in his 30 July 1955 report to the National People's Congress two days before the start of the Geneva talks.[5] Chou underlined Chinese interest in peaceful coexistence and accommodation with the United States. He also pointed to PRC positions that were later to surface in the course of the Geneva discussions.

Chou routinely cited the Taiwan area as the "most tense in the Far East" from the time of the Korean armistice and the agreement on Indochina and automatically placed full blame for this state of affairs on American interference and occupation.[6] On the question of Sino-American confrontation in the Taiwan area stemming from the U.S. "occuaption" of Taiwan, Chou affirmed that tensions could be eased through negotiations. Regarding the question of Peking's "liberation" of Taiwan and the area's reunification with the mainland, Chou declared that Peking was prepared to seek liberation by peaceful means. He stated that, provided the United States did not interfere in China's internal affairs, the probability of the peaceful liberation of Taiwan would continue to increase. Chou even pushed for negotiations with "the responsible local authorities of Taiwan," calling on them to work with the central government in Peking to plan for Taiwan's peaceful liberation. He made it quite clear that Peking would never accept any sort of "two Chinas" settlement.[7]

Concerning the ambassadorial talks, Chou was optimistic that agreement could be reached on the first agenda item, which dealt with the mutual repatriation of detained citizens. Chou averred that "the number of American civilians in China is small, and their question can be easily settled." At the same time, he mildly criticized alleged obstruction by the United States of several thousand Chinese in the United States who wished to return to the Chinese mainland.[8]

Regarding the other agenda item, which involved "discussion and settlement of certain other practical matters now at issue between both sides," Chou emphasized Peking's desire for rapid forward movement in Sino-American relations. Noting Chinese opposition to the presence of American forces in Taiwan, the U.S.-sponsored trade embargo against China, and unspecified "foreign" subversion against China, Chou affirmed that in order to remove these sources of tension, "it is necessary first of all that China and the United States should display sincerity in negotiations, that the two sides establish contacts to increase mutual understanding and trust." He added that "China, for her part, in accordance with its consistent stand for the relaxation of tensions, will endeavor to make the forthcoming Sino-American talks at the ambassadorial level pave the way for further negotiations between China and the United States."[9]

The First Issue: Mutual Return of Detained Citizens

The first sessions of the talks were taken up with the issue of repatriation of citizens, which was discussed for several weeks until an agreement was finally announced following the fourteenth session on 10 September. The agreed announcement elicited positive comment from both the Chinese and American administrations.[10] However, China's subsequent manner of implementing the agreement quickly met with strong public criticism from the American side.[11] The criticism centered on China's contention that the small number of American citizens who had been convicted of crimes and were serving sentences in China would be released only at the discretion of Chinese judicial authorities. The United States demanded an immediate release of all Americans in China, prisoners or not. The repatriation dispute subsequently took on great significance for the future course of the talks, since the American side at first refused to consider other subjects until after it was certain that all Americans had been released. Finally, the Americans reluctantly relented on this point. Washington also persistently criticized China's stance on the repatriation issue in later sessions of the talks.[12]

Contrary to the standard U.S. interpretation of this issue, contained in Kenneth Young's study of the ambassadorial talks,[13] it seems clear that the Chinese felt justified in their position and were not attempting to trick the Americans or to delay the talks over this question. The Chinese had already signaled the importance they placed on encouraging progress in Sino-American relations, and they certainly realized that perfidy in the early sessions would not achieve this end. Although there were no significant public disclosures by either side on the substance of the ambassadorial talks prior to the 10 September announcement, Peking later insisted in authoritative statements that the Chinese side had made clear to the American side that all American citizens who had been convicted of crimes and sentenced under Chinese law could not be immediately released; they would be subject first to Chinese judicial procedures and review before they would be eligible for release.[14] Denying that Peking had made this distinction, the United States supported its call for immediate release by referring to the English-language text of the agreed announcement, which said, "The People's Republic of China recognizes that Americans in the People's Republic of China who desire to return to the United States are entitled to do so and declares that it has adopted and will further adopt appropriate measures so that they can *expeditiously* exercise their right to return."[15]

U.S. spokesmen affirmed that "the Americans sincerely believed that the agreement meant unconditionally that all the Americans in China, including those in jail . . . would be immediately released and returned to the United States in September 1955."[16] The United States interpreted *expeditiously* to mean immediately and denied that the Chinese had done anything in the talks prior to 10 September to make them think otherwise.[17] The Chinese, on the other hand, interpreted *expeditiously* to mean, perhaps, "as soon as possible" and thus attempted to retain the option of continuing to detain, after the date of the announcement, at least some Americans who had been convicted of crimes.

A brief account of the negotiation of the agreed announcement contained in a book of memoirs by Robert Ekvall, the chief U.S. interpreter at the Geneva talks, indicates clearly that the Chinese, in fact, had told the Americans prior to 10 September that they had no intention of releasing all Americans immediately. Ekvall noted that in preparing the English- and Chinese-language versions of the agreed announcement, the Chinese negotiators groped for language that would have allowed Peking to delay the release of some Americans. He stated that, while the Chinese were successful in choosing language for the Chinese version of the announcement which permitted some delay, they chose the word *expeditiously* in the English version under the illusion that it too would reflect their intention to delay some releases. Ekvall's account vividly demonstrates that the American side was indeed well aware of Chinese intentions on the prisoner issue prior to 10 September but that the United States chose to ignore this fact in pursuing a heavy-handed propaganda campaign pressing for the release of all Americans. It also shows that the Chinese did strictly carry out their commitment under the terms of the Chinese-language text of the agreed announcement.[18] According to Ekvall:

> One item of critical importance in the agreement was when and how soon the civilians would "exercise their right to return." Our aim was the immediate, . . . *but the stubborn refusal of the Chinese ruled out immediacy for all, though promising it for some.* . . .
>
> In the English text originally proposed by the United States negotiator, the phrase used was "promptly to exercise their right to return." A Chinese rendering of the word "promptly" was a matter of some difficulty. The word for "promptly" in the most common Chinese use also means "immediately" and *we knew that would not be accepted.* . . . In the English text which the Chinese proposed the phrase "as soon as possible" was one we could not accept. Although "soon" was what we wanted, we did not want it dependent on the "possible" which introduced a new concept, not of time but of possibility. The attention

of both sides then focused on the term used in the Chinese text proposed by the Chinese. It was a compound, CHIN-SU, CHIN, utmost, and SU, fast. It seemed to embody just what we were seeking and I proposed as its English equivalent "very quickly."

The Chinese felt constrained to consult among themselves and after some discussion countered with their own suggestion. . . . In this instance they should have left well enough alone, for they suggested "expeditiously." It was the best of words for us. In addition to the idea of "quickly," *which was all the Chinese had in mind,* it had connotations of efficacy and efficient action far beyond anything we had sought to gain in the word promptly." It was strong, and *as the club they offered us to use "expeditiously" was heavier than we could have hoped for. The weight of the phrase "expeditiously to exercise their right to return" has pressed strongly ever since on a world opinion that still knows English better than Chinese and which has never noticed, if it ever heard, that CHIN-SU only means "utmost speed" with no overtones of efficacy and efficient action.*[19]

The United States subsequently focused on the English-language text of the agreement and demanded the immediate release of all American citizens. Washington began to charge that Peking's delay demonstrated perfidy, disregard for agreements, and lack of concern for human affairs.[20] The Americans of course realized that Peking's interpretation of the agreement gave it a loophole allowing continued detention of some U.S. prisoners. This would have provided an important source of Chinese leverage in later bargaining with the United States. Indeed, Peking could have used the release of American prisoners to prompt U.S. agreement to further improvement in Sino-American relations—something the United States opposed.[21]

The American charges did not alter China's position, but they did demonstrate to Peking that the United States would not compromise its stern posture in the talks. Chinese spokesmen also judged that the U.S. demands were a reflection of its refusal to recognize and deal with China as an equal.[22] The United States was seen as unjustifiably attempting to achieve its ends by holding Peking up to international censure over the issue and by demanding that Peking release American prisoners. The Chinese judged that the American demands were not only unreasonable but also offensive to Peking's recently established national security. Viewed from a historical perspective—and the past was very much in the minds of Chinese leaders of the time—the American demands for release were comparable to the demands made by imperialist powers for special legal treatment in China during the nineteenth and twentieth centuries. The Chinese communists, who had risen to power because they were able to portray themselves as true protectors of China's national sovereignty and rights against outside powers, not surprisingly, were unwilling to capitulate publicly in the face of such affronts to China's national integrity.

The Second Issue: Renunciation of the Use of Force on Taiwan

Divergent Sino-American interpretations of the 10 September agreed announcement on the repatriation issue soon became a bone of contention in the talks, but Peking continued efforts to encourage bilateral agreement on other issues. At the fifteenth session on 14 September, the Chinese side proposed a discussion of the U.S. economic embargo against China.[23] Peking was later to raise this issue on several other occasions in the talks, but it never received a positive response from the Americans.

More importantly, the Chinese also proposed at the fifteenth session a major initiative calling for an agreement to discuss the Taiwan issue at a higher-level conference between the American and Chinese foreign ministers.[24] This proposal was a logical extension of Chou En-lai's offer for Sino-American talks during the Bandung conference and his comments in the 30 July 1955 report to the National People's Congress. Talks with Dulles would have allowed the Chinese their best opportunity to date to establish a workable relationship with the United States. And such meetings would have added considerably to China's international prestige, while undermining the stature of the Chiang Kai-shek government. The Chinese imposed no preconditions for the sessions.

Dulles had no intention of adding to Peking's world stature, which he felt had already received an undesirable boost as a result of Chinese participation in major diplomatic events over the past year. He was determined to keep the talks limited to the ambassadorial level. Dulles was nonetheless compelled to counter the Chinese initiative, which had prompted considerable interest in the United States and abroad.[25] In response, therefore, the American side issued a proposal calling for the mutual renunciation of the use of force in the Taiwan area and made acceptance of the proposal a precondition for further progress in the talks.[26] The proposal was in line with Dulles's longstanding position that the United States could not agree to negotiate differences with the Chinese when American forces and those of their allies were still under the "threat" of Chinese communist attack.

Peking had made clear on a number of occasions Chinese unwillingness to accept such an agreement, calling it a formal restriction of PRC sovereignty over Chinese territory.[27] Thus, the American side almost certainly entertained little hope that the Chinese would accept its new plan. By making acceptance of the proposal a precondition for further progress in the talks, the Americans were, in effect, stalling the discussions. Yet, Washington managed to avoid blame for the stalemate in the talks, since the U.S. "renunciation of force" proposal seemed reasonable to the American people and to a large body of world opinion. Thus Dulles's maneuver adroitly neutralized Peking's request for a higher-level conference and again placed the responsibility for making progress in the negotiations in the hands of the Chinese.

Peking opposed the new American proposal because it confused the international and internal aspects of the Taiwan problem. As Chou had stated on 30 July and on a number of other occasions, the Chinese were willing to deal with the United States over their bilateral confrontation in the area, but there could be no accommodation reached at the expense of Peking's claim to sovereignty over Taiwan. PRC acceptance of the American proposal—which specifically called for renunciation of any use of force in the Taiwan area—would have meant that Peking would be recognizing formally a limitation to its claim to be the legitimate ruler of the island. The Chinese thereafter would not have been able to use force in their attempts to liberate Taiwan, an activity they considered to be strictly an internal affair.

The U.S. proposal, which was formally offered in the talks on 8 October, was not without some benefit for Peking.[28] For example, it granted the Chinese government greater security vis-à-vis the large number of American-backed forces in this area, easing Peking's keen concern over possible U.S.-supported offensives by Chiang Kai-shek's forces. But the proposal clearly had a negative impact on other important communist interests. By endorsing the plan, Peking would have been recognizing the existence of two Chinas. The Chinese government was well aware that unless it maintained the option of using force to liberate Taiwan, it would have only a very remote chance of gaining control of the island, completing the Chinese civil war, and dismantling the rival Chiang Kai-shek government. Thus, Chinese agreement to the American proposal would have marked a formal endorsement of a Taiwan arrangement permanently compromising basic goals of the Chinese communist movement.

Peking was willing to accommodate the United States to the extent of accepting a "renuncitation of force" agreement that avoided an explicit compromise of its claim to Taiwan. The Chinese were anxious to get beyond this hurdle and move forward in the talks. Thus, they proposed measures to accommodate the American demands over Taiwan. Linked to the Chinese proposal of 27 October 1955 calling for an agreement that did not refer specifically to Taiwan was a pledge to hold a Sino-American foreign ministers' conference on relaxing tension in the Taiwan area.[29] Peking's offer also referred to a promise to avoid the use of force against "the territorial integrity and political independence of any state." The latter may have been designed by Peking to challenge the American "use of force" against Chinese territorial integrity involved in the stationing of U.S. troops on Taiwan. At any rate, because of the passage regarding the foreign ministers' conference and the lack of specific reference to the repudiation of Chinese military activity in the Taiwan area, the Chinese offer was promptly rejected by the United States.

Peking then offered its most conciliatory proposal yet concerning the Taiwan issue. On 1 December, the Chinese side presented a terse proposal that called for the two countries to pledge to seek a peaceful resolution to bilateral disputes, without resorting to the threat of or use of force, adding that the two ambassadors should continue their talks "to seek such practical and feasible means for the realization of this common desire."[30] By evading the issue of Taiwan, the proposal avoided setting any formal limitation to what Peking saw as its sovereign rights. Yet, the vague wording of the agreement made it subject to interpretation whether or not the Chinese would have been able to retain the right to use force in Taiwan. Indeed, the proposal called for a Sino-American "renunciation of force" declaration that would have been basically compatible with U.S. interests in the area.

Unlike the 27 October proposal, there was no clause in the December proposal which could have been pointed to by Peking as limiting the right of the United States to station troops in the Taiwan area. Thus, any effort by Peking to even threaten to use force in the Taiwan area could have been challenged by the United States on the basis of the agreement. The Americans could have maintained that such PRC action—threatening American forces stationed in and around Taiwan —repudiated the understanding between the two countries that force would not be used. Washington could have justified the presence of its forces in the area as legal under terms of the U.S. defense treaty and other agreements signed by the "legal" ruler of the area, Taipei. Of course, Peking could have claimed that the presence of the American forces in Taiwan was illegal, but it would have had nothing in the agreement to point to in support of its position. Inasmuch as the bulk of world opinion had consistently favored peaceful settlement of the Taiwan dispute—as opposed to the use of force in the area—it seemed obvious that an American position opposing Peking's resort to military action would have enjoyed wide international backing, while Peking would have been able to find few allies for its militant position. The result would have been the maintenance of the status quo in the Taiwan area, in line with American interests.

Later Chinese comment disclosed that the 1 December proposal for continued talks by the ambassadors to seek practical means of negotiating Sino-American differences did not meet with American approval.[31] According to the Chinese, Washington had judged that the passage implied U.S. agreement to future higher-level PRC-U.S. negotiations along the lines of the foreign ministers' conference proposed earlier by Peking. However, the text of the agreement—though not ruling out such a foreign ministers' meeting—committed the United States to nothing on this score.

In spite of Peking's conciliatory attitude, Washington stuck to its demand that any declaration prohibiting the use of force must specifically refer to the Taiwan area.[32] Washington's stance underscored well the obstinacy of the American position during the talks. It was evident that U.S. agreement to Peking's 1 December proposal would have helped stabilize the Taiwan area, but the United States refused it, making demands concerning Taiwan that it knew Peking could not accept. Such behavior suggests that Washington at that time was more interested in blocking further progress in the talks than in reaching an agreement with Peking on stabilizing East Asia.

The Chinese nevertheless persisted in efforts to meet the U.S. position halfway. Peking media on 4 March 1956 publicized a PRC foreign ministry statement on the ambassadorial talks that for the first time indicated China's willingness to agree specifically to a mutual renunciation of the use of force in the Taiwan area.[33] The agreement was to be made on the condition that the United States consent to hold higher-level talks. A later statement maintained that if the Americans desired prohibition of PRC military activity in Taiwan, then they "must agree to provide specifically in the announcement for the holding of a Sino-American conference of foreign ministers." This stance was formally put forth in an 11 May 1956 Chinese proposal in the talks that linked the renunciation of the use of force in Taiwan with preparations for a foreign ministers' conference. That draft contained a passage affirming principles of "mutual respect for territorial integrity and sovereignty and noninterference in each other's affairs," which may have been designed in part to undercut the legitimacy of the American military presence in Taiwan.[34] Such conditions were not contained in the authoritative statement of 4 March, however. Neither probe met with any success in the United States.

Peking's Altered Approach to the Talks

When it became clear after the first year of negotiations that there was little likelihood of any progress being made concerning major Sino-American issues such as Taiwan, the Chinese still persisted in efforts to find some common ground for agreement with the United States. It was clear that many of China's earlier expectations and aspirations regarding the sessions were not to be achieved. For one thing, the negotiations had not significantly improved China's international image, in part because persisting American charges over the prisoner repatriation question had branded the Chinese leaders as inhumane and untrustworthy. Washington's claims regarding Peking's refusal to renounce the use of force had meanwhile reinforced widespread international suspicion of Peking's alleged aggressive designs in Asia. At the same time, the continuing lack of meaningful progress in the talks, together with persisting U.S. assurances and material aid to the Chinese nationalist government, served to frustrate previous Chinese communist hopes that the talks would substantially upset the Chiang Kai-shek government's position. Perhaps of most importance, the general failure of the discussions along with the continuation of America's containment policy against China seriously diminished Peking's earlier hope that it might be able to establish a working relationship with Washington and reduce the American presence in Asia. Not only was Dulles insistent on an intransigent U.S. position in the talks, but his continued efforts to reinforce ROC military forces and to solidify military-political power around China's periphery showed no signs of abating during the Geneva talks.[35]

In fact, Peking eventually perceived Dulles's policy as one of using military force and intimidation in order to coerce the Chinese to accept American demands in the ambassadorial talks. In an interview in *Life* magazine published in mid-January 1956, Dulles dwelt on the efficacy of using the threat of American nuclear power to counter communist expansion in Asia.[36] Peking protested against Dulles's stance in an 18 January foreign ministry statement, which connected Dulles's remarks with the U.S. efforts in Geneva to force China to agree to a renunciation of the use of force in the Taiwan area. The statement noted that while pushing the American proposal at the talks, the secretary of state "again openly cried out recently that in order to hold on to China's territory and infringe upon China's sovereignty he had no scruples about starting atomic war. The U.S. aggressors imagined that this would frighten the Chinese people into giving up their own sovereign rights."[37]

Faced with Washington's unyielding position, Peking was forced to try to make use of the talks in other ways. One effort centered on emphasizing the negative implications of the Sino-American talks for the Chiang government on Taiwan. The Chinese focused on the U.S. discussion of Taiwanese matters in the talks and on the U.S. military presence in Taiwan as evidence that Chiang Kai-shek only remained in power because of support from the United States. They warned Chiang that the United States might withdraw its support from him at any time, and they called on him to begin cooperating with the PRC before it was too late.

Most notably, Chou En-lai's 30 January 1956 report to the Chinese People's Political Consultative Conference (CPPCC) made a major appeal for PRC-KMT cooperation against the United States.[38] He promised leniency for both military and political personnel of the Kuomintang "no matter who they may be or how serious their past crimes were" if only they would now assist in the completion of Taiwan's "peaceful liberation." This report represented the first public bid by the communists for political collaboration with what they had always called the traitor clique. Reflecting a new approach designed to encourage Taipei to cooperate with Peking, Chou omitted all usual references to the tyrannical and traitorous nature of Chiang's regime and spoke of Taiwan as being "under the armed rule of a foreign power." Invoking the "common patriotic duty" of the Chinese Communist Party and the Kuomintang to throw off the foreign yoke, he recalled past instances of cooperation and had hopes that Taiwan would now rejoin the mainland.

Chou subsequently told the press in Phnom Penh on 1 December 1956 that even Chiang Kai-shek could have an important PRC post, if he were to assist in the peaceful liberation of Taiwan. This statement was not reported in PRC media.[39] In remarks to the press in India on 6 December, carried by NCNA, Chou sidestepped a newsman's query about his remarks concerning Chiang in Phnom Penh, stating simply that "Chiang and his group are Chinese and we as Chinese do not like to see a permanent split among the Chinese people . . . that is why we are making every effort to bring about the peaceful liberation of Taiwan."[40] On 10 December Chou remained equivocal about whether he had specifically offered Chiang a government post. According to NCNA, he told the press in Calcutta that "what actually happened was that one correspondent asked if Chiang would be offered a minister's post. I said a minister's post is too low." Chou then added, "If Taiwan is restored to China, then Chiang Kai-shek would have made a contribution and he could stay in a part of his fatherland according to his wish."[41] Peking media had not previously reflected any specific promises to Chiang Kai-shek, though coverage had not signaled him out for abuse since Chou's January 1956 appeal. Without mentioning Chiang by name, Chou, on 28 June 1956, informed the National People's Congress that "appropriate jobs" would be waiting for those "responsible Kuomintang military and political personnel" who "play an important role in the cause of peaceful liberation of Taiwan."[42]

In a report to the CPPCC on 5 March 1957 concerning Peking's foreign affairs, Chou elaborated further on the need for Kuomintang cooperation with the PRC against the United States. He reiterated that Peking's goal was to attain the peaceful liberation of Taiwan, and he called upon all KMT military and administrative personnel on Taiwan, including Chiang Kai-shek, to contribute to China's unification. Claiming that progress continued to be made toward liberating Taiwan, Chou denounced alleged U.S. attempts to intensify its military control of the island. He charged that the United States was seeking to overthrow the present "authorities on Taiwan" and to replace them by an even more compliant pro-American faction. He asserted that awareness of this aim will enable "patriotic Chinese to see more clearly the U.S. attempts at enslavement."[43]

Meanwhile, Peking also began in 1956 to probe for common ground with the United States over relatively minor issues involving unofficial exchanges.[44] Thus, in the summer and fall of 1956, Peking encouraged American journalists to visit China and formally approved the applications for travel to China of about a score of important American media representatives.[45] Peking formalized this initiative during the ambassadorial talks in September. A PRC foreign ministry statement issued on 16 October 1956 publicized for the first time Peking's 22 September 1956 proposal made during the talks calling for the promotion of Sino-American contacts. After repeating routine Chinese charges that the United States was unjustifiably "dragging out" the Sino-American talks, the statement censured Washington for refusing to discuss the PRC proposal to "promote mutual understanding, . . . resume the traditional friendship between the peoples of China and the United States, . . . [and] eliminate the existing barriers interfering with the freedom of mutual contacts and cultural exchange."[46]

However, the Chinese proposals continued to run up against the American position that contacts could not be considered until the U.S. proposal concerning the use of force in Taiwan was accepted and until a few Americans still held in China were released. American policy makers were well aware that the Chinese in the past had managed to gain favorable publicity and greater international stature as a result of favorable reports from U.S. newsmen in China. The effects of Edgar Snow's reports in the 1930s and those of visiting American journalists in Yenan in the 1940s were still fresh in their memories. Such results were incompatible with Dulles's conception of how China should be handled by the United States in the 1950s.

After several months of persistent American refusal to move ahead, even on minor issues in the talks, the Chinese, by early 1957, could find little reason for continuing the talks. At bottom, Peking seemed to persist in the sessions chiefly to avoid the onus of being the one to break them off. And it wanted to keep open a channel of communication to high-level officials in Washington. Referring to the ambassadorial talks during a 10 December 1956 press conference in Calcutta reported by NCNA, Chou En-lai called attention to Chinese impatience with the lack of accomplishment in the Geneva forum and appealed to Washington to do something to get the talks off dead center. He asserted:

> In the Sino-U.S. talks in Geneva, we made suggestions to lessen and eliminate tension in Taiwan. The best way to do this, we suggested, was to have a conference of the foreign ministers to settle concrete problems; and until such a conference was held, something could be done to improve relations such as lifting the trade embargo, encouraging trade between China and the United States, cultural exchange, and allowing the peoples of China and America to visit each other. But we regret that our efforts received no corresponding response from the U.S. government and did not meet with its approval. . . . If the U.S. government wants to satisfy the desire of the American people for friendship with the peoples of the world, including the Chinese people, they should do something to improve Sino-U.S. relations.[47]

The Americans did not respond to Chou's request and the talks began to take on the signs of a futile diplomatic exercise. The Chinese saw increasingly less room for maneuver. Gaps between meetings lengthened in early 1957 to two months, whereas gaps between the meetings at the start of the talks had only been a few days. Reflecting a hardened Chinese attitude toward Washington, Chou referred to China's proposal for a foreign ministers' conference in a 30 January 1957 press conference carried by NCNA, stating that since China's repeated proposal on this matter had been treated with a very cold attitude by the United States, China did not want to risk being rebuffed again by reiterating the offer. Chou later disclosed in an over-all assessment of the talks that "we have put forward many proposals trying to meet the views of the U.S. side; all these proposals have been rejected. As a result, the Geneva talks are stalemated. This proves that the United States always wants other parties to make concessions while it itself does not want to make any concessions. That is why compromise cannot be reached. Only when both parties move forward can they shake hands. But in the case of the United States even when we extended our hand, they refused to take it."[48]

Not only was Peking discovering little advantage in the ambassadorial talks vis-à-vis the United States, but its efforts to exploit the talks as a lever against the Chinese nationalists also failed. In mid-1957 the famous One Hundred Flowers campaign in China encouraged intellectual dissidence on the mainland and soon triggered a sharp reaction by the regime, culminating in a severe anti-rightist campaign lasting into 1958. Reports of severe political suppression and of purges in the ranks of political, cultural, and other groups served notice to the leaders in Taiwan that now was not the opportune time to consider accommodation with the mainland. The upshot was that Peking's year-an-a-half effort to woo Taiwan's support for peaceful liberation fell flat. The mainland more than ever appeared to be an unattractive alternative to the status quo in Taiwan.

By mid-1957, therefore, the Chinese were aware that their efforts aimed at accommodation with the United States had not borne fruit. Peking had tried various ways to find common ground with Washington but had come up empty-handed. American policy makers under Secretary Dulles's influence were decidedly uninterested in accommodation with Peking. The U.S. containment policy against China remained firm. This situation prompted the Chinese once again to grope for new alternatives to escape their vulnerability and isolation on the international scene and to attain their foreign objectives. A new opportunity was presented by the apparent superiority of Soviet strategic power over the United States, evident after Moscow's rocket successes in late 1957. The Chinese leadership then reverted to the route it had bypassed in early 1955. Peking once again began to prod Moscow to provide China with active support in confronting the United States in East Asia.[49]

CHAPTER FIVE

China's First Overture to the Nixon Administration

Following its disappointing negotiating experience with the United States, which resulted finally in the collapse of the Geneva talks in 1957, Peking adopted a militant policy toward the United States, striving to use new Soviet strategic power to counter the American strength in the East Asian power balance. This new policy was exemplified by Peking's more forceful approach toward Taiwan, which culminated in the famous Sino-American confrontation during the 1958 Taiwan Straits crisis. However, Moscow again disappointed the Chinese by failing to provide effective support for Peking in the face of strong U.S. defense measures during the crisis. Without such assistance, the Chinese were forced to retreat and seek a resumption of the ambassadorial talks, in order to defuse the potentially disastrous confrontation with the United States.

China's disappointment at the lack of Soviet support and at the poor cooperation of the United States during the Geneva talks prompted Chinese planners to move toward becoming more self-reliant. Peking now judged that it could not count on accommodation with Washington nor trust in Soviet support as a means for dealing with the imbalance in the East Asian power equation caused by American containment.

Peking, in any event, gradually devoted less attention to the American presence in Asia over the next decade. For one thing, U.S. containment had proved to be a system supporting the status quo in East Asia, not promoting aggressive attacks against PRC-held territory. Moreover, Peking's leadership was seriously preoccupied with other problems concerning PRC internal developments, such as the Great Leap Forward of the late 1950s and the Cultural Revolution of the mid-1960s, and in foreign affairs it was devoting primary attention

63

to the growing dispute with the USSR. The U.S. build-up in Vietnam in the mid-1960s did generate keen Chinese concern for a time, but Peking was soon satisfied that American protestations of peaceful intent toward China were genuine.

The developing Sino-Soviet dispute in the 1960s did serve notice to American strategists that Washington's earlier assessment stressing Peking's ideological unity with Moscow was incorrect. Many planners now saw that the Chinese were indeed capable of following a policy contrary to Soviet interests. Some judged that Washington should improve relations with China in order to use Peking as a source of leverage against Moscow, thereby establishing a more favorable strategic balance in East Asia for the United States, but this policy evoked little sympathy at the highest levels. The Kennedy administration, enjoying only a slim margin of support in Congress, was loath to alienate the large segment of U.S. opinion which still supported containment as a morally correct effort against the alleged evil of rabid Chinese communism. A deepening of the American involvement in the Vietnam war under Johnson only served to solidify Peking's attitude toward Washington and to harden U.S. opinion against the allegedly uncompromising brand of Asian communism typified by the People's Republic of China.

International pressures and events in the late 1960s finally led the United States—under the newly installed Nixon administration—to put aside its traditional moralistic views and abandon its unrealistic policy. The Sino-Soviet border clashes in 1969 proved to even skeptical Americans that Peking's leadership was an independent international force free from Soviet control. And the failure of the heavy American military involvement in Vietnam vividly demonstrated the limits of U.S. power internationally. Under Nixon, the United States continued past efforts to sustain a favorable balance of power in Asia and seemed determined to use military force and power politics when necessary. But the United States now attempted to exploit existing nationalistic divergencies in Asia to achieve the strategic equilibrium, rather than use American might as the sole balancing force. The major Asian divergence Washington chose to exploit was that between Moscow and Peking. The United States realized that withdrawing troops from forward positions along China's periphery would preserve needed resources for the protection of more vital American interests threatened by Washington's most serious and increasingly powerful adversary, the USSR. Such a move would also prompt closer relations with Peking, leading to the establishment of a favorable equilibrium in the area based on improved Sino-American relations.

Peking's Weak Position at the End of the Cultural Revolution

In mid-1968, Chinese foreign affairs were marked by acute Chinese isolation, stemming from the negative impact of the Cultural Revolution in China on the conduct of Peking's foreign policy. Peking's provocative diplomatic behavior, particularly during 1967 and early 1968, severely weakened China's international stature and isolated it from many of an already limited number of foreign friends. Toward many neighboring states in Asia, for example, Peking adopted an attitude of self-righteous hostility and disdain. Red Guards in Peking launched poster attacks in early 1967 against Korean party leader Kim Il-song, triggering an official Korean protest and further exacerbating China's already strained relations with Pyongyang.[1] Moreover, vexing Chinese diplomatic behavior in Peking and abroad severely alienated several, previously friendly neighboring states, including Cambodia, Nepal, Ceylon, and Burma.[2] Red Guard demonstrations in southern China during mid-1968 resulted in the interruption of vital war shipments to North Vietnam, exacerbating tensions in Sino-Vietnamese relations, which had been introduced by Hanoi's decision to enter the Paris peace talks with the United States in May 1968.[3] Elsewhere, China's proselytizing efforts and shrill polemics alienated a number of nonaligned states, including Kenya, Tunisia, Algeria, the United Arab Republic, as well as many European states. The diplomacy of the Cultural Revolution also affected China's posture toward the Soviet Union and the United States, resulting in a markedly more uncompromising approach toward both superpowers. Chinese demonstrations in front of the Soviet embassy in Peking and abrasive anti-Soviet activity by Chinese representatives abroad were only the most visible Chinese actions serving to widen the Sino-Soviet rift during this period. At the same time, Chinese officials in May 1968 underlined an anti-American stance by suspending the Sino-American ambassadorial discussions, which were taking place in Warsaw. Peking called off the talks for at least six months, ostensibly because it judged that "there was nothing to talk about" with the U.S. representatives.[4] Thus, the Chinese by mid-1968 had pared their international contacts to the point that Peking's circle of foreign influence was limited to a small handful of states, such as Albania, Pakistan, and a few African states.[5]

Prospects for a return to a more effective Chinese international policy also appeared less than promising in 1968. The foreign ministry apparatus, seriously disrupted during the course of the Cultural Revolution, had only begun to show tentative signs of a return to more normal functioning. Foreign Minister Chen I, a number of vice-ministers of foreign affairs, and other high-ranking foreign ministry officials had come under strong Red Guard attack. Many no longer appeared in public, though their positions were not filled by others. Peking had also recalled all but one of its ambassadors abroad, in many cases leaving only extremely junior and inexperienced officials at foreign diplomatic posts.[6]

Beginning in late 1967, the regime attempted to restore a veneer of normality in Chinese foreign affairs. Red Guard demonstrations against foreign embassies in China were halted, and Chinese officials were once more attending some diplomatic functions in Peking. In May 1968, for example, the Chinese gave an effusive welcome to a visiting joint delegation from Guinea and Mali, which had come to China to conclude initial agreements for Chinese assistance to a highly ambitious railway project to join the two African states.[7] In June, President Julius Nyerere of Tanzania was warmly received by the Chinese during a good-will visit, and he conferred at length with Chou En-lai.[8]

More significantly, the Chinese also demonstrated some willingness to overlook recent disagreements with some states in order to rebuild China's international influence. In May, for example, the Chinese improved relations with Nepal by warmly receiving the visiting Nepalese foreign minister.[9] In July, NCNA reported that a Chinese vice-minister of foreign affairs had attended a Cuban anniversary reception in Peking—a noticeably more amicable attitude toward the event than China had expressed in 1967.[10] Also in July, China began to clear up one of its many outstanding disagreements with Great Britain stemming from the Cultural Revolution; Peking permitted a senior British diplomat to leave China, marking the first such occurrence since restrictions were imposed on the British mission in August 1967.[11]

However, Peking's efforts toward establishing a more conventional approach to foreign affairs were extremely slow and halting. There was little change in China's state of international isolation. Moreover, there were signs that some of the efforts to mend relations with certain states were half-hearted. In the case of Burma, for example, the Chinese gradually moderated their public criticism of the Ne Win government during the first half of 1968, and they gave several signs of a more positive approach toward Rangoon. These included a donation of 10,000 yuan by the Chinese Red Cross to the Burmese Red Cross to assist relief operations for hurricane victims in May 1968; participation of the Chinese chargé d'affaires in a 19 July ceremony honoring a Burmese independence leader; and a 1 August PRC Army Day reception at the Chinese embassy in Rangoon, which NCNA reported was attended by Burmese officials.[12] In mid-August, however, the Chinese unexpectedly reversed their course, launching a series of strong statements attacking the "reactionary Ne Win government" and strongly supporting the dissident Burmese Communist Party.[13] By late 1968, relations had once again become severely strained and there was little prospect for rapprochement.

The Chinese leadership also continued to reveal its preoccupation with matters other than foreign affairs. The volume of Peking's media coverage of diplomatic events and foreign issues was still far below what it had been before the Cultural Revolution. Such reports were more than overshadowed by China's public attention to domestic affairs, and to acclamations over such ideological matters as the thought of Mao-Tse-tung. In addition, the Chinese leadership was preoccupied with a number of crucial developments in domestic affairs. As Philip Bridgham pointed out in his study of the period, Peking at this time was striving to complete the formation of provincial administrative structures and was encouraging the army to end civilian disorders, dissolve factions, and restore internal peace in preparation for a number of strong domestic reforms.[14] In this context, Peking's concern over a restoration of China's influence in foreign affairs remained secondary.

Concern over Soviet Intentions

Peking's lack of attention to foreign affairs was not substantially altered until the Soviet incursion in Czechoslovakia on 20 August 1968 and Moscow's formulation of the Brezhnev Doctrine of limited sovereignty within the socialist community prompted a marked change in Chinese foreign policy. China's immediate reaction was to increase considerably its media criticism of Sovet foreign policy, to the point that China's foreign coverage in important media outlets such as *Peking Review* almost equaled output on Chinese domestic affairs.[15] Peking's coverage also reflected several departures from China's view of international affairs evident earlier in the year. In general, these changes can be grouped in three categories: increased concern over Soviet military pressure against China; greater conviction that the Soviet Union was collaborating and colluding with the United States on a number of important international issues contrary to China's interests; and, increased concern over what the Chinese saw as a tightening military-political "ring of encirclement" established by the United States and the Soviet Union in order to stifle China's vital interests in Asia. Against this background, the Chinese showed more interest in improving relations with several countries of critical importance in the Sino-Soviet dispute and a greater willingness to overlook past disagreements with certain nations in order to improve China's diplomatic position vis-à-vis the Soviet Union and to reduce Peking's international isolation.

The rise of Chinese concern over Soviet military intentions was perhaps the most vivid change in China's view of the world after the Soviet occupation of Czechoslovakia. The Chinese showed an awareness that Moscow's new doctrine of limited sovereignty within the socialist community held serious implications for China. Peking, accordingly, began to look more fearfully at the build-up in Soviet forces deployed near the Sino-Soviet and Sino-Mongolian frontiers, which had been going on for several years.

Although solid information regarding the Soviet military expansion in this area has remained scanty,[16] it appears that beginning around 1966 Moscow instigated an active program aimed at bringing its forces stationed in the Far East to a higher state of readiness, equipping them with better and larger amounts of weaponry and augmenting their numbers. During this period, Soviet forces in the Far East received surface-to-surface missiles with nuclear warheads. Furthermore, the Soviet Union signed a new defense agreement with Mongolia in January 1966, which Moscow implied gave it the right to station troops and maintain bases in that country. By 1967, the Russians had apparently increased their troop strength in the border regions by around twenty thousand men. After their agreement with Mongolia, the Russians also began to station sizable contingents of troops there. By early 1969, there was a consensus among Western observers that the Soviet Union had increased its manned strength in the border areas near China by about ten divisions—an increase of about 60 percent over the Soviet strength in the mid-1960s. All these steps by the Soviet Union significantly upset the rough balance of forces—between the Chinese numerical superiority and the Soviet fire-power and military advantages—that had previously existed in the military regions fronting on the border. The Russions now maintained their previous advantages and were continuing to establish a capability in manpower that could impose serious defeat on the Chinese in certain key areas, notably the more weakly defended Inner Asian areas of Sinkiang and Inner Mongolia.

The first public sign of Peking's new concern over Soviet military intentions came on 16 September 1968 in a formal Chinese protest to the USSR over what Peking said were recently intensified Soviet intrusions into China's air space along the frontier.[17] By directly linking Moscow's action to the Soviet invasion of Czechoslovakia, the Chinese demonstrated a new seriousness in their assessment of Soviet military intentions. They protested that "those intrusions by the Soviet military aircraft took place around August 20 when the Soviet Union sent its troops of aggression against Czechoslovakia; and *it is in no way accidental.*" The Chinese protest also maintained that the intrusions "were wholly engineered by the Soviet government in an organized and planned way in support of it activities of aggression against Czechoslovakia and in pursuance of its global strategy of allying with the United States against China."[18]

On 22 September, an article in *People's Daily* underlined the new Chinese concern over the frontier and reiterated China's judgment that Moscow was becoming a growing threat to China's interests in Asia and throughout the world. In particular, the article highlighted China's uneasiness by reversing the usual polemical order used in propaganda attacks against Washington and Moscow and citing the Soviet Union *before* the United States as the chief foreign opponent. Making indirect reference to Moscow's continuing military expansion along the frontier, the Chinese also charged that the USSR was actively engaged in establishing nuclear bases around China to intensify its nuclear threat to the PRC. In conclusion, the article claimed that Moscow's chief aim in "rigging up the anti-China ring of encirclement" was to prepare to launch military provocations against China.[19]

In a 30 September speech before Albanian representatives visiting Peking on China's National Day, Premier Chou En-lai made China's first public reference to the recent expansion of Soviet forces along the frontier.[20] Chou demonstrated once again that Peking saw Moscow's build-up as directly related to its forceful action in Czechoslovakia. After denouncing the Czech invasion and Moscow's subsequent increase in military pressure against Albania, Chou stated: "While intensifying its aggression and threats against Eastern Europe, Soviet social imperialism is also stepping up armed provocations against China. In coordination with U.S. imperialism, it is energetically forming a ring of encirclement against China by stationing massive troops along the Sino-Soviet and Sino-Mongolian border, and at the same time, it is constantly creating border tensions by ever more frequently sending planes to violate China's airspace."[21]

Chou's remarks were echoed by Army Chief-of-Staff Huang Yung-sheng in a 4 October speech commemorating Chinese National Day. Huang condemned the Soviet Union for sending "large numbers of troops to reinforce its forces stationed along the Sino-Soviet and Sino-Mongolian frontiers and for intensifying its armed provocations against China."[22] Vocal Chinese concern over Soviet military pressure did not abate in subsequent months. Huang Yung-sheng again denounced

Moscow's military expansion and provocations along the Chinese border in a speech in Albania in early December.[23] NCNA repeated the condemnation on 14 December.[24] More pointedly, Radio Peking in early February accused the Russians of displaying a "very warlike attitude," intensifying military preparations, and directing a "spearhead" against China.[25]

In addition to concern over Soviet military pressure, Peking demonstrated more serious preoccupation over what it saw as increased Soviet efforts to join with the United States in order to establish an alliance against China. The Chinese had for several years shown sensitivity over Soviet-American world-wide "collusion." Nevertheless, Peking media expanded treatment of this issue—by around 400 percent in one leading propaganda vehicle[26]—during the months following the crisis in Czechoslovakia. Also, Peking now claimed that this collusion was gaining influence in many areas of crucial importance to China and that it was primarily designed to forge a military force to attack China. Thus, the Chinese persistently claimed that the lack of forceful U.S. opposition to the Soviet action in Czechoslovakia was directly related to alleged Soviet efforts to assist the United States in reaching a negotiated settlement at the Paris talks. Peking claimed that this Soviet-American cooperation would lead to a "sell-out" of both Hanoi's and Peking's interest in Southeast Asia.[27] In addition, the Chinese media began to devote expanded attention to allegedly increased Soviet diplomatic and economic initiatives designed to gain influence in Asia at Chinese expense. Thus, the Chinese attacked Soviet dealings with Japan, India, Singapore, Malaysia, Thailand, Burma, and South Korea, claiming that those initiatives were a prelude to the organization of an anti-China alliance in Asia led by Moscow and Washington.[28] The Chinese also claimed to see expanded Soviet-American collusion aaginst China's interests in the Middle East and Europe.[29]

Chinese Initiatives against Moscow

Chinese policy makers now faced important decisions concerning Peking's future foreign policy toward Soviet diplomatic and military pressure. Had Peking maintained its then current approach—making only haphazard progress toward a more conventional foreign posture, while focusing on domestic issues and ideological themes—it would have been relatively powerless against what it saw as increased anti-China pressure on the part of the Russians. The Chinese instead embarked on their most important effort in conventional foreign policy since the start of the Cultural Revolution. Peking's effort was focused against Moscow and had two notable features. On the one hand, the Chinese used standard diplomatic measures, such as increased media releases, speeches by party leaders, and meetings with foreign heads, in an effort to brand Soviet leaders as Russia's "new tsars," who were threatening Eastern Europe and expanding military and political pressure throughout the world. In this way, the Chinese tried to undermine Soviet influence with a number of nations of critical importance in the Sino-Soviet rivalry. At the same time, the Chinese showed greater willingness to overlook past disagreements and to improve ties with a number of strategically important countries—including even the United States—in order to enhance China's leverage in the face of Soviet pressure.

Peking's first significant step after the Czechoslovakia crisis was to sharply increase coverage of events in Czechoslovakia in an effort to portray the Russian leaders before the world as aggressors and "social imperialists." The Chinese also undertook to refurbish their long-neglected relationship with Romania, a nation particularly sensitive to increased Soviet military pressure in Eastern Europe at this time. Foreign Minister Chen I held a private conference with the Romanian ambassador in Peking on 22 August,[30] while Chou En-lai chose to voice his first denunciation of the invasion during a Romanian National Day reception on 23 August. In his speech, Chou pointedly pledged China's strong support for Romania's efforts against the danger of Soviet "intervention and aggression."[31]

In a similar vein, Chou En-lai denounced Moscow during a North Vietnamese National Day reception in Peking on 2 September. Chou not only attempted to discredit Moscow over the Czechoslovakia issue, but he also linked the Russian action to Moscow's "sham support" for the Vietnamese struggle. Chou warned the Vietnamese—who earlier had publicly hailed Moscow's "noble action" in Czechoslovakia—that "it is high time that those who cherish illusions about Soviet revisionism woke up."[32] A harshly anti-Soviet approach was also taken by Chen I at the North Korean National Day ceremonies in Peking on 9 September, when he denounced Moscow for conspiring with the United States in Czechoslovakia and Asia.[33] The Chinese at this time also showed a willingness to put aside some of their recent disagreements with the government of Charles de Gaulle in France. Conflict had arisen over the Chinese propaganda support for the student-worker strikes in Paris earlier in 1968. Thus, Peking media covered favorably the French president's remarks at a 9 September press conference, where he attacked the Soviet Union and the United States for allegedly dividing Europe into spheres of influence.[34]

By mid-October, the Chinese had developed a broader foreign

offensive against Moscow. For one thing, direct Chinese propaganda attacks against the Tito regime in Yugoslavia stopped, marking the first step in China's movement over the next few years to improve its long-strained relations with Belgrade.[35] On 28 November, NCNA reported on the Yugoslav embassy's National Day reception in Peking for the first time since before the start of the Cultural Revolution.[36] Peking, by this time, had also stopped criticizing the "Dubcek revisionist clique" in Czechoslovakia and other leaders in Eastern Europe, stressing, instead, China's support for the "people" in the Soviet bloc countries against the evils of Moscow's "domination" and "oppression."

The Chinese also had begun, by mid-October 1968, to show some signs of abating their harsh disapproval of Hanoi's policies. Thus, on 19 October, they issued their first acknowledgment of Hanoi's participation in the Paris peace talks, which had begun the previous May.[37] By early November, the Chinese had revived favorable coverage of North Vietnamese battle reports, and they promptly reported in matter-of-fact style President Lyndon B. Johnson's bombing-halt message on 2 November and noted the subsequent North Vietnamese reply.[38]

In late November, Peking further improved its diplomatic leverage against Moscow by sending Huang Yung-sheng on a good-will visit to Albania. This marked the first trip abroad by a high-ranking Chinese official in over two years. Huang's statements revealed that the trip was chiefly designed to demonstrate Chinese solidarity with their Albanian allies, but he also used the occasion to enhance Peking's improving relations with Romania. On 27 November, Huang made a stopover in Romania, where he consulted with high-level Romanian military leaders led by General Ion Gheorghe.[39]

In a broad sense, therefore, the Soviet invasion of Czechoslovakia had made the Chinese leadership realize how seriously the strategic balance in East Asia had turned against vital PRC interests. The expansion of Soviet forces on the border had corresponded with the weakening of Chinese strategic power resulting from the Chinese armed forces' heavy involvement in domestic governing chores. Peking now became aware that Moscow might use its strategic advantage against China as it had against Czechoslovakia, and the Chinese felt compelled to take immediate remedial action.

Overture to the United States

By far the most striking departure in China's foreign policy during this period was its approach to the United States. The longstanding Sino-Soviet dispute—fostered by Mao and closely intertwined with

Chinese domestic politics—caused PRC leaders to rule out accommodation with the USSR as a means to remedy China's vulnerable strategic position. Peking nonetheless still had the option of moving closer to the other major power in East Asia—the United States—in an effort to improve its situation. Under the leadership of Chou En-lai and the Chinese foreign ministry, Peking moved in this direction. The Chinese issued a moderate foreign ministry statement calling for revived Sino-American ambassadorial talks after the new Nixon administration took power.[40]

The statement by the spokesman of the Information Department of the foreign ministry was particularly unusual since it contained no criticism of U.S. foreign policy except for one reference to the Taiwan issue. It also proposed for the first time since the start of the Cultural Revolution that Sino-American relations be conducted on the basis of the five principles of peaceful coexistence. Peking's motivation for such a major initiative was undoubtedly complex, but China's overwhelming preoccupation with the Soviet Union at this time indicated that the initiative was designed in part to strengthen Peking's anti-Soviet diplomatic efforts. The Chinese were well aware that the Warsaw meetings had frequently triggered concern in the USSR over a possible rapprochement between China and the United States. As a result, Peking almost certainly judged that the mere revival of the discussions at this time would significantly enhance its leverage against Moscow. At the very least, talks with the United States would allow China to assess more closely the actual extent of what it saw as Washington's and Moscow's increasing efforts to collude against Chinese international interests, and they would permit Peking to better prepare itself for meeting any new Soviet-American challenge.

Apart from Peking's concern over the Soviet Union, Chinese comment at this time showed that China's new willingness to resume the Warsaw talks derived from a judgment that the recently elected Nixon administration might disengage the United States from some of its resistance to China's interests in Asia. Peking's statement on 26 November, for example, clearly linked Chinese readiness to reconvene the Warsaw talks with the American presidential elections and a possible change in policy by the new administration. In proposing a 20 February date for the sessions, the Chinese maintained that "by that time, the new U.S. president will have been in office for more than a month, and *the U.S. side will probably be able to make up its mind.*"[41]

Furthermore, Chinese media commentary on Nixon's foreign policy pledges during the campaign linked his success in the elections with his promises to pull back American military forces around the world, particularly in Asia. One media statement concluded that

"Nixon was elected president after he called for the necessity to 'reduce our commitments around the world in areas where we are overextended,' and to 'put more emphasis on the priority areas,' namely Europe and other areas."[42]

Such comment reflected a judgment that the new administration would be inclined to adopt fresh policies and reduce American involvement in Asia. The Chinese responded with a more flexible approach toward Washington. They hoped to use the revived Warsaw talks to assess future U.S. intentions firsthand and to encourage Washington to disengage from China's periphery in Asia. The Chinese at the same time began to reduce media coverage of sensitive Sino-American bilateral issues and to restrict commentary on other anti-American matters, presumably to foster an improved atmosphere in Sino-American relations prior to the Warsaw meeting. This departure, together with the unexpectedly positive PRC statement of 26 November, triggered a spate of speculation in the Western press whether the Chinese had "turned over a new leaf" in foreign affairs, had abandoned their former truculent opposition to the United States, and were now willing to meet the western power halfway on a number of disputed issues.[43]

However, Peking media indicated that, for the time being, the Chinese were interested only in a carefully limited dialogue with Washington. The commentary underscored the view that persisting disagreements with Washington precluded major compromise in China's attitude toward the United States. The 26 November foreign ministry statement, for instance, demanded that the United States withdraw from Taiwan—an issue that had long been the cornerstone of China's fundamental opposition to Washington. Moreover, the statement also stressed that the Nixon administration could expect no major concessions at the February session, for, after all, "the Chinese government has repeatedly told the U.S. side in explicit terms that the Chinese government will never barter away principles."[44]

Two days before releasing their proposal for talks with the United States, the Chinese issued a new directive from Chairman Mao urging that historical experience be studied and discussed in order to deal with current problems.[45] At the same time, Peking reprinted and gave wide publicity to Mao's report of 5 March 1949 to the second plenary session of the Seventh Central Committee of the Chinese Communist Party. Clearly, the directive and report were designed to be used mainly in solving current domestic problems, but the report also contained an entire section that rationalized entering into diplomatic negotiations with an enemy. This section appeared designed to explain to the Chinese people Peking's abrupt move to revive the Warsaw talks. It also helped explain Peking's recently revised attitude toward

Hanoi's negotiations with the United States in Paris. The report seemed to foretell the message of the 26 November statement, emphasizing that the Chinese were willing to negotiate with adversaries but would remain uncompromising regarding principles. In particular, Mao's report stated: "We should not refuse to enter into negotiations because we are afraid of trouble and want to avoid complications, nor should we enter into negotiations with our minds in a haze. We should be firm in principle; we should also have all the flexibility permissible and necessary for carrying out our principles."[46]

In short, the Chinese noted that they were willing to moderate their posture toward Washington in a limited way and that they wanted to resume the Warsaw discussions. But they carefully indicated that basic disputes between the two sides over matters of principle would continue to impede any fundamental compromise of China's longstanding opposition to the United States.

In the following weeks, Peking's new approach toward the United States did not proceed smoothly. Trends in the Chinese media began to suggest serious disagreement within the Chinese leadership over several aspects of this new policy—a marked contrast to previous Chinese Communist Party initiatives in the 1940s and 1950s. In particular, certain commentaries voiced opposition to any slackening of China's critical coverage of the United States, opposed negotiations with the United States, and emphasized that the only correct way to handle such an enemy as through armed struggle. These opinions were evident in commentaries concerning cultural matters, suggesting that proponents of this harder line—opposed to the moderate approach advocated by the Chinese foreign ministry under Chou En-lai[47]—were loyal to Chiang Ching and her entourage of cultural overseers, who had recently gained tight control of propaganda relating to cultural matters.

The dissenting views were particularly visible in a series of virulent attacks against the already well-discredited foreign policy approach of former Chief of State Liu Shao-ch'i. These articles were ostensibly part of the regime's large-scale anti-Liu campaign, which followed the twelfth plenary session of the Eighth Central Committee of the CCP in October 1968. The campaign had subsided by late November, but in early December—in the immediate aftermath of China's initiative toward the United States—attacks against Liu's foreign approach began to appear in force. In fact, the attacks marked the strongest denunciation of any Chinese leader's foreign policy approach in almost a year. They reached a crescendo in mid-December.

Although one cannot conclusively state that these commentaries were primarily intended as an attack against Chou's flexible attitude toward Washington, it is certain that the articles represented a point of view that was opposed to moderation toward the United States. In particular, a correlation between the development of Peking's adaptable approach toward Washington in late 1968 and the heavy attacks against Liu Shao-ch'i's diplomatic stance toward the United States strongly suggests divergence of opinion within the Chinese leadership over policy toward Washington.

The first forceful attack on Liu's foreign policy came in a series of articles in the Shanghai paper *Wen Hui Pao* on 2 December denouncing a film depicting Liu Shao-ch'i's dealings with foreign officials during a visit to Indonesia in 1963. The criticism generally centered on Liu's alleged betrayal of Chinese concerns in Asia in favor of the interests of the United States during the course of his Indonesian trip. In an apparent effort to call attention to current policy toward the United States, the articles emphasized the recent "widespread, pernicious influence" of the film and added that there had been resistance from an unspecified quarter to the publication of the critical articles. One article charged: "Some cadre hold that this is an old film which we once criticized a good deal, and we have nothing more to say about it. This attitude underestimates the power of the enemy. It is of course incorrect."[48]

Cultural workers in Peking soon echoed this attack, paying particular attention to the specific offenses Liu had allegedly committed by capitulating to the United States during his Indonesian visit. By comparing the thrust of charges against Liu with China's approach toward the United States in late 1968, one can discern a sharp divergence in the views of Peking leaders concerning policy toward the United States. Thus, the articles criticized Liu for not fully exposing the criminal nature of U.S. imperialism. (The Chinese media had sharply reduced anti-American polemics since November 1968). Moreover, they stated that Liu's unwillingness to attack American policy while in Indonesia had "amazed and startled even the bourgeois newspapers and periodicals of the West." (Of course, the Western press in 1968 reacted similarly to China's muting of anti-American propaganda and Peking's conciliatory statement of 26 November announcing its desire to resume the Warsaw talks.) And one article denounced Liu's efforts to deal with the United States through peaceful political means, emphasizing that "only with guns can the whole world be transformed."[49]

Liu was also criticized in an article in *People's Daily* for his compromising approach toward Chiang Kai-shek and the United States in the late 1940s.[50] In general, this article reflected the same themes evident in the criticism of Liu's visit to Indonesia. It denounced Liu because he was not sufficiently critical of the United States and because he proposed the use of negotiations instead of total reliance on armed struggle in dealing with the United States. Contradicting Peking's late 1968 stress on Mao's ideological sanction of 1949 of talks with an enemy such as the United States, the article stated: "Taught by our great leader Chairman Mao, the Chinese people were clear-headed and refused to believe the nice words of the U.S. imperialists and the Chiang Kai-shek bandits. They knew that the people's political power already established must not be lost and must be defended by fighting."[51]

The culmination of the attacks on Liu's foreign policy came in mid-December. Two articles in *People's Daily* dropped the earlier approach of denouncing films concerning Liu Shao-ch'i's visit to Indonesia and virulently attacked Liu's actions themselves during the visit.[52] In particular, they denounced Liu for opposing the resolution of the tenth plenary session of the Eighth Central Committee of the CCP in April 1963, which they claimed had emphasized that China must continue to "hold high the banner of opposing imperialism" and unite with all "peace-loving countries and peoples" against the United States. It is obvious that such charges could also have been leveled against Chou En-lai and the Chinese foreign ministry for their new approach toward the United States in late 1968. Since anti-American polemics were sharply reduced in the wake of the 26 November foreign ministry statement, Peking was obviously not "holding high the banner of opposing imperialism." In fact, it was attempting to rationalize negotiations with this longstanding enemy.

The articles went on to denounce Liu because "he never condemned U.S. imperialist crimes of war and aggression when he referred to China's sacred territory Taiwan, or South Korea [and] South Vietnam." Such criticism could also have been applied to the Chinese policy, in the wake of the 26 November statement, to mute almost completely commentary on issues having sensitive implications in bilateral Sino-American relations. One article added: "The imperialist and bourgeois propaganda machines applauded him loudly. They showered him with praise for 'completely avoiding mention of the United States, to which the Chinese leaders frequently refer, avoiding any direct attack on the United States,' and 'even not accusing the United States of conducting aggression against China.'" This criticism too had obvious parallels in the Western press reaction to Peking's discreet public posture toward the United States in November 1968.

One can never be certain that criticism appearing in media coverage of cultural affairs relates to political concerns of the Chinese leadership. However, revelations of policy disagreements among the Chinese leaders during the Cultural Revolution have shown that comment on cultural affairs frequently has important political significance. It should also be noted that it is never possible to prove with absolute confidence that wide differences of opinion reflected in the media— such as those between the rigid foreign policy approach advocated by Chiang Ching's cultural media and the more moderate approach advocated by Chou's Chinese foreign ministry—actually indicate the existence of serious leadership disagreements over Chinese policy.

Nevertheless, great importance is attached to precise wording in media commentary throughout the communist world, particularly in China. And the Chinese have a peculiar penchant for esoteric communication, well exemplified by the mid-1960s controversy concerning the historical play *Hai Jui Dismissed from Office*. It therefore seems likely that significant policy implications lay behind the differing views of policy toward the United States expressed in 1968 commentary. The timing and the content of the press attacks against Liu-Shao-ch'i's approach to the United States indicate that the assaults were designed to rebut those in the Chinese leadership who wanted to moderate policy toward the United States.[53]

Peking Cancels the Warsaw Meeting

The divergence of opinion within the PRC leadership over policy toward the United States complicated Peking's efforts to formulate a consistently moderate posture toward Washington in November and December 1968. It also appears to have played a role in the Chinese decision to reverse this posture, cancel the proposed Warsaw meeting, and return to a rigid anti-American approach in late February 1969. An analysis of Chinese media trends and concurrent events demonstrates that the decision to cancel the Warsaw session was made only just prior to the 20 February meeting date. It also indicates that Peking's ire over the American role in the defection of a Chinese diplomat in the Netherlands to the United States—the ostensible cause of the cancellation—was clearly not the sole reason for aborting the discussions. And such a study of media coverage and concurrent events also demonstrates that the final decision to cancel was unilateral on China's part and was influenced by considerations other than American actions toward China.

Members of the Chinese leadership who opposed a moderate policy toward the United States presumably played a role in China's decision to cancel the Warsaw session on 18 February 1969. In particular, they may have been able to exploit provocative American actions toward China—such as Washington's involvement in the Chinese defector case—enough to gather sufficient support within the leadership to reverse the earlier moderate initiative taken by the foreign ministry under Chou En-lai. At the least, an inflexible anti-American attitude among certain members of the leadership during the February 1969 deliberations over policy toward the United States clearly moved China's policy toward putting off the Warsaw discussions.

By the end of December 1968, it appeared that the anti-American stress in criticism of Liu Shao-ch'i's foreign policy was beginning to have an impact on Peking's general policy toward the United States. The Chinese media began to voice more criticism of the United States and to snipe at some of President-elect Nixon's avowed domestic and foreign policies, marking a change from Peking's silence on such issues in the aftermath of the 26 November foreign ministry statement. In January, Chinese anti-American statements gradually increased, and late in the month Peking began to denounce the United States over sensitive bilateral issues. On 27 January, *People's Daily* and *Red Flag* issued a joint article assailing Nixon's inaugural speech and attacking Washington's continued military actions in Taiwan and Vietnam.[54] On the next day, NCNA predicted that the United States would stubbornly follow a policy of aggression and war and would continue to oppose the Chinese and other peoples of the world.[55] *People's Daily* on 30 January also charged that the United States had never stopped its sabotage attempts against China and was "still laying its hands" on Taiwan.[56]

Despite this upsurge in polemics, the Chinese media maintained a degree of flexibility toward the United States up to the very day of the cancellation of the Warsaw meeting. In reporting on President Nixon's first press conference in late January, for example, Peking showed notable discretion by avoiding discussion of the president's remark's emphasizing his strong support for the Republic of China's position in the United Nations and his categorical rejection of any change in Washington's position on the China representation issue in the United Nations.[57] Moreover, the Chinese letter of protest to the United States on 6 February denouncing the alleged American role in the defection of the Chinese diplomat in the Netherlands did not place full blame on Washington for the defection. It divided responsibility among the diplomat himself, the Dutch government, and the United States.[58]

More importantly, during the twelve days following the publication of the protest note and prior to Peking's 18 February announcement cancelling the talks, Chinese media continued to show significant moderation toward the United States, particularly over sensitive Sino-

American bilateral issues. In fact, a review of China's coverage of the United States in this period shows a marked decline in the number of criticisms of American actions from the number expressed in January. In particular, Peking avoided repeating charges that the United States was aggressive and hostile toward China and that Washington's occupation of Taiwan was improper. The Chinese also passed over several opportunities to denounce American actions against them. Thus, NCNA's 8 February coverage of President Nixon's press conference held two days before made no mention of the president's claim that the increase in the Chinese nuclear threat was a prime rationale for his administration's support of the installation of an antiballistic missile system in the United States.[59] This omission was particularly noteworthy since the Chinese later demonstrated extreme sensitivity over the issue. In the same NCNA release, Peking duly reiterated its contention that the Nixon administration was colluding with the Soviet Union to divide up the world between them, but it avoided the frequent companion charge that one of the chief goals of this collusion was to oppose China. In addition, *People's Daily* on 11 February denounced U.S. bases in Okinawa, referring to the American use of the bases for military operations in Vietnam, but it refrained from making the frequent Chinese claim that the bases also formed a key link in Washington's containment policy toward China.[60] Finally, NCNA, on 16 February, released a long report describing the misery that people on Taiwan suffered under the "bloody rule of the Chiang Kai-shek gang." In contrast to past practice, the report avoided criticizing the U.S. role in Taiwan, focusing exclusively on ROC policies there.[61]

After the 18 February cancellation, the Chinese pulled out all stops and leveled harsh polemical broadsides against the Nixon administration. In late February, for example, the Chinese initiated a series of shrill personal attacks against the president during his European tour, comparing him to a "rat crossing the street," and accusing him of making "repulsive gestures" during his journey.[62] At the same time, the Chinese overlooked no opportunity to portray the United States as hostile toward China and even went so far as to accuse the Nixon administration of scheduling a news conference in early March in order to demonstrate American support for the Soviet Union against China after the outbreak of Sino-Soviet armed clashes along the Ussuri River frontier on 2 March.[63]

In short, there was a gap in Peking's charges against the United States after the initial Chinese protest of 6 February over the defection of the PRC diplomat. This suggests that Peking was not overly angered at the United States over the defection and that Peking still wanted to limit coverage of sensitive Sino-American issues in order to establish a more favorable atmosphere for the start of the Warsaw discussions. In particular, this trend in Chinese coverage indicated that Peking was still willing to meet with the United States, even up to two days before the cancellation announcement of 18 February. This contention is also supported by evidence released to the Western press by American officials after the Chinese cancellation. For one thing, American officials reacted with great surprise to the Chinese move, adding that they judged that Peking's decision was made at the last minute.[64] They disclosed that after the 6 February protest there had been official communication between the Chinese and American delegations in Warsaw concerning preparations for the 20 February meeting.[65] Since American officials were surprised by the 18 February cancellation, it is almost certain that Chinese officials in Warsaw gave no indication that they might cancel the meeting on account of the defection or any other matter during their interchange with the American side in preparation for the meeting. Moreover, U.S. conviction that the talks would take place was underscored by the disclosure that—only hours before the Chinese announced cancellation—Washington had gone to the expense and inconvenience of sending two of its leading China experts to Warsaw to assist the American ambassador in the 20 February meeting with the Chinese.[66]

In view of this evidence, it seems certain that the Chinese did not initially regard the defection of their diplomat as sufficient grounds for cancelling the Warsaw talks and that they only later decided to use this issue to justify their blocking resumption of the talks. American behavior following the 6 February protest indicates that Washington had done nothing in this period that would have triggered further Chinese anger and prompted a cancellation of the talks. The Chinese statement on 18 February added a new element by accusing the United States of plotting with the Chiang Kai-shek government to send the defector to Taiwan.[67] In fact, the Chinese nationalist embassy on 9 February had predictably invited the diplomat to visit Taiwan, but the United States had remained silent on the issue, and the defector had remained in the United States.[68] As a result, it appears that the final decision to cancel the talks and to resume a harsh approach toward the United States derived from factors other than American actions toward China.

Analysis of earlier Chinese media commentary strongly suggests that certain members of the Chinese leadership disapproved of the projected negotiations in Warsaw and the moderation in China's approach toward the United States initiated by the Chinese foreign ministry under Chou En-lai. It thus seems plausible to argue that this group was able to exploit the defection, and perhaps other U.S. actions,

81

in order to discredit Chou's Warsaw initiative and tip Chinese policy toward uncompromising opposition to Washington.

In a broad sense, the decision to cancel the Warsaw meeting was the work of Chinese leaders who favored a show of firm Chinese resolve against both the United States and the Soviet Union. These leaders, who seemed to center around Chiang Ching, had indicated that they viewed accommodation with the United States as a retreat from Chinese principles and as ideologically deviant behavior. Opposing them were leaders of the Chinese foreign ministry under Chou En-lai, who had tried to soften ideological considerations in order to deal pragmatically with Peking's weak position in the balance of power in East Asia. This group judged that the strategic threat posed by Moscow had made it necessary for the PRC to move expeditiously toward the major countervailing force in the area, the United States. It realized that Peking would have to put aside certain principles and ideological positions in order to move closer to Washington but judged that such action was essential in order to protect China's vital interests and national security in the existing power equation.

The politically charged atmosphere in China during the Cultural Revolution made all Chinese leaders extremely sensitive to the ideological propriety of their policy decisions. It is therefore not surprising that the group of ideologues surrounding Chiang Ching could manage to undercut Chou's pragmatic policy and steer leadership decisions away from accommodation with Washington at this crucial juncture. The reversal of the Chinese stance over the Warsaw talks was a defeat for Chou's realistic, balance-of-power approach to foreign policy. It marked an instance when China's concern for ideological principles and righteousness confounded a pragmatic pursuit of Chinese vital foreign-policy interests on the basis of the East Asian power balance. The result was an unrealistic PRC policy that placed Peking in strident opposition to both superpowers at a time when its national security seemed threatened by Soviet power.

CHAPTER SIX

China's Response to the Sino-Soviet Border Clashes

The pragmatic foreign policy associated with Chou En-lai remained in abeyance throughout most of 1969. Ideological opposition to accommodation with either superpower remained the foundation of the foreign policy of the People's Republic of China. At the same time, the Chinese showed little willingness to broaden the policy begun in late 1968 of improving foreign contacts with smaller nations. As a result, Peking remained diplomatically isolated.

The outbreak of Sino-Soviet border clashes in March 1969—which alerted the outside world to China's dangerously vulnerable position vis-à-vis the Soviet Union—had little immediate impact on Chinese foreign policy. Peking's propaganda line of self-confident defiance before the Soviet menace did not begin to change until late summer, when a combination of thinly veiled Soviet threats to invade China and serious military clashes along the western Sino-Soviet frontier prompted signs of Chinese alarm over Soviet intentions. Under the leadership of Chou En-lai, Peking moved to defuse the border problem by compromising with the USSR. It agreed to proposals for starting negotiations on the Sino-Soviet border conflict, which were offered by Soviet Premier Aleksei Kosygin during an 11 September stopover in Peking airport. At the same time, the Chinese moved rapidly to end Peking's diplomatic isolation and broaden its foreign leverage against the Soviet Union. They improved relations with a number of strategically important nations—a policy which led to a renewed Chinese interest in developing better relations with the United States. Peking's revived desire for a closer association with Washington was also influenced by concurrent U.S. policy changes in Asia, which indicated that the Nixon administration was determined to modify the past American policy of containment of the PRC.

Chou's new moves toward the Soviet Union and the United States were not accomplished without prompting some signs of Chinese leadership debate. As in the case of Chou's late 1968 demonstration of a more amicable attitude toward the United States, the 1969 policy changes elicited commentaries in the Chinese media calling for a continuation of uncompromising opposition to both superpowers. This dissent did not seriously impede the new pragmatic policies, which quickly proved their utility in easing Soviet pressure on China and in widening Peking's international influence.

Peking's Initial Reaction

After the outbreak of armed clashes along the Sino-Soviet border in early March 1969, the focus of Chinese foreign policy shifted from the Warsaw talks and the United States to the more immediate problem of Soviet pressure on China. For the next eight months, Chinese foreign policy was dominated by anti-Soviet concerns; however, the basic Chinese strategy to counter the USSR did not change until late in the period. The Chinese approach involved no major shift in policy but a continuation, and in some instances a moderate expansion, of the policy which had characterized Peking's efforts against Moscow since the Soviet invasion of Czechoslovakia.

Of course, the newly publicized border hostilities caused the Chinese to greatly expand their media coverage of Soviet military actions against China, and the clashes clearly triggered a heightened degree of concern over Soviet military intentions.[1] Furthermore, Peking showed greater uneasiness over the visits by high-ranking Soviet dignitaries to nations adjacent to China, judging them to be evidence of an increased Soviet interest in limiting China's influence in Asia.[2]

In spite of these concerns, however, Chinese foreign initiatives against Moscow were still confined largely to the limited approach that had characterized their posture in late 1968. In fact, Peking's flexibility in this approach was in some ways even more limited than in late 1968. Most notably, the cancellation of the Warsaw talks and subsequent unprecedented Chinese attacks against the Nixon administration signaled that China had ruled out—for the time being, at least—a repetition of the foreign ministry's effort the previous November to use the Warsaw talks to upset Soviet calculations, offset Moscow's pressure against China, and gain greater international leverage against suspected Soviet machinations.

Peking's first reaction to the frontier clashes was to rapidly expand polemical comment against the Soviet Union, portraying the Soviet leaders as the aggressors in the frontier dispute and branding them as practitioners of fascist policies at home and imperialist aggression abroad.[3] At the same time, the Chinese used the opportunities of contacts with foreigners during diplomatic functions in Peking and abroad to undermine Moscow's international stature and to publicize China's side in the dispute. China also attempted to improve its relations with some countries, though not all, that were of crucial importance in the Sino-Soviet dispute.[4] In Eastern Europe, the Chinese adopted a somewhat more flexible policy as part of their continuing efforts to turn Soviet bloc discontent with Moscow to China's advantage. In May, the Chinese sent National Day greetings to Czechoslovakia for the first time in three years and made a pointed reference in the greetings to Chinese support for the "unyielding" people of Czechoslovakia.[5] At the same time, Peking reprinted an Albanian editorial that voiced strong support for the government of Romania.[6] In late May, Peking sent a trade delegation to Czechoslovakia, Romania, and Poland[7]—a move that increased China's influence in these states immediately prior to Moscow's unsuccessful efforts to align them and other communist regimes against China during the Soviet-sponsored World Communist Conference in June. In addition, the Chinese media persisted in attacks against Moscow's political and economic oppression of Eastern Europe, while continuing to be circumspect in criticizing East European governments and their leaders. Meanwhile, Chou En-lai moved to dispel rumors regarding a possible rift between Peking and the newly installed government in Pakistan by sending official greetings to the regime on 5 May.[8]

Despite these and other actions, however, Chinese efforts to expand Peking's international influence against the Soviet Union during most of 1969 did not achieve significant breakthroughs. This failure stemmed in large part from China's continued unwillingness to overlook its differences with a number of nations of crucial importance in the Sino-Soviet dispute. Most significantly, Peking not only maintained a hard line toward the United States, but also showed no sign of moderating its strained relations with two critically important neighbors, North Vietnam and North Korea. In the case of North Vietnam, for instance, the Chinese still refused to moderate their unproductive opposition to Hanoi's negotiations with the United States in Paris—the prime stumbling block to improved relations between the two states.[9] China's general attitude toward North Korea also gave little hint of thaw, and Peking's refusal to support Pyongyang's successful attack against a U.S. military aircraft in April probably acted to sour bilateral relations even more.[10]

Fear of Attack, Compromise with Moscow

It was only in late summer that China's approach to the Soviet Union began to show significant change. Most notably, the Chinese moderated their attitude toward Moscow, compromised their earlier position on border negotiations, and began discussions with the Soviet Union in Peking. In conjunction with these efforts, Peking also showed more flexibility in its general foreign policy, trying to expand China's international leverage against the Soviet Union. This attitude led ultimately to a new overture to the United States. These changes were triggered fundamentally by a sharply altered Chinese perception of the USSR, deriving from Moscow's greatly increased military and political pressure against China at this time. Moscow's pressure vividly demonstrated to Chinese leaders the dangers involved in Peking's isolation. It strengthened the position of Chou En-lai, who advocated expeditious and pragmatic Chinese foreign policy maneuvering in order to adjust to the altered East Asian balance.

A basic factor prompting China's change in attitude was the continuing reinforcement of Soviet forces along the border throughout 1969. By the middle of the summer, it was estimated that the Russians had as many as thirty divisions along the frontier and that their clear superiority in armor, artillery, and air power made them stronger than Peking's forces in most border areas.[11] Western governments appeared generally agreed that Moscow could carry out successful offensive military action against China, even at some of the most sensitive sections of the frontier. Thus, U.S. Secretary of State William Rogers disclosed on 20 August that he judged that Moscow had the military capability to seize a considerable portion of Chinese territory, including Peking.[12]

Not only did Moscow have powerful forces in place, but it had also demonstrated a willingness and ability to employ its military superiority. During the major border clash along the northwestern Sinkiang frontier on 13 August, for instance, the Chinese reported that the battle raged for the good portion of a day and that the Soviet forces employed tanks, planes, and other sophisticated weaponry in the fray.[13] *Pravda* later reported that "several dozen" Chinese soldiers were killed in the clash.[14]

In addition, Moscow applied increasing pressure with a barrage of explicit and implied threats concerning more forceful Soviet military moves against China. The threats seemed designed to intimidate Peking and to compel it to compromise its position in the frontier dispute and to agree to enter border talks on Soviet terms. Moscow's propaganda increasingly attacked Mao Tse-tung personally, likening him to the worst of the Chinese emperors and implying that Moscow considered it a Soviet duty to overthrow his government. In line with this commentary, Radio Moscow on 11 June declared that "the Soviet people are determined to come to the aid of their Chinese brothers."[15] At the same time, the Soviet Union allowed news to reach the international press concerning the steady reinforcement of Soviet troops in the Far East, the major Russian military ground and air exercises there, and the closure of the Trans-Siberian Railroad to civilian traffic because of military movements.[16] In August, a leading Soviet missile specialist was appointed to command the Far East military district bordering on the Amur and Ussuri rivers.[17] Soon afterward, press reports appeared which claimed that Moscow had been quietly inquiring among communist parties of both Eastern and Western Europe as to what their reaction would be if the Soviet Union executed a military strike against China's nuclear installations. The story appeared in the American press on 28 August and undoubtedly helped to intensify the pressure then being felt by the Chinese leadership.[18] Also on the 28th, *Pravda* released what was regarded as the Soviet Union's most authoritative and threatening indictment of Peking to date. The statement suggested that war with China would inevitably necessitate the use of nuclear weapons, and it warned that a conflict with China would involve other nations.[19] At about the same time, Moscow sent a private letter to other major communist parties emphasizing that there was a real danger of a Sino-Soviet war over the frontier dispute.[20]

It was within this context that Chinese press coverage began to show a more intense concern over Soviet intentions. Peking media started to dwell on the ominous possibility that Moscow would soon initiate large-scale hostilities against China. Most significantly, two articles released in August stand out as clear departures from China's earlier, more confident attitude toward Soviet military pressure. Thus, one of the articles included the following:

> Recently, the Soviet revisionist renegade clique, from Brezhnev on down to many military chiefs, have shouted themselves hoarse in war cries on various occasions. Brezhnev vilified China as having staged "armed conflicts." He blustered that the Soviet revisionists would maintain "defense" capability at the highest level, frantically making war threats against China. The Soviet revisionist military chiefs Grechko and Yakubovsky ranted hysterically about so called "military might" and openly threatened to start a nuclear war. Recently other military chiefs . . . published one article after another in the press, raving wildly about launching an "unexpected surprise attack" just as Hitler boasted of the "Blitzkrieg" in his day.[21]

More ominously, Peking media in mid-August released an article which gave China's most detailed description of Soviet military preparations along the frontier to date. It specifically claimed that Moscow's ultimate goal was the occupation of all Chinese territory north of the Great Wall. The remarks focused on the expansion of Soviet missile forces, air bases, and ground forces, and they alluded to continuous planning sessions by Soviet leaders designed to prepare for total war against China. Most startling, the article spoke of alleged Soviet efforts to organize "international columns" composed of Warsaw Pact troops —similar to those used in Moscow's action against Czechoslovakia the year before.[22]

Against the backdrop of heightened concern, the Chinese agreed to receive Soviet Premier Kosygin in Peking on 11 September. According to communist sources, Kosygin proposed to Chou En-lai that talks begin immediately between Sino-Soviet officials at the level of deputy foreign minister to deal with the border situation. He also proposed that Sino-Soviet ambassadorial relations be restored and that trade ties be resumed. Ideological and party matters were to be put aside for consideration later.[23] The Chinese side apparently remained noncommittal at the meeting, and Peking did not publicly respond to the Soviet initiative until almost a month after the session.

In the interim, Moscow continued to apply heavy pressure on the Chinese leadership. On 13 September, a deputy defense minister of the USSR engaged in what was characterized in the West as a "rocket-rattling" speech against China, emphasizing the importance of offensive nuclear missiles in a "Blitzkrieg" attack.[24] Two days later, Peking radio referred to a "black signal" emanating from Moscow concerning an alleged increase in Soviet war preparations against China.[25] On 16 September a widely known Soviet journalist, Victor Louis, published an article in a London newspaper claiming that Moscow was still ready, if necessary, to launch a military strike against China.[26]

In response to such growing Soviet pressure, the Chinese released a new and highly unusual PRC National Day slogan on 16 September. It stressed the likelihood of a nuclear attack against China and urgently called for immediate preparations against nuclear war.[27] Chinese uneasiness was also evident in Chou En-lai's remarks—delivered at a National Day reception on 30 September—which dwelt defensively on Peking's nuclear development. Chou emphasized that China had no intention of using nuclear weapons to attack the Soviet Union or any other country. He stated, "We develop nuclear weapons solely for defense and for breaking nuclear monopoly, and our ultimate aim is to eliminate nuclear weapons."[28] At the same time, Chinese media—in a highly unusual development—muted all commentary on Peking's successful nuclear tests of 23 September and 29 September until after Peking had agreed to Kosygin's proposal to start border talks.[29]

Chinese uneasiness was further reflected in the PRC government statement of 7 October, in which Peking officially responded to the Soviet proposals put forward by Kosygin. The statement was defensive regarding China's nuclear weapons program; it denounced Soviet attempts to vilify China as a cover for alleged Soviet plans for a nuclear war; and it made pointed reference to a "handful of war maniacs" in Moscow who were allegedly planning to raid China's nuclear development and testing sites.[30] More significantly, the statement reflected a clear retreat from Peking's previous position on the border issue. In particular, the Chinese now agreed to drop their demands of earlier in the year that Moscow must meet certain conditions *before* the border talks could begin. For example, a 24 May 1969 Chinese statement on the border situation had listed a series of conditions which it implied Moscow had to accept in order "to make serious negotiations possible." These included: confirmation that the existing border situation was based on "unequal treaties" forced on China by Tsarist Russia, the return "in principle" of virtually all disputed territory to the Chinese, and the withdrawal of Soviet forces from all disputed territory, including such important islands on the frontier as Chen Pao island, the site of the bloody clashes of March 1969, and Heisha Tzu, the large Soviet-held island located at the confluence of the Amur and Ussuri rivers, immediately opposite the strategic Russian city of Khabarovsk.[31]

However, in their statement on the border issue on 7 October and in a PRC foreign ministry statement on the following day, the Chinese clearly demonstrated that Moscow still had not agreed to these conditions.[32] In fact, the Chinese proposed that these issues be the first matters discussed *after* the talks were underway. Such a compromise was certainly distasteful to Peking. Yet the Chinese clearly judged that they had no alternative but to moderate their intransigent position in order to alleviate the border crisis, avoid a potentially disastrous war with Moscow, and reduce Soviet military pressure against China along the frontier and elsewhere around China's periphery. This motivation was emphasized by Peking's 7 October statement, which portrayed China's most urgent goal in the discussions as the disengagement of forces along the frontier. The statement maintained that, "in order to relax the situation along the border between the two countries and enable the Sino-Soviet boundary negotiations to be held free from any threats, the Chinese side put forth the proposal that the Chinese and Soviet sides first of all reach an agreement on the provisional measures for maintaining the status quo of the border, for averting armed conflict, and for disengagement."[33]

After accepting this compromise, however, the Chinese demonstrated that their deep-seated opposition to Moscow over the frontier dispute and other issues would be modified no further. In the 8 October statement, for example, the Chinese refuted an earlier Soviet statement on the border problem and emphasized that any final settlement of the issue must accord to Chinese terms, including a Soviet recognition of the "unequal treaties" and agreement in principle to return disputed territory to China. At the same time, Peking pointed out that China's fundamental differences with Moscow over ideological matters would continue unabated. In short, Peking made a tactical compromise in the face of strong Soviet pressure. The Chinese retreated over the border issue and moderated their posture toward the Soviet Union in a carefully limited way in order to avoid war and to reduce Soviet military pressure against China.

Debate over Policy toward Moscow

At the time of China's decision to moderate its opposition toward the Soviet Union and begin negotiations over the border problem, several articles appeared in Chinese media representing divergent opinion over what constituted the proper approach toward the USSR. In general, the differences focused on issues similar to those debated in Chinese media at the time of China's conciliatory initiative toward the United States in late 1968. The differences centered on two interrelated problems: (1) whether it was justified for the Chinese to enter into negotiations with the Soviet Union and/or the United States, and (2) whether China should avoid such peaceful political dealings with the USSR and the United States, in favor of total reliance on armed struggle and people's war to deal with these adversaries.

In contrast to the division of Chinese opinion into two groups in late 1968, three different opinions were voiced on these problems at this time. Also, in contrast to the 18 February 1969 reversal of China's initiative at the Warsaw talks, this subsequent divergence of Chinese opinion seems to have had no startling effect on the course of Chinese foreign policy. Nevertheless, the differences clearly demonstrated a continuing lack of agreement among the Chinese leaders over important foreign policy matters—a factor which undoubtedly complicated the formulation of Chinese policy toward Moscow at this critical juncture.

The most flexible approach toward the Soviet Union was reflected in two articles released by the Kiangsu provincial media during the week immediately prior to the commencement of border discussions in

Peking on 20 October. The articles were obviously designed to justify China's decision to enter into border negotiations, and they indicated that China could also justify a similar approach toward its other superpower enemy, the United States. They also stressed that negotiations with either the Soviet Union or the United States were evidence of Chinese tactical flexibility and compromise and that such actions did not reflect a basic change in China's longstanding opposition to both these "imperialist" powers.[34]

To justify China's amenability toward the superpowers, the authors cited a 1945 report written by Mao, "On the Chungking Negotiations." The report advocated negotiating with an enemy during a period of protracted struggle. Mao emphasized in the report that to thwart a foe's "counterrevolutionary dual tactics"—involving peace-talk initiatives along with military aggression—the Chinese should adopt "revolutionary dual tactics"—entailing negotiating with the enemy while remaining militarily alert to block any possible surprise attacks. The articles focused specifically on Moscow's current policy toward China, and they advocated China's use of revolutionary dual tactics in order to unmask alleged Soviet machinations and perfidy. At the same time, the articles implied that China could employ similar tactics toward the United States. In particular, one article stated: *"It is our consistent policy to settle problems through peaceful negotiations. . . .* Chairman Mao teaches us, 'How to give tit for tat [during a period of protracted struggle with an enemy] depends on the situation. Sometimes, not going to negotiations is tit for tat; and *sometimes, going to negotiations is also tit for tat.'* This is the method we used in our negotiations in Chungking with the Kuomintang reactionaries. *This is also the method we use in our negotiations with U.S. imperialism and Soviet revisionism."*[35]

The counterview to this flexible approach was evident in a series of commentaries ostensibly concerned with cultural affairs. The writings condemned a number of already well-discredited plays, while praising model plays produced under the guidance of Chiang Ching. Though only a few of the articles explicitly referred to the topic of negotiations with an enemy, those articles were uniformly opposed to such a tactic. Employment of negotiations with an enemy was denounced as a capitulationist policy which was counter to the ideas of Mao Tse-tung. It was also claimed that the act of negotiating with an enemy was an insult to the fighting ability and political quality of the Chinese army and the Chinese people.[36]

Contrary to what might have been expected, these strongly worded criticisms of negotiation did not subside when China began to moderate its posture toward the Soviet Union and started negotiations with Soviet officials in Peking. In fact, a few articles, which appeared immediately before and after the commencement of the Peking border discussions, stridently called for a policy of uncompromising opposition to enemies such as the Soviet Union.[37] For example, Radio Peking on 19 October—the day before the start of the Peking talks—hailed Chiang Ching's model play *Taking the Bandit's Stronghold* and denounced the already soundly discredited play *Beleaguered City*.[38] The article pointedly condemned negotiations with an enemy as an insult to Chinese fighting ability. It emphasized that the only proper way to handle an enemy is through armed struggle and people's war. In particular, it stated: *"Taking the Bandit's Stronghold* uses a beautiful artistic form to praise the brilliant concept of people's war conceived by Chairman Mao and emphasizes the great truth that political power grows from a gun barrel. On the contrary, the reactionary film, *Beleaguered City,* defends the nonsense of relying on glib talk to get the enemy to lay down his weapons and capitulate. This idea openly opposed the concept of people's war." The article went on to state:

> In the big poisonous weed, the "Beleaguered City," there appears [Chiang], director of the department for intelligence work behind enemy lines, . . . he gave no consideration to the military and political strength of our forces. Even less was his consideration to the tens of millions of people under oppression. There was no end to his illusions about the enemy.
>
> He did not rely on people's war to conquer the enemy, but on the existing sharp dissensions within the enemy's ranks. . . . He was a capitulationist who depended on glib talk. This ugly figure is portrayed as an upright person, but he is actually a vanguard for Liu Shao-ch'i and company's restoration of capitalism.[39]

The third approach to negotiations during this period was reflected in China's actual policy toward the Soviet Union. It was less flexible than the posture advocated by the Kiangsu media commentary but more moderate than the rigid position proposed in coverage of cultural affairs. Peking demonstrated that it viewed total reliance on people's war and avoidance of negotiations with the Soviet Union as an unworkable approach at that time. A truculent, rigid attitude toward Moscow had been adopted without success throughout the earlier part of 1969. In fact, such a policy had led China to the brink of a disastrous war. The Chinese leadership demonstrated that they felt tactical compromise and negotiations with Moscow were necessary in order to avoid war, defuse the volatile border situation, and achieve a disengagement of Soviet forces along the frontier.

But the leadership apparently judged that the moderate approach reflected in the Kiangsu media was also inappropriate and potentially embarrassing at this juncture. Although the Chinese felt constrained to compromise their position over the border talks, they showed no desire to call attention to this retreat. As a result, Peking avoided publicizing any ideological rationale similar to that evinced in the Kiangsu media's focus on Mao's "On the Chungking Negotiations." At the same time, the Kiangsu approach also had clearly implied a willingness on the part of the Chinese to negotiate with the United States—something Peking was not yet ready to endorse publicly.[40]

The differences evident in these approaches toward Moscow, like the differences apparent in Chinese commentary on the United States in late 1968, almost certainly complicated efforts to initiate changes in Peking's foreign policy during this period. Thus, in formulating a new policy toward Moscow in 1969, Chou En-lai and other proponents of a more flexible Chinese foreign approach not only had to consider Soviet pressure and the traditional constraints imposed on Chinese foreign policy by ideological, historical, and other differences with the Soviet Union, they also had to contend with some Chinese leaders who were completely opposed to any flexibility in China's stance. They ended up by adopting a policy that helped neutralize Soviet pressure but did not fundamentally undermine China's longstanding position on basic Sino-Soviet differences. The policy struck a balance between the rigid and moderate positions reflected in leadership opinion on the issue.

Diplomatic Initiatives against Moscow

The Sino-Soviet border talks began in Peking on 20 October 1969. While easing concern over an immediate Soviet attack, the talks did little to remove China's more fundamental concern over Soviet military pressure along the frontier. The Chinese were especially fearful that the Soviet Union would now exploit its military superiority in order to force the Chinese to make further concessions, perhaps resulting in a border settlement contrary to their interests. This judgment was most apparent in the only public Chinese commentaries on the talks in the months following the start of the discussions. Two articles on the issue appeared in the English language edition of the authoritative Hong Kong communist newspaper *Ta Kung Pao* in November 1969 and January 1970.[41] The first article is known to have been prepared by the director of the paper and leading communist in Hong Kong, Fei I-min. Fei had reportedly just returned from consultations in Peking.[42] Both articles emphasized that the Chinese were seriously concerned over what they viewed as Soviet attempts to negotiate from a position of strength and thereby force China into a disadvantageous border settlement. At the same time, they underscored the continuing lack of progress in the border talks and emphasized that the Soviet Union still had not agreed to China's urgent proposal for the disengagement of Soviet forces from along the frontier.

Meanwhile, other Chinese comment reflected serious concern over allegedly increasing Soviet efforts to block Peking's interests in Asia and throughout the world. Moscow's foreign policy initiatives in this period toward the United States, Japan, West Germany, and other countries—which were designed to settle outstanding problems such as the nuclear armaments issue, the Middle East crisis, the future of Germany, the balance of power in Europe, and the growing role of Japan in Asia—were seen in this light. Thus, from Peking's point of view, such Soviet efforts were designed by the USSR to settle Soviet disputes elsewhere so that Moscow could then focus more pressure on China.

Because of such continuing strong concerns, a key decision facing the Chinese policy makers at this juncture was what foreign policy to adopt in order to counteract Soviet military and political pressure. One route open to the Chinese was to maintain the relatively rigid approach that had characterized Chinese international efforts against the Soviet Union since late 1968. This approach—involving ideologically based opposition to accommodation with either the United States or the Soviet Union—had left Peking in a vulnerable position within the East Asian power balance. It was an unrealistic stance, which had not only achieved no significant new advances in Chinese international leverage since 1968, but in recent years had left Peking unmistakably weak and passive in the face of Soviet power. Thus, Peking's acute need for countervailing power against Moscow's pressure soon gave the upper hand to pragmatists in the Chinese leadership led by Chou En-lai. They favored a moderation of past rigid Chinese adherence to ideological principles and the assumption of a more conciliatory international posture.

In implementing this policy, the Chinese first of all focused attention on strengthening their influence in key neighboring states and on blocking suspected Soviet initiatives there. Most significantly, the Chinese managed to overlook their past serious differences with the North Vietnamese, adopting a more amicable attitude toward their communist neighbor. Peking, in early fall, muted its criticism of Hanoi's negotiations in the Paris talks and warmly welcomed visiting Vietnamese dignitaries. China's stand on the Vietnam War eventually was brought into agreement with that of North Vietnam.

These changes first became apparent in late September, when the

Chinese gave an especially warm welcome to North Vietnamese Premier Pham Van Dong.[43] Dong had come to China to celebrate Peking's National Day. While Dong held private consultations with Chou Enlai, Vietnamese affairs were prominently and favorably covered in the Chinese media[44]—a sharp contrast with China's almost complete omission of Vietnamese matters during coverage of PRC National Day celebrations in 1968. At the same time, the Chinese media began to use such terms as *warm* and *friendly* to describe Sino-Vietnamese ties —a practice that had characterized Peking's propaganda approach toward Hanoi prior to the 1968 rift over the start of the Paris talks. Most significantly, NCNA reported on 4 October that the Chinese ambassador had indicated during an embassy reception in Hanoi that Sino-Vietnamese solidarity was back to normal. He did so by using such formulations as: China and Vietnam are "as close as lips and teeth," and the Chinese and Vietnamese are "brothers sharing the same weal and woe." Such comments had been absent from Peking publications during the past year.[45]

Soon after, Chou En-lai signaled the beginning of the end of China's opposition to the Paris talks by toning down previous demands for unswerving protracted war in Vietnam. He drew attention instead to China's new support for Hanoi's maximum demands concerning a negotiated settlement of the war. During an 8 October speech before a visiting National Liberation Front-Provisional Revolutionary Government (NLF-PRG) delegation, he maintained, ". . . the sole correct road to genuine settlement of the Vietnam question is the unconditional withdrawal of all U.S. aggressor troops and its vassals' troops from South Vietnam, so that the people of South Vietnam may tackle their own problems without any outside interference."[46]

A 16 October Sino-Vietnamese communiqué marking Chinese discussions with the NLF-PRG delegation demonstrated a further compromise in Peking's position. While reiterating Chou's earlier support for the Vietnamese communists' maximum demands in the Paris talks, the Chinese also gave indirect support to the NLF-PRG ten-point proposal for a peaceful settlement of the Vietnam conflict. Specifically, Peking reported in full the NLF-PRG contention in the communiqué, which stated that "the basis for a settlement of the South Vietnam question is the ten point document for a total solution put forward by the NLF-PRG."[47]

Meanwhile, the Chinese also demonstrated a new willingness to overlook differences and restore good relations with the North Korean government. Most importantly, Peking warmly welcomed a high-ranking Korean delegation to China's 1969 National Day celebrations, constituting China's friendliest action toward Pyongyang since before the

95

start of the Cultural Revolution.[48] The Chinese then continued efforts to demonstrate their solidarity with Pyongyang by exploiting anti-Japanese themes designed to underscore common Chinese cause with the Korean government.[49] Most notably, the Chinese called great attention to the Nixon-Sato communiqué of November 1969, which had expressed particularly strong Japanese interest in developments in South Korea and Taiwan. Peking focused on the communiqué as an indication of the need for common efforts by Peking and Pyongyang against the Japanese.[50] The Chinese even went so far as to reprint North Korean commentary critical of the communiqué, the first such favorable Chinese reiteration of Korean comment in several years.[51] At the same time, the Chinese moved to solidify their unsteady relationship with the Sihanouk government in Cambodia. During National Day ceremonies, for instance, Peking welcomed the highest-level Cambodian delegation to visit China since before the Cultural Revolution and gave it a friendly reception, including a private meeting with Chou En-lai.[52]

China' new flexibility was not limited to neighboring Asia. In the Middle East, for example, Peking overlooked its past differences with the Algerian government and warmly welcomed a visiting delegation from Algiers to China's National Day ceremonies.[53] Later in the month, the Chinese reciprocated by sending a special delegation to Algeria's National Day celebrations for the first time since the start of the Cultural Revolution.[54] Peking also made further efforts to improve its position in Eastern Europe at the expense of the USSR. Most importantly, it was announced in November that the Chinese had agreed to restore ambassadorial-level relations with the government of Yugoslavia, ending a hiatus of over a decade during which relations were conducted by chargés d'affaires.[55] In addition, NCNA reported in early October that a vice-minister of foreign affairs had attended East Germany's National Day reception in Peking—a considerably more favorable Chinese treatment than in 1968, when the Peking media ignored the reception.[56] And, *People's Daily* in late December released a stinging critique of Moscow's alleged collusion with the Bonn government, which declared strong support for the state sovereignty of both East Germany and Poland and accused Moscow of sacrificing such sovereignty for the sake of better relations with the West. The article marked one of the most emphatic Chinese statements in support of Soviet bloc states in several years.[57]

Peking's New Overture to the United States

By far the most substantial change in China's international posture at this time was its revival of a moderate approach toward the United States, culminating in China's agreement in December 1969 to resume ambassadorial meetings in Warsaw. China's continued serious concern over Soviet pressure, its persistent fear of Soviet-American collusion against Chinese international interests, and its preoccupation with gaining foreign leverage against the Soviet Union at this time—all set the stage for this attempt to enhance China's position vis-à-vis the Soviet Union through utilization of the American connection.

Peking almost certainly judged that the renewal of the talks at this time would significantly strengthen and secure its interests in the face of Soviet military and political pressure. In order to upset the Soviets and ensure security in the talks, the Chinese agreed to abandon the meeting hall used in the Sino-American talks in Warsaw in the past. That hall was provided by the Poles and was widely believed to be "bugged" by both the Polish and Soviet authorities.[58] Instead, Peking agreed to hold the talks alternately in the more secure confines of the Chinese and American embassies in Warsaw. The Chinese were well aware of the traditional Soviet suspicion and nervousness over any private contacts between the United States and China, and they presumably agreed to this unprecedented step in Warsaw in order to increase Soviet uneasiness. At the same time, they also realized that such private meetings with the United States might cast doubt on American motives in Soviet eyes. In particular, they might serve to complicate efforts by Moscow to reach agreement with Washington over a number of issues contrary to China's interests. At any rate, China's move had a clear and unmistakable impact on Moscow; Soviet media viewed the discussions as complicating border negotiations with the Chinese as well as their nuclear armaments discussions with the United States. Soviet commentators even charged that Peking, fearful of Soviet intentions, might be seeking to come to terms with the United States, in order to play one nuclear power off against the other.[59]

Chinese press and private commentary demonstrated that, aside from its anti-Soviet motivation, Peking's approach toward the United States also originated with its judgment that the Nixon administration was moving toward a more relaxed foreign policy in East Asia. Since mid-summer 1969, the Chinese media had been uncharacteristically silent on several U.S. initiatives in Asia. Most significantly, the Chinese did not condemn persistent American calls for the resumption of the ambassadorial talks in Warsaw. They discreetly avoided all commentary on Washington's step-by-step efforts to improve the atmosphere surrounding U.S.-PRC relations by means of reducing American trade and travel restrictions with the mainland government.[60] At the same time Peking consistently delayed comment on Washington's announced troop withdrawals from Vietnam, usually for several weeks after each American announcement.[61]

China's media also maintained a highly unusual five-day silence in coverage of President Nixon's Asian tour in late July and August 1969. This reticence seemed to suggest some uncertainty in China's approach toward Washington at this time.[62] In particular, the Chinese delayed for a week official comment on the president's remarks during a news conference on Guam. Nixon had used the forum to advocate a reduced American military role in Asia and to lay the foundation of what was to become known as the Nixon Doctrine.[63] More strikingly, the Chinese media made only one passing reference to the simultaneous trip by Secretary of State William Rogers to sensitive Asian areas such as Taiwan and Hong Kong.[64] This approach contrasted sharply with the harsh Chinese attacks against Rogers's visit to Southeast Asia during May 1969.[65]

In September, Peking issued an authoritative article on policy toward the United States which appeared to represent a sharp turn toward moderation. While the article reviewed familiar themes concerning Peking's resistance against American "aggression" over the past twenty years, it was largely written in the past tense. Significantly, it left the impression that the Chinese no longer considered Washington to be a strong threat to Chinese security and vital foreign policy interests. In addition, the article affirmed the existence of recent changes in American policy toward China and stated that Washington had become "more and more passive" toward China in recent years.[66]

This line was further developed in subsequent months. In a speech in late October, for example, Chou En-lai stressed Washington's feeble international condition and underscored the Chinese contention that the United States had been defeated and was on the retreat in Vietnam. He stated: "U.S. imperialism has suffered disastrous defeat although it has thrown more than 500,000 U.S. troops into the South Vietnam battlefield, employed enormous manpower and natural resources, and resorted to all means of war short of atomic weapons. . . . At present, the struggle of the people of the world, including the American people, against U.S. aggression in Vietnam is daily surging forward, while the U.S. ruling clique is riddled with contradictions and bogged down with ever more serious political and economic crisis."[67]

Furthermore, NCNA comment on the U.S. posture in the annual Chinese representation debate in the United Nations during 1969 emphasized China's reduced concern over American actions and pointed out that Washington had become more passive toward China.

It observed that "the debate in the UN General Assembly clearly showed that U.S. imperialism's policy of hostility toward China was widely denounced and it has landed itself in a predicament of increasing isolation and passivity."[68] Even China's virulent commentary against the Nixon-Sato communiqué of November focused chiefly on the alleged aggressive designs of Japan, stressing that Washington was forced to rely on Tokyo because of its weakened position in Asia.[69]

In short, Chinese coverage of the United States reflected a clear Chinese appreciation of American efforts to reduce military commitments along China's periphery in Asia. It also showed an unwillingness to criticize American moves to resume the Warsaw talks or to reduce longstanding restrictions on interaction with the Peking government. The Chinese viewed the United States as less of a threat to China. They saw U.S. resolve to block China's interests in Asia and elsewhere as weakening, and they even saw signs of change in the United States' China policy. At the same time, Chinese officials used private conversations with foreign diplomats in Peking to voice a strikingly more moderate approach toward the United States. They showed particular interest in Washingtons' unilateral decision to ease trade and travel restrictions against China.[70] In short, it seems fair to conclude that the Chinese adopted their newly flexible approach to Washington and agreed to reopen the Warsaw talks at least partly in order to assess first hand the actual significance of these recent American changes toward China. The Chinese especially wanted to encourage what they saw as a weakening of American containment in East Asia.

Debate over U.S. Policy

By late 1969, therefore, China's attitude toward the United States was becoming increasingly more flexible and moderate. However, there appeared in the Chinese media at this time a number of indications that not all Chinese leaders were completely satisfied with this new approach. Most importantly, a few articles appearing in the national and provincial media seemed to dispute the new Chinese posture. As in articles which had appeared to oppose China's moderation toward the United States in late 1968, and those which had appeared to be against China's entry into negotiations with the USSR in 1969, the current commentaries took a completely rigid position. The articles condemned those who perceived a change toward moderation and relaxation in the American foreign policy, particularly in the United States' China policy. They implied that any peaceful political interaction or negotiation with Washington was not in China's best interests.

Comparison of the major points of these articles with the concurrent Chinese policy toward the United States reveals clear differences in judgment as to what constituted a proper Chinese approach toward the United States at this time. On 14 September, for example, an article in *People's Daily* pointedly attacked Soviet party chief Brezhnev over his allegedly sanguine assessment of U.S. foreign policies.[71] Although this article may have been designed solely to discredit the opinions of the Soviet leader, the nature of the charges against Brezhnev and the timing of the attack suggested that it may have been intended to discredit those in Peking who were advocating a more moderate Chinese approach toward Washington. In any case, the article's avowed attitude toward the United States was in sharp contrast to the more moderate tone of most Chinese comment on the United States at this time.

The article ridiculed those who held that Washington had altered its international posture. It emphasized what it called the continuing dangerous, predatory, and warlike nature of U.S. imperialism. By contrast, China's general coverage of the United States at this time had affirmed that Washington's position in Asia had weakened. It had also indicated that the United States was in a state of increasing internal and international crisis and confusion and, accordingly, was less of a threat to China.

The article denounced as "political frauds" all efforts by the United States to seek improved relations with revolutionary states such as China. Peking media, however, had remained discreetly silent on all recent U.S. speeches and substantive initiatives designed to improve relations with China, implicitly showing an interest in such American efforts. The article also strongly focused on alleged recent American efforts to expand military oppression around the world, particularly against China. The general Chinese media, however, had indicated that Washington was weakened in its opposition to China. Finally, the article disputed the contention that the Nixon administration had done anything to change the warlike international approach of the United States. Peking's general commentaries regarding the United States, however, had already recognized a moderation in the Nixon administration's policy toward China.[72]

A more strikingly divergent line was evident in an article appearing in the Anhwei provincial media on 19 November 1969.[73] By this time, the general Chinese media line toward the United States had clearly moderated. High-level Chinese spokesmen led by Premier Chou En-lai had publicly endorsed the view that the United States was less of a threat to China and was retreating in the face of defeat in Asia. More importantly, Chinese officials by this time had begun to show a keen interest in recent American moves to relax tensions with China, and they were privately querying foreign diplomats in Peking regarding these changes in American policy. Despite the reduction of hostility, the Anhwei article condemned Chinese moderation toward the United States. It used the technique of repudiating a foreign policy associated with deposed head of state Liu Shao-ch'i, condemning Liu's alleged schemes for coming to terms with the United States, and it strongly denounced the "towering, unforgivable crimes" committed by the United States against China. The article insisted that the United States was stepping up efforts to oppose China, in marked contrast to the Chinese press statements at this time, which generally presented the United States as more passive toward China. While the article made no direct reference to the topic of negotiations with an enemy such as the United States, it clearly implied that China could successfully deal with Washington only through armed struggle. The article also implied that there should be no abatement in China's public opposition to the United States and that Peking should fully expose the "aggressive, man-eating features" of the United States.

In what may have been a covert attack on advocates of a more moderate Chinese posture toward the United States, the article severely criticized those who judge that there are clear-minded officials in Washington who do not favor war. In particular, it attacked Liu Shao-ch'i, because he stated that "even within the ruling groups of the USA, there are people who are more clear minded and will gradually understand that a war policy may not be in the interests of the USA." The article also warned that any moderation in China's posture toward Washington would lead to disaster for China. The article summarized its case against moderation toward the United States by concluding:

> Liu Shao-ch'i . . . vigorously spread the theory that within the ruling groups of the USA there are people who are more clear minded. His particular aim is to make us relax our vigilance against the aggressive nature of U.S. imperialism and social imperialism and thereby enable him to serve the war policy of U.S. imperialism and social-imperialism.
>
> If we were so easily fooled by the lies of Liu Shao-ch'i, we would find ourselves unarmed and helpless in the face of a war of aggression waged by U.S. imperialism and social-imperialism, and we would be at their mercy. This we absolutely cannot accept. The heinous ambition of Liu Shao-ch'i to bring a wolf into the house must not be allowed to materialize.

The apparent divergence between this rigid approach and that of China's concurrent moderate and flexible posture toward the United States indicates that some members of the Chinese leadership continued up to late 1969 to strongly oppose a flexible policy toward the

United States. It seems almost certain that the presence of such opinions among the ruling Chinese group acted to complicate China's positive movement toward Washington at this time. During leadership deliberations leading to this new policy toward the United States, therefore, advocates of flexibility such as Chou En-lai doubtlessly had to contend with and perhaps accommodate the views of those who opposed change in Chinese policy toward Washington.

Nevertheless, by the end of the year, it was increasingly evident that the influence of such hard-line opinions had been reduced. The decline in U.S. pressure and the increase in Soviet pressure had reached a point where Peking came to judge that its previous rigid posture toward both superpowers was no longer workable. The Chinese now felt impelled to adopt at least a tactically flexible policy toward both powers and to enter into negotiations with them in order to neutralize the serious increase in Soviet pressure against China and to encourage the moderation of American containment in Asia. As a result, advocacy of an uncompromising Chinese approach to either power became an increasingly unattractive position and disappeared in Chinese comment.

In short, the pragmatic approach of Chou En-lai had successfully defended China's security and vital interests in a dangerous situation. By contrast, the previous ideological stance opposed to both the United States and the Soviet Union had led China to the brink of disaster. Chou's realistic appraisal of the situation thus had gained the upper hand in leadership councils. The developing power balance in East Asia, and Soviet pressure on China in particular, had demonstrated vividly that sustained reliance on ideological principles as a basis for foreign policy was too dangerous for vital Chinese concerns.

CHAPTER SEVEN

Sino-American Rapprochement in the 1970s

Peking's new policies toward the Soviet Union and the United States and its more flexible posture in international affairs proved to be extremely beneficial for China's national interests over the next few years. Following the pragmatic strategy begun by Chou En-lai in the late 1960s, Peking rapidly expanded diplomatic contacts and improved relations with many nations during the first years of the 1970s. The Chinese advance was highlighted by Peking's entrance into the United Nations in October 1971, President Nixon's visit to China in February 1972, and the normalization of Sino-Japanese relations during Prime Minister Kakuei Tanaka's trip to China in September 1972. These developments testified to China's emergence as a new force in international politics, and they served to offset what Peking viewed as the anti-China designs of its main adversary—the Soviet Union.

The prevailing East Asian balance of power warranted Chinese pursuit of a differentiated approach to the two superpowers. Persisting Soviet military and political pressure against China underlined Moscow's continued unwillingness to meet Chinese demands over the sensitive border dispute. Moscow's concurrent diplomatic and propaganda initiatives—especially those centered on the Soviet proposed Asian Collective Security System, an implicitly anti-Chinese proposition first propounded by Brezhnev in 1969—appeared designed to check Peking's emergence on the world stage after the Cultural Revolution.[1] By contrast, the United States demonstrated increasingly that it was less of a threat to Chinese interests and that it could provide the Chinese wih a useful source of leverage in competition with the USSR. The result was that the establishment of an improved relationship with the United States came to seem increasingly attractive to the Chinese leaders as a potentially effective way to safeguard and enhance vital

103

military and political interests of the People's Republic of China in East Asia.

As in the early 1940s and mid-1950s, the Chinese leaders concluded that their security and independence were closely tied to the improvement of Sino-American relations. At bottom, the Soviet Union posed an immediate military threat to China's security, as well as a long-term impediment to its desire for an independent foreign posture. The United States appeared to hold the key that would allow Peking to escape its vulnerability vis-à-vis Moscow. At the same time, Peking was well aware that its longstanding efforts to complete the Chinese civil war, reunify Taiwan with the mainland, and dismantle the rival Chiang Kai-shek regime were closely related to U.S. policy in East Asia.

As in the early 1940s, the Chinese Communist Party leaders now saw some signs that the United States might be more open and flexible toward the communists than it had been in the past. In particular, the United States was moving away from Dulles's stress on containing China and was taking steps to ease longstanding trade and travel restrictions with the PRC. In addition, the United States appeared anxious to strengthen bilateral communication with China in the ambassadorial talks in Warsaw. But of particular importance to Peking, the United States demonstrated the sincerity of its announced intention to ease U.S. military pressure in Asia through the unilateral withdrawal of American forces from Indochina and other areas around China's periphery. Most notable on this score was the American decision to stop its past practice of having ships of the U.S. Seventh Fleet patrol in the Taiwan Straits.[2]

American policy toward the Chinese communists had indeed changed markedly from what it had been in the 1940s and the 1950s. Washington now approached the Peking leaders because they could help the United States maintain power interests in East Asia. The United States had begun to pursue a policy of realistic power politics in the existing nation-state system in East Asia. The Nixon administration had largely put aside the ideological baggage and political moralism that had impeded U.S. policy in the past. In pursuing a pragmatic policy, Washington now wished to use whatever sources of international leverage were available, even if they came from a communist state. In this context, the Nixon administration considered dealing with the Peking leaders to be compatible with American power interests in East Asia and began to view China as the main bulwark against Soviet dominance on the Asian mainland.

Thus, reflecting a growing awareness of congruent Sino-American interests in East Asia, Chinese leaders soon responded positively to

American calls for closer cooperation. Peking's new policy developed slowly in response to persisting U.S. initiatives—in contrast to the more direct CCP approach toward the United States in the 1940s and the 1950s. The Chinese only haltingly showed interest in meeting with American leaders, and they withheld full approval of an accommodation with Washington until after the July 1971 secret trip to China of President Nixon's national security adviser, Henry A. Kissinger.

Chinese caution almost certainly derived in part from the frustration that had met Peking's previous futile efforts to accommodate the United States. Peking's new approach avoided significant displays of openness or flexibility until American intentions were clarified. Another factor inclining Chou En-lai and other architects of the PRC strategy to proceed slowly was probably the continued lack of unanimity among the Chinese leaders concerning policy toward the United States. Chou had seen his initiative of 26 November 1968 abruptly turned aside by internal opposition, and he fully realized that the groundwork for a departure from the current attitude toward the United States would have to be prepared very carefully.

Early Reflections of Peking's New Posture

Peking's interest in reconciliation with the United States was apparent in its early stages largely through subtle changes in Chinese media coverage of the United States. The media continued sharp criticism of American leaders and their policies but reduced the number of personal attacks on President Nixon and avoided denouncing the administration's policies on certain sensitive bilateral issues including Taiwan. At the same time, Peking departed from its past appraisal of international affairs as being dominated by Soviet-American collusion and began to differentiate between the two superpowers and to take advantage of signs of division between them. Peking, thus, began to portray the Soviet Union as the most dangerous enemy of China and the developing world while viewing the United States as less threatening. Peking also revived attention to Mao tracts, written thirty years earlier, that had justified Chinese reconciliation with a secondary enemy—such as the United States—in order to isolate and destroy the main adversary —in this case, the USSR.

The subtlety of the Chinese approach was apparent in the coverage of President Nixon's annual message to Congress in early 1970. The Chinese depicted the United States as skidding irreversibly from a position of dominance after World War II to a state of crisis at home and diminished power abroad. The overall thrust of the comment suggested that the Nixon administration, while persisting in its predecessors' aggressive intentions, was subject to powerful pressures to accommodate itself to changing realities, in which U.S. global commitments were vastly overextended and resources severely strained.[3]

Peking's comment was marked by a confidently mocking tone, contrasting the formerly preeminent power of the United States, basking in the "American Century," with present conditions, in which the president was constrained to deliver low-key messages pervaded with a sense of decline and trouble. After NCNA's 31 January commentary characterizing the state of the Union address as conceding that the United States faced a "terrible mess" at home and abroad,[4] NCNA reports in early February discussed the president's economic report and budget messages presented on 2 February.[5]

According to NCNA, a new economic crisis was looming at a time when U.S. resources were inadequate to meet the demands of American domestic and foreign policies. Analyzing the budget, NCNA interpreted the president's reference to "difficult choices" in allocating resources as indicating that the United States was locked in a series of dilemmas arising out of conflicting desires to both expand its military capabilities and alleviate its economic woes. Despite these difficulties, the agency added, the president "does not want to give up his ambitions of aggression" and has stressed that the United States wants to maintain sufficient military power to meet its international commitments. NCNA also observed that the administration intended to expand its nuclear force and to engage in "nuclear blackmail." Peking nonetheless did not mention China in discussing U.S. nuclear arms policy and did not report on the president's 30 January press conference, in which he announced a new phase in antiballistic missile construction as a defense against PRC nuclear attack.

Peking's reaction to the president's foreign policy report of 18 February again consisted of a mocking description of diminished American power, as evidenced by the president's acknowledgements of a changing world situation.[6] But Peking carefully avoided subjecting the president to vituperative personal attack, as it had the previous year. A 28 February NCNA commentary provided Peking's most direct response to U.S. overtures to the PRC up to that time. While the article derided the president's advocacy of negotiations and accused him of being hypocritical in expressing a desire to improve relations with the PRC, it mentioned only his reaffirmation of the American treaty commitment to the Republic of China. No mention was made of Nixon's references to the Warsaw talks or to the unilateral measures taken by the United States in an effort to normalize relations. NCNA went on to scorn the president's proposed desire for peace as reflecting an intent to "forcibly occupy the world" and to suppress revolutionary movements, but it failed to develop the once standard image of the United States as an aggressive power menacing the Asian peoples and seeking to encircle China.[7]

The absence of the encirclement theme was conspicuous in NCNA's discussion of the president's remarks on Soviet-American relations. NCNA maintained that the president's report indicated an intention to intensify Washington's contention and collusion with the USSR. Significantly, unlike earlier Chinese comment, which had stressed collusive and congruent Soviet and American policies, the NCNA discussion focused on elements of contention and thus implicitly pointed to the possibility of the PRC's advancing its interests by playing on the contradictions between the two superpowers.

The U.S.-backed incursion into Cambodia in May 1970 compelled Peking to interrupt the Warsaw talks with the United States. Peking's 18 May 1970 announcement differed significantly from the previous cancellation announcement of 18 February 1969 in its implications for the future of the talks and for Chinese intentions toward the United States.[8]

The 1969 announcement had used the occasion to denounce the "vicious features" of the Nixon administration and to accuse it of following its predecessors in "making itself an enemy" of the Chinese. The announcement said nothing about rescheduling the meeting, and subsequent Chinese comment took a hard line on Sino-American relations. By contrast, the May 1970 announcement avoided naming the Nixon administration and did not refer to the state of Sino-American relations. Unlike the February 1969 announcement, it also broached the subject of rescheduling the meeting, saying this question would be decided upon later through consultations among the liaison representatives of the two sides. The announcement thus managed to register protest against American actions in Indochina, while indicating that Sino-American contacts would continue.

More notable in signaling Chinese flexibility toward the United States was Peking's comment in late June marking the twentieth anniversary of the outbreak of the Korean War and the American "occupation" of Taiwan. Using the occasion to reaffirm their determination to recover Taiwan and to put on record their first comment on the Warsaw talks since the meetings had resumed in January, the Chinese did not exhibit a strong sense of urgency in pledging the liberation of Taiwan and pointedly expressed their interest in normalizing Sino-American relations on the basis of the five principles of peaceful coexistence. PLA Chief of Staff Huang Yung-sheng referred to the Warsaw talks during a 27 June address in Pyongyang.[9] He cited two principles

—that the United States must withdraw all its troops from Taiwan and that Sino-American relations must be based on the five principles of peaceful coexistence—that had been formulated in the 26 November 1968 PRC foreign ministry statement proposing that talks be resumed after the inauguration of Richard M. Nixon. Significantly, Huang's call for peaceful coexistence with the United States was Peking's first since the November 1968 statement.

Comment on the anniversary showed flexibility in another respect; it continued the trend of moving away from portraying the Soviet Union and the United States as conspiring to contain China. Although the Chinese used the occasion of the Korean War anniversary in 1970 to take several digs at the Soviets for their dealings with the United States and Japan, there was no attempt like those of the previous years to depict the international environment as being dominated by joint Soviet-U.S. efforts to encircle the PRC.

Over the next year, Peking continued to adopt a more adaptable approach toward the United States but did not follow through with a resumption of the suspended Warsaw negotiations. By this time, U.S. and PRC leaders were involved in the direct official communication that was to pave the way for Dr. Kissinger's journey in July 1971.[10] The significance of the breakthrough already made in Sino-American relations was as yet unpublicized by either side. In late 1970, however, the Chinese leaders indirectly but unmistakably indicated their keen interest in better relations with the United States. Three months after after the event, and in the wake of communications with President Nixon, Peking chose to belatedly draw attention to the early October 1970 visit to China by Edgar Snow.[11] On Christmas Day, NCNA reported that Mao had "recently" met with Snow for a "cordial and friendly" talk,[12] and Peking radio disclosed on the same date that a picture of Mao and Snow reviewing the 1 October parade from Tienanmen rostrum had been placed on the front page of the 25 December *People's Daily*.[13] Peking's decision to focus on the visit of Snow—who had made the initial breakthrough in CCP-U.S. relations in the mid-1930s—served to communicate Mao's approval of a new move to improve relations with the United States.

The Chinese produced an ideological rationale for their new approach to Washington in July 1971. They authoritatively endorsed for current use the pragmatic policies called for in two Mao tracts, "On the Chungking Negotiations" and "On Policy." The implications of the former tract were that Peking should adopt flexible tactics, including the use of negotiations, in order to deal with an adversary such as the United States. The latter work suggested that the Chinese should unite in a broad front with other nations, including even former imperialist enemies of China such as the United States, in order to isolate and counteract the principal enemy—the USSR. Foretelling the thrust of Chinese international strategy over the next few years, the tracts also served to recall the citation of Mao's "On the Chungking Negotiations" that had been made in a Kiangsu provincial broadcast immediately prior to the commencement of the Sino-Soviet border talks in October 1969. The broadcast had quoted from the Mao work in order to justify flexible negotiations with both the United States and the Soviet Union, but it had been countered by another media line stressing the impropriety of negotiation and compromise with an imperialist enemy such as Moscow or Washington. In contrast, the adoption of a policy of flexibility in 1971 seemed to bear the full stamp of approval of the Chinese leadership. This approval of the new approach was expressed in the 1 July 1971 joint editorial marking the fiftieth anniversary of the CCP, and the concurrence of opinion seemed to suggest that disagreement within the leadership over policy toward the United States was no longer a major problem.[14]

The Nixon Visit

The Sino-American reconciliation had its official beginning with President Nixon's 21–28 February 1972 visit to China. The visit was important to China for several reasons: (1) it marked an end to U.S. containment of China and all but eliminated Chinese concern over American forces stationed in Asia; (2) it reflected a reduction in U.S. support for the Taipei government, thus providing greater leverage and new opportunities for Peking in its continuing effort to gain control of Taiwan; and (3) it enhanced China's rising international stature and established a set of Sino-American principles that would govern future developments in East Asia.

The two sides' agreement in their final communiqué on the need for cooperation in building a new order in East Asia was a significant step for Peking in its efforts to counter its main enemy, the USSR. The communiqué stated that the two sides disavowed any intention to seek hegemony in East Asia and opposed any effort in that direction by any third country as well. They also formally pledged not to collude with another country against a third.[15]

These agreements gave China the opportunity to have a more relaxed stance on its eastern and southern flanks and put the United States on record as opposing any effort by Moscow on the north to dominate China. Meanwhile, the mutual agreement to avoid collusion in international affairs served to ease Peking's longstanding concern that the United States and the Soviet Union might find common ground in opposition to China. Peking now obtained an assurance that Washington, while continuing to negotiate with the Soviet Union on a wide range of issues, would not seek to accommodate the USSR at China's expense.

In short, the route Mao and Chou charted for China in the new order in East Asia was based to a great degree on the policy, strength, and influence of the United States. Peking looked to Washington for at least two things: it expected the United States to abide by its pledges in the Nixon Doctrine and withdraw gradually from strategic positions around China's periphery, thereby permitting China to emerge as an increasingly dominant power in East Asia; and, at the same time, it expected the United States to remain an adversary of the USSR and be particularly vigilant against Soviet penetration into areas sensitive to both Chinese and American interests in Asia. Peking was worried that Moscow might attempt to move into Asian areas along China's eastern and southern borders, especially as the United States withdrew from its forward positions there. It expected the United States, while withdrawing gradually, to remain vigilant against any such Soviet encroachment.

Peking, at the same time, preferred to leave the major role in maintaining the strategic balance against Moscow in East Asia to the United States. While China continued efforts to widen its diplomatic contacts abroad, the thrust of Chinese leadership attention turned inward and focused mainly on the problems of developing Chinese internal wealth and power. The Chinese presumably expected to be able to undertake, over the longer term, a more prominent effort in sustaining the East Asian balance against Moscow. But in 1972 Peking seemed satisfied to rely on U.S. power as the main strategic guarantee.

The United States was quite willing to accept the role in Asia envisioned in the Shanghai communiqué and the Nixon Doctrine. The Western power had now signaled an end to its previous policy of sustaining the Asian balance against communist expansion, and it was developing a new strategy in Asia designed to foster a favorable balance of power through the exploitation of Sino-Soviet differences. The United States now relied on friendship with China, as well as on continued American military resolve, to prevent East Asia from coming under the dominant influence of an unfriendly power—the USSR.

Clearly, the United States judged that the reconciliation with China would also reduce the likelihood of a repetition of the past Sino-American confrontations over Korea, Indochina, and Taiwan. And, most importantly, talks with Peking prompted anxiety in Hanoi over the reliability of China's support and served to pressure the Viet-

110

namese to reduce their demands and accept a compromise peace settlement agreeable to American interests.

Peking had reason to be satisfied with Washington's fulfillment of its Shanghai communiqué pledges over the next three years. In implementing the Nixon Doctrine, the United States gradually withdrew forces from forward positions in Indochina, Southeast Asia, Taiwan, and Japan. At the same time, the United States repeatedly emphasized that its withdrawal should not be interpreted as a sign of American weakness and that Washington remained firmly opposed to any power's attempt to gain a dominant position in East Asia. The Nixon administration kept sufficient force on hand to support its stance.

Peking's satisfaction was registered in growing moderation of heretofore routine Chinese criticism of the United States and in effusive Chinese media comment on the expanded interchange between the two countries. Although the Chinese press continued to attack the Nixon administration for its "aggression" in Indochina, Peking media ceased echoing Vietnamese protests against the United States and dropped personal attacks against Nixon when transmitting Vietnamese statements.[16] Moreover, the previous level of routine Chinese media coverage of strikes, riots, and other internal difficulties in the United States was significantly reduced.[17] Meanwhile, Sino-American exchanges, such as the 1972–73 tour of the Shenyang acrobats in the United States, prompted an outpouring of Chinese reportage stressing the growth of friendship between the two countries.[18]

The signing of the Vietnam peace agreement in Paris in January 1973 enhanced Sino-American relations. Most notably, withdrawal of U.S. combat forces from Vietnam eliminated a major Sino-American disagreement cited in the Shanghai communiqué. Reflecting Chinese satisfaction, Peking gave an especially warm welcome to Dr. Kissinger during a visit to China in February, agreeing to his proposal that official liaison offices be established in Washington and Peking.[19]

In the wake of the Nixon visit, the Chinese exhibited increasing satisfaction with their position vis-à-vis the Soviet Union. China's new prestige and closer relationship with the United States caused Moscow to give greater weight to the possible international response to any heavy pressure on China. The Soviet Union was unable to use the threat of force to compel China to accept its terms over the border issue or other points in contention, and Peking was able to maintain an uncompromising position vis-à-vis the USSR. As tensions along the Sino-Soviet frontier gradually eased, the Chinese felt confident enough over the alleged Soviet threat to alter their propaganda line in a way that minimized the immediate danger from Moscow. Thus, Chou En-lai indicated a reduction in Chinese concern over Soviet military power in a report to the Tenth Chinese Communist Party Congress in August 1973. He declared that the USSR was merely making a "feint to the East" while preparing to attack the West in Europe. The Chinese concurrently de-emphasized the previous propaganda stress on domestic war preparations against the Soviet threat.[20]

Sino-American Difficulties during the Ford Administration

The first serious crisis in the new Sino-American relationship occurred after the collapse of U.S.-supported regimes in Indochina in spring 1975. From Peking's viewpoint, the stability of the new East Asian order—based in large part on the Sino-American understandings set forth in the 1972 Shanghai communiqué—had met with a significant setback. Although the Chinese had obviously expected the United States to withdraw eventually from Indochina, the precipitous American departure had serious implications for China's interests. Most importantly, the United States had suffered a serious defeat at a time when American leadership and resolve abroad had already been called into question because of the leadership crisis stemming from the Watergate scandal and because of the serious economic consequences of the 1974–75 recession in the United States.[21]

Peking also realized that the U.S. losses in Indochina had serious ·implications for Taiwan. Faced with defeats in Southeast Asia, conservatives in the United States were unwilling to accept the loss in American prestige that allegedly would follow a break in U.S. ties with Taiwan. As a result, the Ford administration indicated that a break with Taipei and the establishment of full diplomatic relations with Peking could come only after the 1976 U.S. presidential elections.

It now seemed to the Chinese that the American defeats in Indochina had cast some doubt on key premises of the Shanghai communiqué—especially on the ability of the United States to serve as the primary strategic guarantee for the PRC against suspected Soviet encroachment in East Asia. Chinese media content demonstrated that Peking judged that the United States had indeed been weakened by the events in Indochina and that the American strength and resolve in East Asia were significantly reduced. Shifts in media treatment reflected an altered Chinese perception of the balance of power in the area. The Chinese indicated that they saw the United States as less influential in Asia: they viewed Washington's utility as a bulwark against future Soviet expansion as compromised.

The Chinese responded to this perception of an altered East Asian situation in several ways. They demonstrated continuing interest in

Sino-American cooperation in a new East Asian order as set forth in the Shanghai communiqué. But, whereas Peking had relied mainly on American strength to sustain the favorable balance in the past, the Chinese now began to take on a greater responsibility in their own right for shoring up East Asian positions against Soviet expansion.

For one thing, Peking moved quickly to solidify China's relations with and to cement anti-Soviet feelings in the two noncommunist states in East Asia most affected by the collapse of the American positions in Indochina—the Philippines and Thailand. The establishment of diplomatic relations with both countries prompted in each instance a joint communiqué testifying to mutual opposition to international hegemony.[22] The Chinese also strove to reassure both Manila and Bangkok of their security and stability in the wake of the U.S. defeat. Such reassurances were designed to dissuade Manila and Bangkok from moving toward Moscow in a hasty search for a powerful ally in the new Southeast Asian situation.

Peking repeatedly acknowledged that the United States had been "beaten black and blue" in Indochina and noted that the Asian people, especially those in Southeast Asia, were increasingly successful in efforts to drive the "wolf"—the United States—from the "front gate." But the Chinese clearly indicated that they were opposed to any unilateral, rapid U.S. withdrawal from international involvement as a result of this setback. Instead, they wished the United States to remain heavily involved and strategically vigilant against the USSR in Europe, the Middle East, and Asia. Peking went so far as to stress a propaganda line that portrayed the American defeats in Indochina as presenting an opportunity for the United States to withdraw from such "secondary" areas, where it was overextended, in order to serve more effectively as a strategic bulwark against suspected Soviet expansion in more "vital" areas abroad. Peking reduced its criticism of the U.S. military presence and political influence in Asia. It gave unusually favorable play to American statements of resolve to retain strong ties with Japan and maintain a strong naval presence in the Western Pacific and the Indian Ocean.[23]

The Chinese also adopted a more active policy against the USSR, concentrating on blocking attempts by Moscow to advance along China's flanks as the United States was forced to withdraw. In particular, the Chinese launched a major propaganda campaign to warn Asian states of the danger posed by the ravenous Soviet "tiger"—lurking at the rear door as the Asians pushed the American "wolf" through the front gate. Peking also laid special stress on criticizing Moscow's plan for a collective security system in Asia as a thinly veiled Soviet effort to achieve political hegemony. The Chinese portrayed the Soviet

113

proposal as the complete antithesis of the anti-hegemony front fostered by China and the United States.[24]

By the end of 1975, Chinese comment evinced more confidence that Moscow's alleged desire to fill the vacuum caused by the rapid American withdrawal from Southeast Asia had been blunted. Peking saw that U.S. forces—especially naval and air forces—would remain active in the region, and Chinese media noted in particular the activities of U.S. forces on the Indian Ocean Island of Diego Garcia and at Cockburn Sound in Australia. At the same time, Peking saw that most nations in Southeast Asia were wary of Soviet overtures, noting in particular the efforts by members of the Association of Southeast Asian Nations to resist big power interference. And the Chinese considered their own growing influence in the region to be a brake to Soviet ambitions. Since early 1975, Peking had warmly entertained top-level leaders from every Southeast Asian state except Malaysia and Indonesia, thereby greatly increasing China's leverage in the area.[25]

Renewed Chinese confidence in Asia did not translate into a reduction of Chinese concern over the United States, however. Peking media at this time began to depict the Ford administration, especially Secretary of State Henry Kissinger, as overly anxious to accommodate the Soviet Union. They implied that the United States administration was increasingly trying to appease Moscow at the expense of the interests of other countries. Low-level media coverage even equated the Ford administration policy with that followed by British Prime Minister Neville Chamberlain in the face of Hitler's threats at the Munich conference prior to World War II. Comment focused particular criticism on American accommodation of Soviet interests at the August 1975 European Security Conference summit meeting in Helsinki, and on President Gerald R. Ford's dismissal of Defense Secretary James R. Schlesinger—reportedly because of Schlesinger's forthright views on the Soviet strategic threat.

The implications were clear: Peking saw signs that the United States intended to accommodate Soviet interests, especially in Europe. This possibility apparently prompted Chinese planners to question whether the United States could be counted on to provide a strategic guarantee against Soviet dominance and to continue to honor the intent of the Shanghai communiqué. If the United States was willing to appease the USSR in Europe, might it not follow the same type of policy at the expense of Chinese interests in Asia? At the same time, the continued slow pace of the normalization of Sino-American relations prompted a series of Chinese criticisms of American policies on sensitive bilateral issues, which had not been discussed since the signing of the Shanghai communiqué. Most notably, the Chinese media

114

publicized low-level PRC protests in April, September, and October 1975, which, for the first time, explicitly accused the United States of violating the provisions of the Shanghai communiqué. The protests focused respectively on U.S. policy on Taiwan, U.S. resistance to PRC support for Puerto Rico's independence, and alleged U.S. support for movements favoring Tibet's independence from Peking control.[26]

Peking was not yet prepared to alter its relationship with Washington, but the Chinese were worried over the implications of what they considered to be a lack of American resolve against Moscow. They took advantage of opportunities presented by Secretary Kissinger's October 1975 visit to China, Secretary Schlesinger's departure from the Pentagon in November, and President Ford's 1–5 December visit to Peking to register their views. PRC Foreign Minister Chiao Kuan-hua's toast at a 19 October welcoming banquet for the Kissinger delegation reflected Chinese irritation with American policy. Chiao departed from past practice by omitting introductory words of welcome for the Secretary; instead, he launched a warning—not seen before during a Kissinger visit—that détente was an illusion that should not blind the world to Soviet hegemonism.[27]

A widely publicized 7 November 1975 NCNA dispatch reporting critical comment on the dismissal of Defense Secretary Schlesinger emphasized Chinese concern over U.S. policy toward the USSR. Although NCNA carefully refrained from commenting in its own name, the dispatch departed from Peking's past circumspect treatment of President Ford, by repeating comments that the firing of Schlesinger was a clear sign of the Ford administration's determination to speed up détente with the Soviet Union and was also a decision detrimental to U.S. national security.

While the NCNA dispatch focused on the Schlesinger firing as an indication of the determination of the president and Kissinger to "ease tensions" with Moscow, it did not follow the heretofore standard Chinese media practice of also noting the American leaders' countervailing determination to resolutely maintain U.S. security interests against alleged Soviet encroachment. NCNA replayed British press comment calling Kissinger the "arch-architect" of détente with Moscow. And again citing the British press, NCNA quoted the observation that President Ford's decision to release Schlesinger while retaining Kissinger "shows clearly which side he takes in the argument about 'detente.' "

NCNA reported comment by Senator Henry M. Jackson and others praising Schlesinger and criticizing his dismissal as "a loss to the nation . . . in the pursuit of a prudent defense and foreign policy." It cited statements that the firing had upset West European leaders and could serve to weaken NATO strength against the Warsaw Pact. The dispatch replayed Soviet and U.S. comment highlighting Moscow's pleasure over Schlesinger's departure and speculating that "the shuffle in Washington will certainly be regarded by the Kremlin as a step in the right direction." It concluded by citing *Washington Post* reports that the Schlesinger dismissal would broaden the "already widening debate in the United States over the pros and cons of detente with the Soviet Union."[28]

On the same day that NCNA reported Schlesinger's dismissal, it carried two "international reference material" articles explaining respectively the significance of the 1938 Munich Agreement and the 1940 Dunkirk evacuation. The articles were also published in *People's Daily* and broadcast by Peking radio. The articles focused on the disastrous results of the Munich policy of appeasement followed by the Western leaders in "conniving with the aggressive acts" of the fascists in order to divert the "spearhead of aggression toward the East." One report concluded by noting that "since then, people have often described similar schemes by several major powers in conniving at aggression and betraying other countries as a 'Munich' or 'Munich plot.' "[29]

Underscoring Peking's concern, Vice-Premier Teng Hsiao-ping devoted unusual attention to the need for American resolve against the Soviets during his 1 December welcoming banquet speech for President Ford. While Teng echoed stock Chinese opinion on the state of Sino-American bilateral relations, he focused on "a more important question." Although not explicitly mentioning the Soviet Union, Teng harshly attacked "the country which most zealously preaches peace" as "the most dangerous source of war," and he added that "the crucial point is what line or policy" the United States and China would pursue in the face of this mutual threat. Teng exhorted his audience to follow Peking's example, not to fear such hegemonism, but to form a broad international front against it and wage "tit-for-tat struggle." He added that the USSR was "weak by nature" and "bullies the soft" but that it "fears the tough." Teng underlined the need for continuing the common Chinese-American cause against Moscow by characterizing as "an outstanding common point" the Shanghai communiqué's call for opposition to international hegemony.[30]

Impact of PRC Leadership Changes

The deaths of Chou En-lai in January 1976 and of Mao Tse-tung in September of that year removed the two Chinese leaders most responsible for the current Sino-American rapprochement. The passing of Mao and Chou also set the stage for serious upheavals in the Chinese leadership, which resulted in the April 1976 demotion of Vice-Premier Teng Hsiao-Ping and the October 1976 arrest of four leftist Chinese Politburo members—Wang Hung-wen, Chang Chun-chiao, Chiang Ching, and Yao Wen-yuan. Those currently in control in Peking are led by the new CCP Chairman Hua Kuo-feng, a new-comer to PRC foreign affairs, who is backed by moderate military and government leaders such as Yeh Chien-ying and Li Hsien-nien, two close associates of Chou En-lai who have long supported China's rapprochement with the United States.

Thus, the current leadership situation in Peking suggests that China's intentions regarding Sino-American relations will not change appreciably. The present leaders have repeatedly stressed their deter-mination to continue the previous foreign policy line; Chinese media comment continues to emphasize Peking's longstanding bias against the USSR and its favorable approach toward the United States.[31] There was some evidence in 1976 that leftists in the Chinese leadership were inclined to adopt a harder line against the United States on ideological questions and on sensitive bilateral issues such as Peking's determina-tion to liberate Taiwan,[32] but the recent elimination of the four leftist leaders in the Politburo seems to have checked that potential threat to Sino-American cooperation.

The current Chinese leadership seems generally satisfied with the gains China has made as a result of its move toward the United States. It realizes that turning against Washington would have serious ramifi-cations, including severe complications in PRC relations with Japan and other noncommunist Asian states, and that it also would remove an important pillar supporting China's security in the face of the Soviet threat. At the same time, the leaders in Peking judge that it would be foolhardy to make any significant alterations in China's for-eign policy at a time when the domestic situation is far from settled. In late 1976, Peking faces numerous serious internal problems. There is a need to appoint replacements for leaders who have died or been purged from party, government, and military ranks. The spring 1976 campaign against Teng Hsiao-ping must be reevaluated and a decision reached on how to proceed with the campaign against Teng's enemies, the four leftist Politburo members. Finally, steps must be taken to rehabilitate China's economy, which was severely weakened by the disastrous earthquake in north China in the summer of 1976. These problems presumably will continue to preoccupy the Chinese leader-ship for some time to come, thereby reducing the likelihood that any significant changes in the foreign policy of the People's Republic of China will occur in the near future.

117

CHAPTER EIGHT

Conclusion

The evolution of Sino-American relations over the past three decades vividly demonstrates that strategic factors have played the most important role in bringing about the current rapprochement. Changes in the balance of power in East Asia have compelled the United States and the People's Republic of China to see that, despite years of hostility and distrust, their vital interests in East Asia are best served by cooperation. For Peking, the new relationship with the United States has provided a guarantee against Soviet domination. It has brought an end to American efforts to contain Chinese influence in East Asia and in fact has accelerated the development of that influence. It has also strengthened Peking's position in its longstanding efforts to regain control of Taiwan. For the United States, cooperation with China has helped maintain a balance of power in East Asia that is favorable to the United States, without necessitating massive outlays of U.S. wealth and power. It has also provided Washington with an important source of international leverage in its ongoing competition with the Soviet Union.

Both sides have come to value their new, strategically beneficial relationship sufficiently to put aside concern over many of the disputes that still divide them. Thus, Peking and Washington rarely call attention to the periods of intense Sino-American hostility during the Chinese civil war, the Korean War, and the two-decade U.S. containment effort against the PRC. Peking has sharply reduced propaganda support for "revolution" within the United States, and Washington has similarly cut back its efforts to promote the "cause of freedom" behind the "bamboo curtain." Both sides have also worked hard to ensure that areas of continued Sino-American friction in East Asia—such as

118

Taiwan and Korea—do not seriously undermine the now cordial relationship between the two countries.

In short, Sino-American relations have reached a new stage, in which both sides for the first time see their national interests as best served by continuing cooperation. To appreciate just how extensive the change in U.S. relations with China has been, it is worth measuring the progress made in overcoming traditional obstacles toward a rational China policy that have persistently plagued American policy makers. Those deficiencies in the U.S. approach to the PRC have been documented by a number of scholars, most notably John K. Fairbank and Tang Tsou. The latter, in his authoritative history of the American failure in China during the 1940s, asserts that U.S. policy has suffered from an "imbalance between ends and means." On the one hand, he argues, American policy up to 1947 frequently demonstrated an unwillingness or inability to use military power purposefully to achieve political objectives in China. This failing was overcome at the start of the Cold War, when the United States showed that it was quite prepared to use military power to back up its political objectives in the area—a policy demonstrated vividly during the Korean War, the Taiwan Straits crisis, and the Indochina conflict.

On the other hand, according to Tsou, U.S. policy after 1947 was characterized by a disinclination to abandon unattainable goals and thus avoid entanglement in a hopeless cause in East Asia. Indeed, this failing continued to mark U.S. policy until the late 1960s, when the full impact of the Vietnam involvement forced American planners to reassess strategy in East Asia and abandon the unrealistic goal of singlehandedly blocking communist expansion in Asia.[1]

The new stage in Sino-American relations also marks an advance beyond the problems in Sino-American relations cited in the writings of John K. Fairbank. Fairbank has argued eloquently that the United States has failed to understand China and has therefore committed a number of errors in its policy toward Peking. He has noted that in the past the United States has typically neglected to view China in a realistic light, but has perceived it as "the object simply of our curiosity, our philanthrophy, or our fear."[2]

For the past several years, however, American strategists have demonstrated that they no longer think of China in this traditional fashion. After a long history of misjudgments on Chinese affairs, Washington has made great strides toward a clearer, more realistic view of both PRC and U.S. concerns in East Asia. Washington understands how these two sets of interests affect each other, and it has tailored American policy in the region to ensure continued compatibility between the United States and China. Of course, this is not to say that the United States fully understands China or that the Chinese fully understand the United States; these are ideals that are far from being achieved on either side of the Pacific. But, both sides do fully understand how their vital interests within the East Asian balance of power can best be served by accommodation with one another.

The remarkable progress of the last few years does not at all mean that the current cooperation will continue to develop smoothly. Immediate problems include the fact that China thinks the United States is overly solicitous of Soviet interests in developing East-West détente. It fears that since Washington tends to appease the USSR and is less vigilant against Soviet international expansion, China must bear more of the burden in shoring up an anti-Soviet international balance. Peking at the same time has also shown impatience over the slow pace of Sino-American normalization, demonstrating particular irritation over continued U.S. support for the Taipei government.

The history of East Asian relations also provides a clear perspective on some of the weaknesses of the Sino-American cooperation. In modern times, there have been only a few such bilateral understandings or alliances between a major East Asian power and a major Western power, and none have lasted long. The most notable were the Sino-Soviet alliance of the 1950s, the German-Japanese alliance during World War II, and the Anglo-Japanese alliance of 1902–22.

The Anglo-Japanese relationship seems to parallel most closely the current Sino-American understanding.[3] Like the more recent rapprochement, the Anglo-Japanese alliance was based chiefly on the two sides' strategic interests in the balance of power in East Asia. Japan in 1902—like China today—was faced with a serious strategic threat from Russia and was anxious to ally with another power in order to gain greater international leverage against its major adversary. Great Britain in 1902—like the United States today—had become increasingly aware of its relative weakness in East Asia. In contrast to the British dominance in East Asia in the nineteenth century, Britain was no longer able to maintain, by itself, a balance of power in East Asia that would favor its interests there. Recent Russian expansion in Asia, and particularly the likelihood of Russian domination in Northeast Asia, seemed to pose a major threat to British interests. As there were few strategic disagreements between Japan and Britain at the time, the balance of forces in East Asia encouraged their leaders to form the alliance based chiefly on their mutual opposition to Russian expansion in East Asia.

Since there were few other ties holding the two sides together, as the East Asian balance of power changed substantially over the next two decades, so did Anglo-Japanese relations. In particular, British power in East Asia continued to decline, Russian strategic power was undermined by the 1917 revolution, and Japan and the United States became the major competitors for power in the region. Britain became more concerned with Japan's military encroachments throughout the region and was made increasingly aware of growing American concern over the apparent Japanese threat in East Asia. London finally decided that it would be more in its own interests to abandon the alliance with Japan and join with its close American ally in order to check further advances of Japanese influence in East Asia.[4]

In conclusion, therefore, it is important to note that the most serious limiting factor on the Sino-American cooperation derives from the fact that the current cooperation is based almost exclusively on strategic grounds. There are few other ties—such as trade relations, moral affinity, or common heritage—that hold the two sides together. And, of most importance, there is little likelihood that the two sides will be able to expand these non-strategic ties significantly in the future. Thus, for example, Peking's stress on China's economic self-reliance and Washington's insistence on balanced U.S. foreign trade will probably translate into a continuing low level of Sino-American trade. Substantial cultural interchange will continue to be blocked by the fact that China views most of the American culture as decadent and depraved, while the United States considers many of the PRC cultural efforts to be puritanical and dull. Moreover, the two societies are so different that the general public in the United States finds it hard to identify with the average Chinese whose work consists of agricultural manual labor and who is guided by a tightly knit political party inspired by the thoughts of the godlike Mao Tse-tung. On the other hand, Chinese citizens almost certainly find it difficult to comprehend the goals and desires of the average American family.

In short, Sino-American cooperation will continue to have a narrow base; the U.S. rapprochement with China will depend heavily on the forces which brought it about in the first place—the evolving balance of power in Asia. At present, U.S. and PRC interests in East Asia coincide. But, if the balance of power were to change substantially, it is probable that American and Chinese concerns would also change, leading to a shift in their bilateral relations. For example, fear of the Soviet Union is an important element motivating China to maintain close relations with the United States. If Moscow were to significantly moderate its policy toward China and reduce its military power along the Sino-Soviet border, Peking might find less need for close ties with the United States as a hedge against the Soviet threat. Under these new circumstances, China would be free to adopt an even-handed policy, playing one superpower off against the other.

121

Moreover, if American strength in East Asia were to decline substantially in the near future, the United States would be less useful to China as a guarantor against Soviet domination. Faced with continued serious Soviet pressure, Peking might see its interests best served by an accommodation with the USSR rather than a reliance on the increasingly weak United States. Finally, the Soviet Union could offer major concessions to the United States over strategic arms issues, Asian or European affairs, or other matters, prompting Washington to determine its interests would be best served by close cooperation with Moscow, regardless of the damage this would do to Sino-American cooperation.

These hypothetical examples should sufficiently demonstrate that the current Sino-American understanding is on shaky ground; it is only as stable as the international balance of power in East Asia. To sustain such cooperation in the future, Washington will be in the most influential position if it remains powerful in East Asia. Such strength would provide the necessary leverage to allow the United States to help guide the balance of power there in directions agreeable to both American and Chinese interests. At the same time, Peking will be more likely to respect the United States and deal with it fairly if it realizes that a deliberate Chinese affront of the United States could lead to U.S. countermeasures that would have serious consequences for PRC interests in East Asia. As to the settlement of bilateral problems such as the Taiwan question, Peking has repeatedly stressed that it expects the United States to proceed toward normalization of relations based on the principles of the Shanghai communiqué. It has set no official deadline by which time normalization must be completed but has suggested that slow, steady progress toward that goal would be acceptable.

Notes

Abbreviations used in notes

DR China   Foreign Broadcast Information Service (FBIS), *Daily Report.* Depending on the date cited, this abbreviation refers to: *Daily Report: Far East,* 1953–67; *Daily Report: Communist China,* 1967–71; *Daily Report: People's Republic of China,* 1971–. These publications are available at the Library of Congress.

FRUS China   U.S., Department of State, *Foreign Relations of the United States: Diplomatic Papers.* Depending on the date cited, this abbreviation refers to: *Diplomatic Papers, 1942: China* (Washington, 1952); *Diplomatic Papers, 1943: China* (Washington, 1957); *Diplomatic Papers, 1944: China* (Washington, 1967); *Diplomatic Papers, 1945: The Far East and China* (Washington, 1969).

SCMP   U.S. Consulate General, Hong Kong, *Survey of China Mainland Press,* 1950–76. This serial publication is published by the Department of State and is available at the Library of Congress.

Chapter Two

1. For evidence of these trends, I have relied heavily on a general review of CCP statements on foreign affairs made through the propaganda organs of the Comintern, as well as on statements made by CCP leaders in conversations with Western newsmen during this period. For specific examples, see below. For accounts of Western journalists' interaction with CCP leaders in this period, see bibliography.

2. Central Committee of the Chinese Communist Party, "Against the Offensive of Japanese Imperialism in North China," *International Press Correspondence* 34 (1934): 904.

3. For example, see the response to the Comintern's developing "united front" propaganda line in Wang Ming, "Fifteen Years of Struggle for Independence and Freedom of the Chinese People," *The Communist International,* October 1936, pp. 1341–60.

4. See "The International Situation and China's War of Emancipation: From an Interview with Mao Tse-tung," *International Press Correspondence* 49 (1939):

1029; and Mao Tse-tung, *Selected Works* (London, 1954), 4:23. A CCP statement supporting the pact is cited in Tang Tsou, *America's Failure in China, 1941–1950* (Chicago, 1963), pp. 212–13.

5. This interpretation is put forth notably in Tsou, *America's Failure*, pp. 208–19.

6. For a general study of the CCP view of the United States during this period see Warren I. Cohen, "The Development of Chinese Communist Policy toward the United States, 1922–1933," *Orbis* II (1967): 219–37.

7. See Kan-Sen, "The Sixth KMT Offensive and the Victory of the Chinese Red Army," *The Communist International*, January 1934, pp. 24–28; *International Press Correspondence* 37 (1930): 739–40; 30 (1930): 1–2; 40 (1933): 895. See also Central Executive Committee of the Chinese Soviet Republic, "The New Imperialist Invention against Soviet China," *International Press Correspondence* 44 (1933): 970–71. And see *FRUS 1930* 2:141–54, 165.

8. See Kenneth E. Shewmaker, *Americans and Chinese Communists, 1927–1945: A Persuading Encounter* (Ithaca, 1971). See also Dorothy Borg, *The United States and the Far East Crisis of 1933–38* (Cambridge, Mass., 1964).

9. Prominent examples of the CCP campaign during this period are contained in *FRUS 1942 China*, pp. 227, 265; *FRUS 1943 China*, pp. 192, 202, 214, 230, 257.

10. *FRUS 1942 China*, pp. 226–28.

11. Ibid., pp. 265–66.

12. *FRUS 1943 China*, pp. 192–93.

13. Ibid., pp. 201–3.

14. Ibid., pp. 214–15.

15. Mao Tse-tung, *Selected Works*, 4:23.

16. For example, see Central Committee of the Chinese Communist Party and Central Executive Committee of the Soviet Government of China, "Appeal to the Whole People of China to Resist Japan and Save the Country," *International Press Correspondence* 64 (1935): 1957. This marked a shift in CCP policy toward the imperialist powers then in China, focusing CCP enmity on Japan alone. This line was elaborated in Wang Ming, "The Basis of the New Policy of the Communist Party of China," *International Press Correspondence* 71 (1935): 1751.

17. See Mao Tse-tung, "Tasks of the National Anti-Japanese United Front in China," *The Communist International*, November 1937, p. 828. Also see Wang Ming, "The New Stage of Japanese Aggression and the New Period of Struggle of the Chinese People," *The Communist International*, October 1937, pp. 719–36.

18. See Herbert Feis, *The China Tangle* (Princeton, 1953), pp. 3–13.

19. Lo Chia, *Chung-kuo Ke-ming Chung Ti Wu-chang Tou-cheng* (Shanghai, 1954), pp. 40–42.

20. For example, see *FRUS 1943 China*, pp. 201–3.

21. For example, see Ibid., pp. 194, 201–3.

22. Ibid., pp. 249–51. For more detailed American records on this issue, see U.S. diplomatic papers dealing with China in category number 761.93 at the United States National Archives, Washington D.C.

23. Such factors were reflected throughout U.S. reports of American-Communist interaction in Chungking and later in Yenan from 1942–44. Most notably, see Mao's lengthy interview of 23 August 1944 with John S. Service that is discussed below. (See note 52.)

24. See same Mao interview below.

25. *FRUS 1943 China*, pp. 193–99.

26. Ibid., pp. 203–8.

27. Ibid., p. 208.

28. Ibid., pp. 258–66.

29. Feis, *The China Tangle*, p. 100.

30. *FRUS 1943 China*, pp. 263–64.

31. Ibid., p. 264.

32. Ibid., p. 265.

33. Ibid., p. 266.

34. See ibid., pp. 317–20. See also U.S., Department of State, Division of Far Eastern Affairs memo of 19 May 1944—document number 761.93/1779—in U.S. diplomatic papers relating to China, National Archives, Washington, D.C.

35. *FRUS 1943 China*, pp. 275–78.

36. Ibid., p. 278.

37. Ibid., p. 275.

38. Ibid., p. 279.

39. Ibid., pp. 277–78.

40. See, for instance, ibid., pp. 283–84, 314–15, 316. See also Feis, *China Tangle*, pp. 86–87; and Tsou, *America's Failure*, p. 158. It should be noted that the sudden rise of Soviet press comment and diplomatic initiatives concerning Chinese internal affairs appeared to be closely related to the termination of the Comintern— the Soviet backed organ that had previously served as the prime communist sounding board supporting the CCP.

41. See *FRUS 1944 China*, pp. 516–20. Many of John S. Service's reports from Yenan are published in U.S. Senate, Committee of the Judiciary, Subcommittee to Investigate the Administration of the Internal Security Act and Other Internal Security Laws, *The Amerasia Papers: A Clue to the Catastrophy of China* (Washington, 1970). Service has reviewed his personal assessment of this period in John S. Service, *The Amerasia Papers: Some Problems in the History of U.S.-China Relations* (Berkeley, 1971).

42. *FRUS 1944 China*, pp. 515–16, 539, 541, 576–77.

43. Ibid., pp. 599–614.

44. The offensive is described in Charles F. Romanus and Riley Sunderland, *United States Army in World War II, China-Burma-India Theatre, Stilwell's Command Problems* (Washington, 1956), pp. 407–13.

45. The Stilwell imbroglio has been well covered in Tsou, *America's Failure;* Feis, *China Tangle;* and more recently in Barbara Tuchman, *Stilwell and the American Experience in China, 1911–1945* (New York, 1970).

46. See most notably reports of John P. Davies in *FRUS 1944 China*, pp. 667–71. Davies has written a personal account of this period in his book *Dragon by the Tail* (New York, 1972). See also Service's report in *FRUS 1944 China*, pp. 615–18.

47. For example, see *FRUS 1944 China*, p. 668.

48. See, for example, Service, *The Amerasia Papers.*

49. This expansion is discussed in Lyman P. Van Slyke, ed., *The Chinese Communist Movement* (Stanford, 1968), chap. 4.

50. Mao stressed these points in his 23 August 1944 interview with Service. (See note 52.)

51. In November 1944, Stalin publicly denounced Japan as an aggressor, as a prelude to renouncing the Soviet neutrality pact with Tokyo in the spring of 1945. See Tsou, *America's Failure*, p. 263.

52. See in particular Mao's proposals to Service in *FRUS 1944 China*, pp. 604–14.

53. Yet U.S. observers such as Davies virtually precluded this possibility and thus assessed that the CCP leaders were securely confident of their positions in China. See notably *FRUS 1944 China*, pp. 667–71. John Service took it for granted that the United States would not aid Chiang in a civil war against the CCP. See ibid., p. 617.

54. This American effort is discussed in Feis, *China Tangle*, pp. 204–5.

55. See, for instance, the resolution of U.S. Military planners at this juncture with regard to the timing of the defeat of Japan. Discussed in Feis, *China Tangle*, pp. 236–39.

56. This issue is discussed in a report by Davies in *FRUS 1944 China*, pp. 725–26.

57. Even Davies's optimistic assessment of CCP prospects tended to assume

that the CCP's area of immediate control would be restricted to north China. See ibid., pp. 667–71.

58. The CCP military strength during this period is examined in notable detail in Van Slyke, *The Chinese Communist Movement,* pp. 177–82.

59. Davies, in particular, was emphatic on this score, though he saw CCP motivation from a somewhat different angle. See *FRUS 1944 China,* pp. 668–69.

60. Ibid., pp. 623–26.

61. Ibid., pp. 631–32, 696–97.

62. Ibid., pp. 669–70, 695–97. The continuing U.S. concern with checking Soviet expansion in East Asia, while defeating Japan, was reflected most notably in a 23 April 1945 report by George Kennan concerning Soviet objectives in Asia. See *FRUS 1945 China,* pp. 342–43. See also a 1 March 1945 State Department memo in ibid., p. 59; and a 19 April 1945 report by Averell Harriman in ibid., p. 341. For further evidence of U.S. concern with suspected Soviet expansion in China, see a State Department memo of 19 May 1944 in U.S. diplomatic papers, document number 761.93/1779, at National Archives, Washington D.C. The general category 761.93 includes documents giving a useful overview of U.S. strategy toward the USSR in China during this period.

63. For a discussion of the various changes among high-level U.S. personnel and shifts in strategy during this time, see Feis, *China Tangle,* pp. 208–12.

64. Ibid., chap. 20; Tsou, *America's Failure,* pp. 176–81.

65. Feis, *China Tangle,* chap. 22.

66. This continuing thrust was most vividly pointed up in a 29 January 1945 memo written by senior U.S. China specialist John Carter Vincent summarizing American policy toward China for the benefit of the newly named Undersecretary of State Joseph Grew. Though he urged flexibility in the American approach toward the Chinese internal situation over the longer term, Vincent affirmed that the likely result of withdrawal of U.S. support for Chiang Kai-shek would have to be "chaos" in China. He averred that, ". . . with regard to the short term objectvies, Chiang appears to be the only leader who now offers a hope for unification. The alternative to the support of Chiang for the attainment of our immediate objective might be chaos." See *FRUS 1945 China,* pp. 37–78. See also ibid., p. 74.

67. *FRUS 1944 China,* p. 697.

68. *FRUS 1945 China,* pp. 59, 341, 864–65.

69. This assessment was voiced most notably by General Hurley, but it was also a basic U.S. judgment implied in memos stressing that Chiang was the only Chinese leader capable of keeping China united. See ibid., pp. 37–38.

70. See *FRUS 1944 China,* pp. 674–90. For a vivid description of Hurley's involvement in the drafting of the five-point plan, by an eye witness on the scene in Yenan, see David D. Barrett, *Dixie Mission: The U.S. Army Observer Group in Yenan, 1944* (Berkeley, 1970), chap. 4.

71. *FRUS 1944 China,* p. 699.

72. Ibid., pp. 706–7.

73. Ibid., pp. 727–32.

74. Discussed in Feis, *China Tangle;* Tsou, *America's Failure;* Service, *The Amerasia Papers;* Davies, *Dragon.*

75. Mao, *Selected Works,* 4:328–29; cited in Tsou, *America's Failure,* p. 192.

Chapter Three

1. The origins of this divergence between Chinese and Soviet propaganda is traced in Foreign Broadcast Information Service (FBIS), *Survey of Far East Broadcasts,* 6 May 1954, p. 7; and in "Sino-Soviet Differences on Responsibility for 'Stabilizing' the Far East," FBIS, *Radio Propaganda Report,* 20 May 1954, pp. 1–6.

2. Cited in FBIS, *Radio Propaganda Report,* 20 May 1954, p. 2. (Italics added.)

3. Ibid., p. 3.

4. Mao's anniversay message was transcribed by NCNA and appears in *SCMP* 747, p. 1. (Italics added.)

5. Malenkov's message was reprinted by NCNA and appears in ibid., p. 2. (Italics added.)

6. Ibid., p. 5.

7. FBIS, *Survey of Far East Broadcasts,* 6 May 1954, p. 7.

8. On Japan, see *SCMP* 920, p. 17; on the Netherlands, see *SCMP* 932, p. 6.

9. See, respectively, *SCMP* 831, p. 40; *SCMP* 824, p. 27; *SCMP* 835, p. 27; *SCMP* 833, p. 52; *SCMP* 835, p. 28.

10. For a discussion of the military aspects of the campaign, see Stewart Alsop, "The Story behind Quemoy: How We Drifted Close to War," *Saturday Evening Post,* 13 December 1958, pp. 26–27. See also Alice Langley Hsieh, *Communist China's Strategy in the Nuclear Era* (Englewood Cliffs, New Jersey, 1962).

11. See, for example, criticism of Winston Churchill's stance on Taiwan in the 23 July 1954 *People's Daily* editorial in *SCMP* 855, p. 1.

12. See, in particular, *SCMP* 775, p. 1.

13. Alsop, "Story behind Quemoy," p. 87. See also Joyce Kallgren, "Nationalist China's Armed Forces," *The China Quarterly* 15 (1963):35–36.

14. *SCMP* 843, p. 2.

15. The text of the editorial appears in *SCMP* 845, pp. 28–30.

16. A description of the propaganda campaign on the Taiwan issue appears in "Current Chinese Propaganda on the Liberation of Formosa," FBIS, *Radio Propaganda Report,* 29 July 1954, pp. 1–10.

17. See *SCMP* 850, p. 1; *SCMP* 855, p. 1; *SCMP* 856, p. 1; and *SCMP* 858, p. 1.

18. *SCMP* 860, p. 4.

19. Ibid., p. 3.

20. Ibid., pp. 4–5.

21. Cited in FBIS, *Survey of Far East Broadcasts,* 12 August 1954, p. 4.

22. See *SCMP* 882, pp. 1–2.

23. Cited in FBIS, *Survey of Far East Broadcasts,* 10 September 1954, p. 3.

24. *SCMP* 882, pp. 1–2.

25. Ibid., p. 1.

26. Ibid., p. 2.

27. Khrushchev's commentaries during his visit to China are discussed in FBIS, *Radio Propaganda Report,* 13 October 1954, pp. 1–5.

28. The speech is transcribed in *SCMP* 902, pp. 1–3.

29. Cited in FBIS, *Survey of Far East Broadcasts,* 7 October 1954, p. 2.

30. Ibid., p. 3.

31. See *SCMP* 900, p. 16.

32. Cited in FBIS, *Survey of Far East Broadcasts,* 7 October 1954, p. 4.

33. See *SCMP* 907, p. 7.

34. Cited in FBIS, *Survey of Far East Broadcasts,* 7 October 1954, p. 1.

35. Ibid., p. 2.

36. This aspect of the campaign is treated in "Development of the Formosa Liberation Campaign," FBIS, *Radio Propaganda Report,* 12 January 1955, pp. 3–4.

37. See, for example, the *People's Daily* editorial of 5 December 1954 on the U.S.-ROC treaty in *SCMP* 941, p. 2.

38. See ibid.

39. *SCMP.* 944, p. 3.

40. Cited in FBIS, *Radio Propaganda Report,* 12 January 1955, p. 4.

41. *SCMP* 965, p. 11.

42. Cited in FBIS, *Radio Propaganda Report,* 12 January 1955, p. 4.

43. The text of Chou's statement is given in *SCMP* 974, pp. 1–2.

44. Ibid., p. 2.
45. Ibid., p. 1.
46. *SCMP* 979, pp. 1–2.
47. Cited in FBIS, *Survey of Far East Broadcasts,* 10 March 1955, p. 1.
48. This editorial is discussed in detail in FBIS, *Survey of Far East Broadcasts,* 10 March 1955, pp. 1–2.
49. Ibid.
50. Ibid.
51. Italics added.
52. This issue is discussed in FBIS, *Survey of Far East Broadcasts,* 25 February 1955, p. 2.
53. Ibid.
54. *SCMP* 987, p. 24.
55. Ibid., p. 9.

Chapter Four

1. Kenneth T. Young, *Negotiating with the Chinese Communists* (New York, 1968).
2. Ibid., pp. 47–49.
3. Ibid., pp. 58–59.
4. *Department of State Bulletin* 32, no. 814 (31 January 1955): 191. See also Alsop, "Story behind Quemoy."
5. For the text of Chou's report, see *DR China,* 1 August 1955, pp. AAA1–AAA10.
6. Ibid., p. AAA7.
7. Ibid., p. AAA8.
8. Ibid., p. AAA9.
9. Ibid., p. AAA10.
10. On the U.S. side, see the response of Deputy Undersecretary of State Robert Murphey, contained in *Department of State Bulletin* 33, no. 848 (26 September 1955): 606. On the PRC side, see the 12 September 1955 *People's Daily* editorial in *SCMP* 1128, pp. 1–2.
11. See, in particular, U.S. Ambassador Alexis Johnson's remarks made soon after the agreement was announced, contained in *Department of State Bulletin* 33, no. 848 (26 September 1955): 489. See also Secretary Dulles's press conference remarks of 18 October and 6 December 1955, contained in *Department of State Bulletin* 33, no. 853 (31 October 1955): 689–90; and *Department of State Bulletin,* 33, no. 860, (19 December 1955): 1008.
12. For a discussion of U.S. behavior on this matter, see Young, *Negotiating,* pp. 75–90.
13. Ibid., pp. 1–22.
14. See, for instance, PRC foreign ministry spokesman's statement of 16 December 1955 in *SCMP* 1192, p. 22.
15. See NCNA English text of the agreed announcement in *SCMP* 1127, p. 1. (Italics added.) On American citation of the English-language text, see Dulles's 18 October press conference remarks in *Department of State Bulletin* 33, no. 853 (31 October 1955): 689–90.
16. Cited in Young, *Negotiating,* p. 64.
17. Ibid., p. 87.
18. The following passages are taken from Robert B. Ekvall, *Faithful Echo* (New York, 1960), pp. 87–91. They are quoted at length so as to provide evidence from an American observer supporting the Chinese position on this important issue. (All italics have been added.)

19. The practice of having divergence in the English and Chinese texts of a specific bilateral agreement signed by the PRC is hardly unprecedented. Indeed, Ekvall also pointed to additional textual differences between the English and Chinese texts of the same agreed announcement on the issue of how third countries were to assist in repatriating civilians (pp. 91–92). Further, Young pointed out that in the exchange of ostensibly identical messages between the two sides marking the start of the discussions, the Chinese side employed the Chinese word for Peking in referring to the PRC capital, while the English-language text used by the United States employed the word *Peiping* (p. 51).

More recently, in the 13 March 1972 Sino-British communiqué raising their bilateral relations to the ambassadorial level, the English text stated that London *acknowledged* Peking's position that Taiwan is a province of the PRC; by contrast, the Chinese text used a much stronger term signifying London's *recognition* of Peking's position on Taiwan. For a discussion of this latter communiqué, see FBIS, *Trends in Communist Propaganda*, 15 March 1972, pp. 14–15.

20. See, for instance, *Department of State Bulletin* 33, no. 861 (26 December 1955): 1049–50; 34, no. 865 (23 January 1956): 125; 34, no. 866 (30 January 1956): 166.

21. Note Peking's release of U.S. fliers just prior to the start of the ambassadorial talks and its more recent practice of granting lenient treatment to convicted U.S. agents John Downey and Richard Fecteau as a result of the Sino-American rapprochement in the early 1970s. See also discussion in Young, *Negotiating*, pp. 63–64.

22. See most notably a series of statements from the Chinese foreign ministry and foreign ministry spokesman in late 1955 and in the first half of 1956. They are repeated in *SCMP* 1192, p. 22; *SCMP* 1205, p. 24; *SCMP* 1213, p. 2; *SCMP* 1217, p. 3; *SCMP* 1242, p. 18; *SCMP* 1247, p. 20; and *SCMP* 1310, p. 2.

23. *SCMP* 1130, p. 1.

24. Ibid.

25. See Young, *Negotiating*, pp. 309–10.

26. *SCMP* 1213, p. 3. See also Young, *Negotiating*, pp. 92, 94.

27. See especially Chou-En-lai's rebuttal of Dulles's cease-fire proposal for the Taiwan area of January 1955 in *SCMP* 974, pp. 1–2.

28. For the text of the proposal, see Young, *Negotiating*, pp. 414–15.

29. See *SCMP* 1213, pp. 3–4.

30. Ibid., p. 5.

31. *SCMP* 1242, p. 19.

32. *SCMP* 1213, p. 5.

33. *SCMP* 1242, pp. 18–20. See also discussion in FBIS, *Survey of Far East Broadcasts*, 8 March 1956, p. 1.

34. *SCMP* 1310, p. 3.

35. See, for instance, *New York Times*, 13 December 1955.

36. Cited in *SCMP* 1212, pp. 32–34.

37. *SCMP* 1213, p. 2.

38. For the text of Chou's report, as carried by NCNA's English service, see *DR China*, 31 January 1956, pp. AAA1–AAA32. His specific references to the Taiwan issue are discussed in FBIS, *Survey of Far East Broadcasts*, 9 February 1956, pp. 1–2. See also FBIS, *Radio Propaganda Report*, 8 February 1956, pp. 1–2.

39. Cited in FBIS, *Survey of Far East Broadcasts*, 13 December 1956, p. 4.

40. *SCMP* 1428, p. 31.

41. *SCMP* 1430, p. 29.

42. Cited in FBIS *Survey of Far East Broadcasts*, 13 December 1956, p. 4.

43. For the text of Chou's report, see *DR China Supplement*, 6 March 1957, pp. 1–27. The speech is also discussed in FBIS, *Survey of Far East Broadcasts*, 7 March 1957, p. 1.

44. This issue is discussed in Young, *Negotiating*, pp. 116–34.

45. See, notably, *SCMP* 1350, p. 18; and 1361, p. 23.
46. *SCMP* 1393, p. 16.
47. *SCMP* 1430, p. 29.
48. *SCMP* 1464, p. 29.
49. This shift in Chinese policy is discussed in Richard Wich, "Chinese Allies and Adversaries," in *The Military and Political Power of China in the 1970s*, ed. William W. Whitson (New York, 1972), pp. 293–97.

Chapter Five

1. *Washington Post,* 29 January 1968.
2. For an analysis of Peking's relations with these states during the Cultural Revolution, see Melvin Gurtov, "The Foreign Ministry and Foreign Affairs during the Cultural Revolution," *The China Quarterly* 40 (1969): 65–102.
3. Harold Hinton, *China's Turbulent Quest* (New York, 1970), pp. 157–58.
4. NCNA, 28 May 1968 in *DR China,* 28 May 1968, p. A4.
5. For a general discussion of this turbulent period in PRC foreign affairs, see Gurtov, "The Foreign Ministry," and Hinton, *Quest,* pp. 127–64.
6. See Gurtov, "The Foreign Ministry." See also Daniel Tretiak, *The Chinese Cultural Revolution and Foreign Policy* (Waltham, Mass., 1970).
7. NCNA, 18 May 1968 in *DR China,* 20 May 1968, pp. A1–A4.
8. NCNA, 17, 18 June 1968 in *DR China,* 19 June 1968, pp. A1–A8.
9. NCNA, 24, 25 May 1968 in *DR China,* 27 May 1968, pp. A3–A4.
10. NCNA, 26 July 1968 in *DR China,* 30 July 1968, p. A4.
11. Agence France Presse (AFP), 31 July 1968.
12. Gurtov, "The Foreign Ministry," p. 93.
13. See notably NCNA, 11 August 1968 in *DR China,* 13 August 1968, p. A6; and NCNA, 15 August 1968 in *DR China,* 16 August 1968, pp. A3–A5.
14. Philip Bridgham, "Mao's Cultural Revolution: The Struggle to Seize Power," *The China Quarterly* 41 (1970): 1–25.
15. This phenomenon remained in effect for about six weeks following the invasion.
16. Information in this paragraph is taken from *The Military Balance* (London) (1960–69). Also see *The Economist,* 22 March 1969; and T. W. Robinson, "The Sino-Soviet Border Dispute, Part I," manuscript (Santa Monica, Calif., September 1969).
17. *Peking Review,* 20 September 1968, p. 41.
18. Italics added.
19. The article was repeated by NCNA's English service on 22 September 1968. See *DR China,* 23 September 1968, pp. A1–A2.
20. The text of Chou's speech, as carried by NCNA's English service, is given in *DR China,* 1 October 1968, pp. A1–A3.
21. Ibid., p. A3.
22. *Peking Review,* 11 October 1968, p. 7.
23. *Peking Review,* 13 December 1968, p. 8.
24. NCNA, 14 December 1968 in *DR China,* 16 December 1968, pp. A6–A8.
25. Peking radio in Vietnamese to Vietnam, 1 February 1969 in *DR China,* 5 February 1969, pp. A4–A5.
26. This figure is based on a survey concerning this question in *Peking Review* during the two months prior to the invasion of Czechoslovakia, and the two months following the invasion. Coverage of this issue tended to be focused on the front pages of this journal during the period following the Czechoslovakia events, while earlier it had been limited chiefly to the back pages.
27. See, for example, *Peking Review,* 25 October 1968, p. 9.

28. See, for instance, Peking Domestic Service article of 20 January 1969 in *DR China*, 23 January 1969, pp. A4–A6.

29. See, for instance, *Peking Review*, 18 October 1968, pp. 14–18.

30. NCNA, 22 August 1968 in *DR China*, 23 August 1968, p. A10.

31. NCNA, 23 August 1968 in *DR China*, 26 1968, pp. A1–A3.

32. The text of Chou's speech is contained in *DR China*, 2 September 1968, pp. A2–A4.

33. Chen's remarks are cited in *DR China*, 10 September 1968, p. A2.

34. NCNA, 13 September 1968 in *DR China*, 13 September 1968, pp. A1–A2.

35. For several months preceding the Czechoslovakia crisis, attacks against the Tito government appeared on a regular basis—about one every other week.

36. NCNA, 28 November 1968 in *DR China*, 29 November 1968, p. A15.

37. *Peking Review*, 25 October 1968, p. 12.

38. Cited in *DR China*, 4 November 1968, p. A1.

39. NCNA, 28 November 1968 in *DR China*, 29 November 1968, p. A3.

40. The text of the statement, released by the "spokesman of the information department" of the PRC ministry of foreign affairs and carried by NCNA's English service, is transcribed in *DR China*, 26 November 1968, pp. A1–A2.

41. Ibid. (Italics added.)

42. NCNA, 8 November 1968 in *DR China*, 12 November 1968, p. A1.

43. See, for instance, *New York Times*, 28 and 29 November 1968; and 1 and 8 December 1968.

44. See *DR China*, 26 November 1968, p. A1.

45. NCNA, 24 November 1968 in *DR China*, 25 November 1968, p. B8.

46. Ibid., p. B1.

47. For a discussion of Chou's close control of the foreign policy apparatus at this time, see Gurtov, "The Foreign Ministry."

48. Cited in Shanghai City Service, 2 December 1968 and repeated in *DR China*, 5 December 1968, pp. B4–B5.

49. Cited in Peking Domestic Service, 6 December 1968 and repeated in *DR China*, 7 December 1968, p. B3.

50. Cited in NCNA, 4 December 1968 and repeated in *DR China*, 5 December 1968, pp. B1–B4.

51. Ibid., p. 3.

52. Cited in NCNA, 13 December 1968 and repeated in *DR China*, 16 December 1968, p. B1.

53. This condition of uncertainty stems largely from our continuing lack of reliable information concerning the motivations and thinking of members of the CCP leadership. It should also be noted that none of the criticisms of Liu's foreign approach gives any precise information as to who in the leadership was encouraging this divergent stance. One can only report that this systematic critique was confined largely to media outlets concerned with cultural affairs, suggesting that Chiang Ching and her aides probably supported the campaign. In any case, during the emergence of similar signs of divergence, following China's move toward moderation with the USSR in the latter half of 1969, Chiang's name is to be prominently mentioned in support of a position, advocating an uncompromising approach to both Moscow and Washington.

54. *People's Daily* and *Red Flag*, 27 January 1969 in *DR China*, 27 January 1969, pp. A1–A5.

55. NCNA, 28 January 1969 in *DR China*, 29 January 1969, pp. A1–A2.

56. NCNA, 30 January 1969 in *DR China*, 31 January 1969, pp. A9–A10.

57. NCNA, 28 January 1969 in *DR China*, 29 January 1969, pp. A1–A2.

58. NCNA, 6 February 1969 in *DR China*, 7 February 1969, p. A1–A2.

59. NCNA, 8 February 1969 in *DR China*, 10 February 1969, pp. A1–A2.

60. *People's Daily*, 11 February 1969; NCNA, 11 February 1969 in *DR China*, 12 February 1969, p. A1.

61. NCNA, 16 February 1969 in *DR China*, 17 February 1969, pp. A8–A9.

62. See, for instance, NCNA, 27 February 1969 in *DR China*, 28 February 1969.

63. NCNA, 5 March 1969 in *DR China*, 6 March 1969, pp. A1–A2.

64. *Washington Post*, 19 February 1969.

65. Ibid.

66. *New York Times*, 19 February 1969.

67. NCNA, 18 February 1969 in *DR China*, 18 February 1969, p. A8.

68. *New York Times*, 19 February 1969; *Washington Post*, 19 February 1969.

Chapter Six

1. See, for example, Lin Piao's "Report to the Ninth Congress of the Chinese Communist Party," in NCNA, 27 April 1969, text given in *DR China Supplement*, 29 April 1969, pp. 1–25.

2. See, for instance, Chinese reaction to a Soviet military delegation's visit to India, in NCNA, 11 March 1969, repeated in *DR China*, 12 March 1969, pp. A10–A11.

3. See NCNA coverage of the USSR in the week following the 2 March border clashes in *DR China* for that period.

4. See, for instance, NCNA, 3 March 1969 coverage of a harsh denunciation of the USSR by a Chinese vice foreign minister at a Moroccan embassy reception in Peking, repeated in *DR China*, 4 March 1969, pp. A7–A8.

5. NCNA, 8 May 1969 in *DR China*, 9 May 1969, p. A1.

6. NCNA, 7 May 1969 in *DR China*, 9 May 1969, pp. A4–A7.

7. NCNA, 31 May 1969 in *DR China*, 2 June 1969, p. A1.

8. Karachi Domestic Service, 5 May 1969, cited in *DR China*, 7 May 1969, p. A1. Also in this period, the Chinese showed more interest in the conduct of foreign affairs by beginning to appoint ambassadors abroad for the first time since the start of the Cultural Revolution. This move, however, had long been expected and did not appear to be directly related to China's increased concern over the USSR.

9. This situation remained basically unchanged until early fall. See, for example, the 1 September 1969 message of the Chinese leadership to North Vietnam, repeated in *DR China*, 2 September 1969, pp. A1–A2.

10. For Peking's coverage of this incident, see NCNA, 22 April 1969, repeated in *DR China*, 22 April 1969, pp. A1–A2.

11. For an assessment of the Soviet reinforcement at this time, see the magazine *Strategic Survey* (London) (1969), pp. 67–72.

12. *New York Times*, 21 August 1969.

13. NCNA reports of 13 August 1969 in *DR China*, 13 August 1969, p. A1, and 14 August 1969, p. A1.

14. *New York Times*, 17 August 1969.

15. Cited in *Strategic Survey* (London) (1969), p. 67.

16. Ibid.

17. *New York Times*, 8 August 1969.

18. See, *New York Times*, 28 August 1969 and 29 August 1969.

19. *New York Times*, 28 August 1969.

20. Hinton, *Quest*, p. 318.

21. NCNA, 14 August 1969 in *DR China*, 15 August 1969, p. A1.

22. Peking Domestic Service, 14 August 1969 in *DR China*, 15 August 1969, pp. A2–A3.

23. For a discussion of these sources, see *The China Quarterly* 40 (1969): 180. Also see Hinton, *Quest*, p. 319.

24. *New York Times*, 14 September 1969.

25. Peking Domestic Service, 15 September 1969 in *DR China*, 18 September 1969, pp. A5–A8.

26. *New York Times*, 18 September 1969.

27. Slogan number 22 in NCNA, 16 September 1969, repeated in *DR China*, 18 September 1969, p. B1.

28. NCNA, 30 September 1969 in *DR China*, 1 October 1969, p. B11.

29. First Peking mention of the tests occurred in NCNA, 4 October 1969; see *DR China*, 6 October 1969, p. B1.

30. The text of the statement, as carried by NCNA's English service, is given in *DR China*, 8 October 1969, pp. A1–A2.

31. See *DR China*, 26 May 1969, pp. A1–A10.

32. See *DR China*, 9 October 1969, pp. A1–A11.

33. *DR China*, 8 October 1969, p. A2.

34. Kaingsu Provincial Service, 17 October 1969 in *DR China*, 20 October 1969, pp. A2–A4.

35. (Italics and insert are added.) Also, between these two excerpts, the article stated: "Through negotiations we can further expose the ugly features of the enemy and educate the people to see through the cunning nature of imperialism, revisionism, and all reaction, thereby placing the enemy in an even more isolated position." See *DR China*, 20 October 1969, pp. A3–A4.

36. In late August, for example, *Red Flag* condemned a number of plays that advocated negotiating with an enemy. It stated that these plays "opposed Chairman Mao's military line and thinking on people's war, and misrepresented the revolutionary army and revolutionary people; . . . Furthermore, they advocated winning victory through negotiations and attributed our victory to the righteousness and reasonableness of the enemy." See NCNA, 31 August 1969, repeated in *DR China*, 8 September 1969, pp. B1–B8.

37. See, for example, Anhwei Provincial Service, 13 October 1969 in *DR China*, 17 October 1969, pp. B11–B12. Also see Inner Mongolia Regional Service, 28 October 1969 in *DR China*, 30 October 1969, p. F5. These articles also appear to reflect signs of disagreement within the leadership over whether to rely on people's war or modern military armament and tactics in repelling an enemy. Also see, for another example, Inner Mongolian Regional Service, 9 November 1969. For a discussion, see the *Washington Post*, 19 December 1969.

38. Peking Domestic Service, 19 October 1969 in *DR China*, 28 October 1969, pp. B2–B4.

39. Ibid., p. B3.

40. Interestingly, this Mao work, "On the Chungking Negotiations," was to provide the basis for study material rationalizing to the Chinese Peking's overt move toward the United States in the early 1970s. (See Chapter 7, note 14.)

41. *Ta Kung Pao*, 6 November 1969 in *DR China*, 6 November 1969, p. A1; *Ta Kung Pao*, 9 January 1970 in *DR China*, 9 January 1970, p. A1.

42. AFP, 10 November 1969. For a discussion of the reliability of these articles, see *The China Quarterly* 41 (1970): 178–79; and 42 (1970): 184–85.

43. See, for example, NCNA, 27 September 1969 in *DR China*, 29 September 1969, p. A2.

44. See, for example, Chou En-lai's reception for Pham Van Dong in NCNA, 27 September 1969, repeated in *DR China* 29 September 1969, p. A3.

45. NCNA, 4 October 1969 in *DR China*, 7 October 1969, p. A4.

46. NCNA, 8 October 1969 in *DR China*, 9 October 1969, p. A15.

47. NCNA, 16 October 1969 in *DR China*, 16 October 1969, pp. A1–A3. While the Chinese demonstrated no further compromise in their position on the Vietnam question, they continued to increase conventional diplomatic efforts in order to improve ties with the Vietnamese communists. Most notably, the Chinese, after the departure of the NLF-PRG delegation from Peking, soon welcomed again Premier Pham Van Dong from Hanoi. After consultations with Dong, the Chinese issued a communiqué that once again indirectly endorsed the Vietnamese communists' ten-

point program regarding a negotiated settlement of the war. See NCNA, 25 October 1969 in *DR China*, 27 October 1969, pp. A1–A3.

48. NCNA, 1 October 1969 in *DR China*, 1 October 1969, p. A9.

49. See, for example, NCNA, 28 October 1969 in *DR China*, 28 October 1969, p. A3.

50. NCNA, 23 November 1969 in *DR China*, 24 November 1969, pp. A2–A4.

51. A reprint of an article from *Nodong Sinmun in NCNA*, 27 November 1969 in *DR China*, 1 December 1969.

52. NCNA, 29 September 1969 in *DR China*, 30 September 1969, p. A9.

53. NCNA, 30 September 1969 in *DR China*, 1 October 1969, p. A10.

54. NCNA, 30 October 1969 in *DR China*, 31 October 1969, p. A7.

55. *Le Monde*, 22 November 1969. The announcement was made by Yugoslavia.

56. NCNA, 7 October 1969 in *DR China*, 8 October 1969, p. A22.

57. *People's Daily*, 22 December 1969; NCNA, 22 December 1969 in *DR China*, 22 December 1969, p. A9.

58. *Washington Post*, 14 December 1969.

59. *New York Times*, 21 January 1970. For a more lengthy discussion of Soviet uneasiness, see the *Washington Post*, 2 March 1970.

60. For background on U.S. deliberations leading to this initiative, see the *New York Times*, 22 July 1969.

61. See NCNA, 30 June 1969 in *DR China*, 30 June 1969, p. A2. See also NCNA 20 November 1969, repeated in *DR China*, 21 November 1969, pp. A1–A3.

62. Peking's coverage of the tour stopped abruptly after commentary on the president's initial stops in the Philippines and Indonesia appeared. See NCNA, 27 July 1969 in *DR China*, 28 July 1969, p. A1. It did not resume until the tour was completed.

63. See NCNA, 5 August 1969 in *DR China*, 6 August 1969, pp. A1–A3.

64. NCNA, 6 August 1969 in *DR China*, 6 August 1969, p. A1.

65. See NCNA, 31 May 1969 in *DR China*, 2 June 1969, p. A4.

66. NCNA, 29 September 1969 in *DR China*, 30 September 1969, pp. A15–A19.

67. NCNA, 23 October 1969 in *DR China*, 24 October 1969, pp. A2–A3.

68. NCNA, 16 November 1969 in *DR China*, 17 November 1969, pp. A8–A11.

69. See, for instance, a *People's Daily* editorial of 28 November 1969 carried by NCNA, 28 November 1969, repeated in *DR China*, 28 November 1969, pp. A1–A4.

70. *New York Times*, 9 October 1969.

71. NCNA, 14 September 1969, repeated in *DR China*, 16 September 1969, pp. A4–A8.

72. Most strikingly, the article stated: "When has the Nixon administration shown moderation? It is precisely Nixon who has raised military spending to a record high in the history of the U.S., who has clamoured that U.S. imperialism will 'continue to be a source of world leadership,' and who has stepped up his collusion with the Soviet revisionists and reactionaries in various countries in an attempt to knock together a military ring of encirclement around China."

73. Anhwei Provincial Service, 19 November 1969 in *DR China*, 20 November 1969, pp. A4–A5.

Chapter Seven

1. Evidence of Soviet pressure was reflected in Moscow's continued military build-up along the frontier, in the two Chinese leaks through the Hong Kong communist paper *Ta Kung Pao* shortly after the start of the talks (see chapter 6, note 41) and in revived Sino-Soviet polemics at this juncture. The prolonged absence of the

chief Soviet negotiator in the border talks from Peking in late 1969 also seemed to indicate a Soviet effort to pressure China into a more accommodating position. For a discussion of this latter issue, see FBIS, *Trends in Communist Propaganda*, 7 January 1970, pp. 11–13.

2. The termination of regular U.S. patrols in the Taiwan Straits at this time is discussed in *U.S. News and World Report*, 17 April 1972, pp. 76–79.

3. For a discussion of Peking's response to the message see FBIS, *Trends in Communist Propaganda*, 4 February 1970, p. 24; and 11 February 1970, pp. 23–24.

4. NCNA, 31 January 1970 in *DR China*, 2 February 1970, pp. A1–A3.

5. NCNA, 5 February 1970 in *DR China*, 5 February 1970, pp. A1–A2; NCNA 7 February 1970 in *DR China*, 9 February 1970, pp. A2–A4.

6. Discussed in FBIS, *Trends in Communist Propaganda*, 4 March 1970, pp. 20–21.

7. NCNA, 28 February 1970 in *DR China*, 2 March 1970, pp. A1–A4.

8. See NCNA, 18 February 1969 in *DR China*, 18 February 1969, p. A8; and NCNA, 19 May 1970 in *DR China*, 19 May 1970, p. A1.

9. The address is repeated in NCNA, 27 June 1970, in FBIS, *Daily Report Asia and Pacific: Supplement*, 6 July 1970, pp. 13–16.

10. *Life*, 30 April 1971, pp. 46–48.

11. NCNA, 30 September 1970 in *DR China*, 1 October 1970, pp. B1–B3; NCNA, 1 October 1970 in *DR China*, 2 October 1970, pp. B3–B11.

12. NCNA, 25 December 1970 in *DR China*, 28 December 1970, p. A1.

13. Peking Domestic Service, 25 December 1970 in *DR China*, 28 December 1970, p. A1.

14. See, notably, a 1 July joint editorial article on the CCP's fiftieth anniversary repeated in *DR China*, 1 July 1971, pp. B1–B23. Also see a *Red Flag* article repeated by Peking Domestic Service, 16 August 1971; it appears in *DR China*, 18 August 1971, pp. B1–B7.

15. NCNA, 27 February 1972 in *DR China*, 28 February 1972, pp. A10–A13.

16. See Peking media's mild response to the late 1972 U.S. bombing raids against North Vietnam.

17. Such coverage, which had been a staple in PRC media coverage in the past, appeared on the average only once or twice a week.

18. See NCNA, 17 January 1973 in *DR China*, 18 January 1973, pp. A1–A3.

19. See NCNA, 22 February 1973 in *DR China*, 23 February 1973, p. A1.

20. NCNA, 24 August 1973 in *DR China*, 31 August 1973, p. B1.

21. See Vice Premier Li Hsien-nien's acknowledgment of the "profound crisis" in the U.S. economy on 9 September 1974, cited in *DR China*, 10 September 1974, p. A8. NCNA's first notice of the Watergate affair came in its report of the Nixon resignation on 9 August 1974, cited in *DR China*, 12 August 1974, p. A1.

22. The Sino-Philippines communiqué was repeated by NCNA, 9 June 1975 and carried in *DR China*, 9 June 1975, p. A16. The Sino-Thai communiqué was replayed by NCNA, 1 July 1975 and was carried in *DR China*, 1 July 1975, p. A18.

23. Peking Domestic Service, 16 June 1975 in *DR China*, 19 June 1975, p. A1.

24. See FBIS, *Trends in Communist Media*, 25 June 1975, p. 5.

25. See 21 December 1975 NCNA review of Asian situation in *DR China*, 30 December 1975, p. A4.

26. See *DR China*, 3 April 1975, p. A1; 16 September 1975, p. A4; and 14 October 1975, p. A1.

27. See *DR China*, 20 October 1975, p. A3.

28. See *DR China*, 10 November 1975, p. A1.

29. See *DR China*, 11 November 1975, p. A2; and 12 November 1975, p. A16.

30. See *DR China*, 2 December 1975, p. B3.

31. See 2 November 1976 PRC announcement on foreign policy in *DR China*, 2 November 1976, p. A1.

32. See report of Vice Premier Chang Chun-chiao's "frank" talk with U.S. Senator Hugh Scott in *DR China*, 14 July 1976, p. A2.

Chapter Eight

1. Tsou, *America's Failure*, pp. ix–x.

2. John K. Fairbank, *Chinese-American Interactions* (New Brunswick, N.J., 1975), p. 78.

3. See William L. Langer, *The Diplomacy of Imperialism* (New York, 1951), pp. 747–86.

4. See Akira Iriye, *After Imperialism* (Cambridge, 1965).

Bibliography

Discussion of Source Material

The analytical methods used in this study have varied somewhat, depending on the type of documentation available for use in each instance. In reviewing Sino-American relations in the 1940s, I have made much use of recently declassified U.S. documents reporting on American officials' interaction with the CCP leadership. These reports, which provide considerable information on the positions taken by Yenan spokesmen toward The United States throughout this period, have been used in particular to substantiate an analysis of the goals and aspirations of the Chinese communist leaders as they attempted to attain closer ties with the United States—an area of historical research that has not been as closely studied as other aspects of Sino-American relations of this crucial time. Recently declassified American documents have also pointed up—more strongly than material released earlier —the pronounced anti-Soviet suspicions that lay at the base of American China policy in the latter part of the Pacific war and that complicated Washington's interaction with and assessment of the Chinese communist movement. In reviewing CCP-U.S. attitudes from the late 1920s until Washington's entrance into the Pacific war, I have relied on some secondary sources as well as such stock primary sources as CCP pronouncements, made through the propaganda organs of the Comintern, and U.S. State Department reports. These two latter sources have been useful particularly in describing early encounters and confrontations between American forces in China and armed bands of CCP troops.

For the remainder of the study, I have examined the Chinese side largely through the means of "propaganda analysis," or "media analysis." This method has entailed a systematic review of the controlled output of the Chinese media channels to ascertain trends and patterns that point to directions and intentions in Chinese policy. In this endeavor, I have been aided considerably by a series of reports over the past twenty-five years on China's, and other communist states', media output; these reports have been produced under the auspices of the Foreign Broadcast Information Service and have been recently declassified by the U.S. government. For my purposes, the reports, which include weekly, biweekly, and special articles, provided especially useful information with regard to the state of Sino-Soviet relations following the Korean War and China's approach toward the liberation of Taiwan in 1954–55. (The formal titles of these publications have changed over time. The more recent serial publications are known as *Survey of Communist Propaganda* and *Trends in Communist Propaganda*. Earlier serial publications were divided by geographical area; of these, the one I found most useful in dealing with the period of the mid-1950s was *Survey of Far East Broadcasts*. Special articles appeared irregularly; in the 1950s they were called *Radio Propaganda Reports*, changed to *Special Memorandum* in the 1960s.)

To understand American strategy in the 1950s, I have undertaken a general review of U.S. policy statements and actions and have also made use of the accounts of Americans who themselves interacted with the Chinese. A survey of these materials, along with a review of the major Chinese pronouncements of the period, reveal major discrepancies with the prevailing American analysis of the Geneva talks contained in Kenneth T. Young's study *Negotiating with the Chinese Communists*. Major differences center on the issue of the agreed announcement on the mutual release of civilians. In assessing more recent U.S. policy, I have generally used conventional contemporary sources such as newspaper reports and other accounts of American policy pronouncements.

Acheson, Dean. *Power and Diplomacy*. Cambridge: Harvard Univ. Press, 1958.

――――. *Present at the Creation*. New York: W. W. Norton & Co., 1969.

Agence France Presse Wire Service (AFP), 1965–76.

Alsop, Stewart. "The Story behind Quemoy: How We Drifted Close to War." *Saturday Evening Post*, 13 December 1958, pp. 26–27.

Band, Claire, and William Band. *Dragon Fanges: Two Years with the Chinese Guerrillas*. London: G. Allen & Urwin, 1947.

Banno, Masataka. *China and the West, 1859–1861; The Origins of the Tsung-li Yamen*. Cambridge: Harvard Univ. Press, 1964.

Barnett, A. Doak. *Communist China and Asia: Challenge to American Policy*. New York: Vintage Books, 1961.

――――. *Cadre, Bureaucracy and Political Power in Communist China*. New York: Columbia Univ. Press, 1967.

――――. *China After Mao*. Princeton: Princeton Univ. Press, 1967.

――――. *A New U.S. Policy Toward China*. Washington, D.C.,: Brookings Institution, 1971.

――――, ed. *Chinese Communist Politics in Action*. Seattle: Univ. of Washington Press, 1969.

Barnett, A. Doak, and Edwin O. Reischauer, eds. *The United States and China: The Next Decade*. New York: Praeger Pubs., 1970.

Barrett, David D. *Dixie Mission: The U.S. Army Observer Group in Yenan, 1944*. Berkeley: Univ. of California Press, 1970.

Beal, John R. *Marshall in China*. Garden City, N.Y.: Doubleday & Co., 1970.

Belden, Jack. *China Shakes the World*. New York: Harper & Row Pubs. 1949.

Beloff, Max. *The Foreign Policy of Soviet Russia, 1929–1941*. London: Oxford Univ. Press, 1947.

Berton, Peter, and Eugene Wu. *Contemporary China: A Research Guide*. Stanford, Calif.: Hoover Institution Press, 1967.

Bertram, James M. *First Act in China: The Story of the Sian Mutiny*. New York: Viking Press, 1938.

——. *Unconquered*. New York: John Jay Co., 1939.

Blum, Robert. *The United States and China in World Affairs*. New York: McGraw-Hill Book Co., 1966.

Boorman, Howard L.; Alexander Eckstein; Philip E. Mosely; and Benjamin Schwartz. *Moscow-Peking Axis: Strengths and Strains*. New York: Harper & Row Pubs. 1957.

Boorman, Howard L., and Richard C. Howard. *Biographic Dictionary of Republican China*. 4 vols. New York: Columbia Univ. Press, 1967–71.

Borg, Dorothy. *The United States and the Far East Crisis of 1933–38*. Cambridge: Harvard Univ. Press, 1964.

——. *American Policy and the Chinese Revolution, 1925–1928*. New York: Octagon Books, 1968.

Borkenau, F. *World Communism: A History of the Communist International*. New York: W. W. Norton & Co., 1939.

Bowie, Robert R., and John K. Fairbank. *Communist China, 1955–1959: Policy Documents with Analysis*. Cambridge: Harvard Univ. Press, 1962.

Boyd, R. G. *Communist China's Foreign Policy*. New York: Praeger Pubs., 1962.

Brandt, Conrad. *Stalin's Failure in China, 1924–1927*. Cambridge: Harvard Univ. Press, 1958.

Brandt, Conrad; Benjamin Schwartz; and John K. Fairbank, eds. *A Documentary History of Chinese Communism*. Cambridge: Harvard Univ. Press, 1952.

Bridgham, Philip. "Mao's Cultural Revolution: The Struggle to Seize Power." *The China Quarterly* 41 (1970): 1–25.

Brzezinski, Zbigniew K. *The Soviet Bloc: Unity and Conflict*. Cambridge: Harvard Univ. Press, 1960.

Buhite, Russell D. *Nelson T. Johnson and American Policy toward China, 1925–1941*. East Lansing: Michigan State Univ. Press, 1968.

——. *Patrick J. Hurley and American Foreign Policy*. Ithaca, N.Y.: Cornell Univ. Press, 1973.

Bulletin of Atomic Scientists. *China after the Cultural Revolution*. New York: Random House, 1970.

Bundy, McGeorge, ed. *The Pattern of Responsibility*. Boston: Houghton Mifflin Co., 1952.

Butow, Robert J. C. *Tojo and the Coming of the War*. Princeton: Princeton Univ. Press, 1961.

Carlson, Evans F. *Twin Stars of China*. New York: Dodd, Mead & Co., 1940.

Ch'en, Jerome. *Mao and the Chinese Revolution*. London: Oxford Univ. Press, 1965.

Chen Kung-po. *The Communist Movement in China*. New York: Octagon Books, 1960.

Chi, Madeleine. *China Diplomacy, 1914–1918*. Cambridge: Harvard Univ. Press, 1970.

Chiang Kai-shek. *China's Destiny*. New York, Macmillan Pub. Co., 1947.

The China Quarterly (London), 1960–76.

Clubb, O. Edmund. *Communism in China as Reported from Hankow in 1932*. New York: Columbia Univ. Press, 1968.

———. *China and Russia: The Great Game*. New York: Columbia Univ. Press, 1970.

Clubb, O. Edmund, and Eustace Seligman. *The International Position of Communist China*. New York: Oceana Pubs., 1965.

Cohen, Jerome A., ed. *Taiwan and American Foreign Policy: The Dilemma in U.S.-China Relations*. New York: Praeger Pubs., 1971.

Cohen, Warren I. "The Development of Chinese Communist Policy toward the United States, 1922–1933." *Orbis* 11 (1967): 219–37.

———. *America's Response to China*. New York: John Wiley & Sons, 1971.

The Communist International, 1930–40.

Crowley, James B. *Japan's Quest for Autonomy*. Princeton: Princeton Univ. Press, 1966.

Current Background (Hong Kong, U.S. Consulate General), 1950–76.

Dallin, David J. *Soviet Russia and the Far East*. New Haven: Yale Univ. Press, 1948.

———. *Soviet Foreign Policy after Stalin*. Philadelphia: J. B. Lippincott Co., 1961.

Davies, John Paton. *Dragon by the Tail*. New York: W. W. Norton & Co., 1972.

Dennett, Tyler. *Americans in Eastern Asia: A Critical Study of the Policy of the United States with Reference to China, Japan, and Korea in the 19th Century*. New York: Macmillan Pub. Co., 1922.

Department of State Bulletin 32–34 (1955–56).

Douglas, Bruce, and Ross Terrill. *China and Ourselves: Explorations and Revisions by a New Generation*. Boston: Beacon Press, 1969.

Dulles, John Foster. "Policy for Security and Peace." *Foreign Affairs* 32 (1954): 353–64.

———. "The Evolution of Foreign Policy." *Department of State Bulletin* 30:107–10.

———. "Report from Asia." *Department of State Bulletin* 32:459–64.

Dutt, Vikya Prakash. *China and the World; An Analysis of Communist China's Foreign Policy*. New York: Praeger Pubs., 1966.

Eastman, Lloyd. *Throne and Mandarins: China's Search for a Policy during the Sino-French Controversy, 1880–1885*. Cambridge: Harvard Univ. Press, 1967.

The Economist, 1968–77.

Eisenhower, Dwight D. *Mandate for Change.* New York: New American Library, 1965.

Ekvall, Robert B. *Faithful Echo.* New York: Twayne Pubs., 1960.

Epstein, Israel. *The Unfinished Revolution in China.* Boston: Little, Brown & Co., 1947.

Fairbank, John K. *Trade and Diplomacy on the China Coast: The Opening of the Treaty Ports, 1842–1854.* Cambridge: Harvard Univ. Press, 1953.

———. *China: The People's Middle Kingdom and the U.S.A.* Cambridge: Harvard Univ. Press, 1967.

———. *The United States and China.* Cambridge: Harvard Univ. Press, 1971.

———. *Chinese-American Interactions: A Historical Summary.* New Brunswick, N.J.: Rutgers Univ. Press, 1975.

———, ed. *The Chinese World Order.* Cambridge: Harvard Univ. Press., 1968.

Fairbank, John K., and K. C. Liu. *Modern China: A Bibliographical Guide to Chinese Works, 1898–1937.* Cambridge: Harvard Univ. Press, 1950.

Fairbank, John K.; Edwin O. Reischauer; and Albert Craig. *East Asia: The Modern Transformation.* Boston: Houghton Mifflin Co., 1965.

———. *East Asia: Tradition and Transformation.* Boston: Houghton Mifflin Co., 1973.

Feis, Herbert. *The Road to Pearl Harbor.* Princeton: Princeton Univ. Press, 1950.

———. *The China Tangle.* Princeton: Princeton Univ. Press, 1953.

Fifield, Russell H. *Woodrow Wilson and the Far East: The Diplomacy of the Shantung Question.* New York: Thomas Y. Crowell Co., 1952.

Fitzgerald, C. P. *Chinese View of Their Place in the World.* London: Oxford Univ. Press, 1969.

Foreign Broadcast Information Service. *Daily Report: Asia and Pacific.* 1967–. Springfield, Va., National Technological Information Service (NTIS).

———. *Daily Report: Communist China, 1967–1971.* Springfield, Va., NTIS.

———. *Daily Report: Far East, 1953–1967.* Springfield, Va., NTIS.

———. *Daily Report: People's Republic of China.* 1971–. Springfield, Va., NTIS.

———. *Radio Propaganda Reports, 1953–1966.* 15 vols. Springfield Va., NTIS.

———. *Survey of Far East Broadcasts, 1950–1959.* 11 vols. Springfield, Va., NTIS.

———. *Survey of USSR Radio Broadcasts, 1947–1958.* 43 vols. Springfield, Va., NTIS

———. *Trends in Communist Propaganda.* 1968–. 16 vols. Springfield. Va., NTIS.

Foreign Relations of the United States: Diplomatic Papers, 1942: China. Washington, D.C., Government Printing Office, 1952.

Foreign Relations of the United States: Diplomatic Papers, 1943: China. Washington, D.C., Government Printing Office, 1957.

Foreign Relations of the United States: Diplomatic Papers, 1944: China. Washington, D.C., Government Printing Office, 1967.

Foreign Relations of the United States: Diplomatic Papers, 1945: The Far East and China. Washington, D.C., Government Printing Office, 1969.

Forman, Harrison. *Report from Red China.* New York: Henry Holt and Co., 1945.

Freidman, Edward, and Mark Selden, eds. *America's Asia.* New York: Pantheon Books, 1971.

Gaddis, John L. *The United States and the Origins of the Cold War, 1941–1947.* New York: Columbia Univ. Press, 1972.

Gelder, Stuart. *The Chinese Communists.* London: Victor Gollancz, 1946.

George, Alexander L. *The Chinese Communist Army in Action: The Korean War and Its Aftermath.* New York: Columbia Univ. Press, 1969.

Gittings, John. *The Role of the Chinese Army.* London: Oxford Univ. Press, 1967.

———. *Survey of the Sino-Soviet Dispute.* London: Oxford Univ. Press, 1968.

———. "The Great Power Triangle and Chinese Foreign Policy." *The China Quarterly* 39 (1969): 41–54.

Gray, Jack, and Patrick Cavendish. *Chinese Communism in Crisis: Maoism and the Cultural Revolution.* New York: Praeger Pubs., 1968.

Griffith, Samuel B. *Peking and People's War.* New York: Praeger Pubs., 1966.

———. *The Chinese People's Liberation Army.* New York: McGraw-Hill Book Co., 1967.

Griffith, William E. *Sino-Soviet Rift.* Cambridge, Mass.: M.I.T. Press, 1964.

———. *Sino-Soviet Relations 1964–1965.* Cambridge, Mass.: M.I.T. Press, 1967.

———. *Cold War and Coexistence: Russia, China and the United States.* Englewood Cliffs, N.J.: Prentice-Hall, 1971.

Griswold, A. Whitney. *The Far Eastern Policy of the United States.* New Haven: Yale Univ. Press, 1962.

Gurtov, Melvin. *First Vietnam Crisis: Chinese Communist Strategy and United States Involvement, 1953–1954.* New York: Columbia Univ. Press, 1968.

———. "The Foreign Ministry and Foreign Affairs during the Cultural Revolution." *The China Quarterly* 40 (1969): 65–102.

———. *China and Southeast Asia: The Politics of Survival.* Lexington, Mass.: Lexington Books, 1971.

Halperin, Morton H. *China and the Bomb.* New York: Praeger Pubs., 1965.

———, ed. *Sino-Soviet Relations and Arms Control.* Cambridge, Mass.: M.I.T. Press, 1967.

Halpern, A. M. "Communist China and Peaceful Coexistence." *The China Quarterly* 3 (1960): 16–31.

———, ed. *Policies toward China: Views from Six Continents.* New York: McGraw-Hill Book Co., 1965.

Hilsman, Roger. *To Move a Nation.* New York: Doubleday & Co., 1967.

Hinton, Harold C. *China's Relations with Burma and Vietnam: A Brief Survey.* New York: Institute of Pacific Relations, 1968.

———. *Communist China in World Politics.* Boston: Houghton Mifflin Co., 1966.

———. *China's Turbulent Quest.* New York: Macmillan Pub. Co., 1970.

———. *Bear at the Gate: Chinese Policymaking Under Soviet Pressure.* Washington, D.C.: American Enterprise Institute for Public Policy Research, 1971.

Ho Ping-ti, and Tang Tsou, eds. *China in Crisis.* 2 vols. Chicago: Univ. of Chicago Press, 1968.

Hofstadter, Richard. *The Paranoid Style in American Politics.* New York: Vintage Books, 1967.

Hsieh, Alice Langley. *Communist China's Strategy in the Nuclear Era.* Englewood Cliffs, N.J.: Prentice-Hall, 1962.

Hsiung, James Chieh. *Law and Policy in China's Foreign Relations: A Study of Attitudes and Practices.* New York: Columbia Univ. Press, 1972.

Hsu, Immanuel C. Y. *China's Entrance into the Family of Nations, The Diplomatic Phase, 1858–1880.* Cambridge: Harvard Univ. Press, 1960.

———. *The Ili Crisis, A Study in Sino-Russian Diplomacy, 1871–1881.* Oxford: Clarendon Press, 1965.

Hu, Chiao-mu. *Thirty Years of the Communist Party in China: An Outline History.* London: Lawrence & Wishart, 1951.

Hucker, Charles O. *China: A Critical Bibliography.* Tuscon: Univ. of Arizona Press, 1962.

International Press Correspondence (Moscow), 1927–39.

Iriye, Akira. *After Imperialism: The Search for a New Order in the Far East, 1921–1931.* Cambridge: Harvard Univ. Press, 1965.

———. *Across the Pacific.* New York: Harcourt, Brace & World, 1967.

Isaacs, Harold R. *Tragedy of the Chinese Revolution.* Stanford, Calif.: Stanford Univ. Press, 1971.

Joffe, Ellis. *Party and Army: Professionalism and Political Control in the Chinese Officer Corps, 1949–1964.* Cambridge: Harvard Univ. Press, 1965.

Johnson, Chalmers. *Peasant Nationalism and Communist Power.* Stanford, Calif.: Stanford Univ. Press, 1962.

———, ed. *Ideology and Politics in Contemporary China.* Seattle: Univ. of Washington Press, 1973.

Johnston, Douglas M., and Hung-dah Chiu. *Agreements of the People's Republic of China, 1949–1967: A Calendar.* Cambridge: Harvard Univ. Press, 1968.

Kallgren, Joyce. "Nationalist China's Armed Forces." *The China Quarterly* 15 (1963): 35–44.

Kennan, George F. *American Diplomacy, 1900–1950.* New York: Mentor Books, 1952.

———. *Realities of American Foreign Policy.* New York: W. W. Norton & Co., 1966.

———. *Memoirs.* Boston: Little, Brown & Co., 1967.

Kerr, George H. *Formosa Betrayed.* Boston: Houghton Mifflin Co., 1965.

Kissinger, Henry A. *A World Restored: Metternich, Castlereagh and the Problems of Peace, 1812–1822.* Boston: Houghton Mifflin Co., 1957.

———. *Nuclear Weapons and Foreign Policy.* New York: Harper & Row Pubs., 1957.

———. *Necessity for Choice.* New York: Harper & Row Pubs., 1961.

———. *The Troubled Partnership.* New York: McGraw-Hill Book Co., 1965.

———. *American Foreign Policy: Three Essays.* New York: W. W. Norton & Co., 1969.

Klein, Donald W. "The Management of Foreign Affairs in Communist China." Manuscript prepared for the Conference on Government in China, 18–23 August 1969, in Cuernavaca, Mexico.

Klein, Donald W., and Anne B. Clark. *Biographic Dictionary of Chinese Communism, 1921–1965.* 2 vols. Cambridge: Harvard Univ. Press, 1971.

Knapp, Wilfred. *A History of War and Peace, 1939–1965.* London: Oxford Univ., Press, 1967.

Koen, Ross Y. *The China Lobby.* New York: Harper & Row Pubs., 1974.

LaFeber, Walter. *America, Russia, and the Cold War.* New York: John Wiley & Sons, 1967.

Lall, Arthur. *How Communist China Negotiates.* New York: Columbia Univ. Press, 1968.

Langer, William L. *The Diplomacy of Imperialism, 1890–1902.* 2 vols. New York: Alfred A. Knopf, 1951.

Lenin, V. I. *Imperialism, The Highest Stage of Capitalism.* Moscow: Foreign Languages Publishing House, 1947.

Leopold, Richard W. *The Growth of American Foreign Policy.* New York: Alfred A. Knopf, 1962.

Lewis, John W. *Leadership in Communist China.* Ithaca, N.Y.: Cornell Univ. Press, 1963.

———, ed. *Party Leadership and Revolutionary Power in China.* London: Cambridge Univ. Press, 1970.

Li, Tien-yi. *Woodrow Wilson's China Policy, 1913–1917.* Kansas City, Mo.: Twayne Pubs., 1952.

Lifton, Robert. *Revolutionary Immortality: Mao Tse-tung and the Chinese Cultural Revolution.* New York: Random House, 1968.

Lindbeck, John M. H. "Research Materials on Communist China: United States Government Sources." *Journal of Asian Studies* 18 (1959): 357–63.

———, ed. *China: Management of a Revolutionary Society.* Seattle: Univ. of Washington Press, 1971.

Lindsay, Michael. *North China Front*. London: China Campaign Committee, 1944.

MacFarquhar, Roderick, ed. *China under Mao*. Cambridge, Mass.: M.I.T. Press, 1966.

McLane, Charles B. *Soviet Policy and Chinese Communists, 1931–1946*. New York: Columbia Univ. Press, 1958.

Malozemoff, Andrew. *Russian Far Eastern Policy, 1881–1904*. Berkeley: Univ. of California Press, 1958.

Mao Tse-tung. *Selected Works*. 4 vols. London: Lawrence & Wishart, 1954.

Maxwell, Neville. *India's China War*. London: Jonathan Cape, 1970.

May, Ernest R. *Imperial Diplomacy*. New York: Harcourt, Brace & World, 1961.

————. *Lessons of History: The Use and Misuse of the Past in American Foreign Policy*. London: Oxford Univ. Press, 1973.

May, Ernest R., and James C. Thomson. *American–East Asian Relations: A Survey*. Cambridge: Harvard Univ. Press, 1972.

Mehnert, Klaus. *Peking and Moscow*. New York: New American Library, 1964.

The Military Balance (London, Institute for Strategic Studies), 1960–69.

Moorstein, Richard, and Morton Abramowitz. *Remaking China Policy: U.S.-China Relations and Governmental Decisionmaking*. Cambridge: Harvard Univ. Press, 1971.

Morgenthau, Hans J. *In Defense of the National Interest*. New York: Alfred A. Knopf, 1951.

————. *Politics among Nations*. New York: Alfred A. Knopf, 1967.

————. *A New Foreign Policy for the United States*. New York: Praeger Pubs. 1969.

Morse, Hosea B. *International Relations of the Chinese Empire*. 3 vols. London: Longmans, Green & Co., 1910, 1918.

Mozingo, David. *China's Foreign Policy and the Cultural Revolution*. Ithaca, N.Y.: Cornell Univ. Press, 1970.

Neuhauser, Charles. *Third World Politics, China and the Afro-Asian People's Solidarity Organization, 1957–1967*. Cambridge: Harvard Univ. Press, 1968.

New York Times, 1950–76.

Nixon, Richard M. *United States Foreign Policy for the 1970's: Building for Peace*. New York: Harper & Row Pubs., 1971.

North, Robert C. *Kuomintang and Chinese Communist Elites*. Stanford, Calif.: Stanford Univ. Press, 1952.

————. *Moscow and the Chinese Communists*. Stanford, Calif.: Stanford Univ. Press, 1963.

————. *Foreign Relations of China*. Belmont, Calif.: Dickenson Pub. Co., 1969.

Ojha, Ishwer. *Chinese Foreign Policy in an Age of Transition*. Boston: Beacon Press, 1969.

Oksenberg, Michael C., ed. *China's Developmental Experience*. New York: Praeger Pubs., 1973.

Peck, Graham. *Two Kinds of Time*. Boston: Houghton Mifflin Co., 1967.

Peking Review, 1965–76.

Pye, Lucian. *The Spirit of Chinese Politics*. Cambridge, Mass.: M.I.T. Press, 1968.

Rice, Edward E. *Mao's Way*. Berkeley: Univ. of California Press, 1972.

Robinson, Joan. *Cultural Revolution in China*. Harmondsworth: Penguin Books, 1969.

Robinson, T. W. "The Sino-Soviet Border Dispute, Part I." Manuscript dated September 1968 and available at East Asian Research Center, Harvard University.

———, ed. *The Cultural Revolution in China*. Berkeley: Univ. of California Press, 1971.

Romanus, Charles F., and Riley Sunderland. *United States Army in World War II, China-Burma-India Theatre, Stilwell's Mission to China*. Washington, D.C.: Department of the Army, 1953.

———. *United States Army in World War II, China-Burma-India Theatre, Stilwell's Command Problems*. Washington, D.C.: Department of the Army, 1956.

Rosinger, L. K. *China's Wartime Politics, 1937–1944*. Princeton: Princeton Univ. Press, 1944.

Salisbury, Harrison E. *War between Russia and China*. New York: W. W. Norton X Co., 1969.

Schlesinger, Arthur M. *A Thousand Days*. New York: Crest Books, 1967.

Schram, Stuart. *Mao-Tse-tung*. New York: Simon & Schuster, 1966.

———. *Basic Tactics*. London: Pall Mall Press, 1967.

———. *The Political Thought of Mao Tse-tung*. New York: Praeger Pubs., 1969.

Schrecker, John E. *Imperialism and Chinese Nationalism*. Cambridge: Harvard Univ. Press, 1971.

Schurman, Franz. *Ideology and Organization in Communist China*. Berkeley: Univ. of California Press, 1968.

Schwartz, Benjamin I. *Chinese Communism and the Rise of Mao*. Cambridge: Harvard Univ. Press, 1951.

———. *Ideology in a Flux*. Cambridge: Harvard Univ. Press, 1968.

Selections from China Mainland Magazines (Hong Kong, United States Consulate General), 1954–76.

Service, John S. *The Amerasia Papers: Some Problems in the History of U.S.-China Relations*. Berkeley: Univ. of California Press, 1971.

Shewmaker, Kenneth E. *Americans and Chinese Communists, 1927–1945: A Persuading Encounter*. Ithaca N.Y.: Cornell Univ. Press, 1971.

Schulman, Marshall. *Stalin's Foreign Policy Reappraised*. Cambridge: Harvard Univ. Press, 1963.

Smith, Gaddis. *American Diplomacy during the Second World War, 1941–1945*. New York: John Wiley & Sons, 1965.

Snow, Edgar. *The Battle for Asia*. New York: Random House, 1941.

———. *Random Notes on Red China, 1936–1945*. Cambridge: Harvard Univ. Press, 1957.

————. *The Other Side of the River*. New York: Random House, 1962.

————. *Red Star over China*. New York: Grove Press, 1968.

————. "A Conversation with Mao." *Life* 70 (1971): 16:46–48.

————. *Journey to the Beginning*. New York: Random House, 1972.

————. *Long Revolution*. New York: Random House, 1972.

Snow, Helen Foster. *My Yenan Note Books*. Madison, Conn., 1961.

Solomon, Richard H. *Mao's Revolution and the Chinese Political Culture*. Berkeley: Univ. of California Press, 1971.

Spanier, John. *American Foreign Policy since World War II*. New York: Praeger Pubs., 1973.

Steele, A. T. *The American People and China*. New York: McGraw-Hill Book Co., 1966.

Stein, Gunther. *The Challenge of Red China*. New York: Whittlesey House, 1945.

Steiner, H. Arthur. "Mainsprings of Chinese Communist Foreign Policy." *American Journal of International Law* 44:69–99.

Strategic Survey (London, Institute for Strategic Studies), 1969.

Survey of the China Mainland Press (Hong Kong, United States Consulate General), 1950–76.

Tang, Peter S. H. *Communist China Today*. New York: Praeger Pubs, 1957.

————. *Russian and Soviet Policy in Manchuria and Outer Mongolia, 1911–1931*. Durham, N.C.: Duke Univ. Press, 1959.

Taylor, George. *The Struggle for North China*. New York: Institute of Pacific Relations, 1940.

Terrill, Ross. *The 800 Million*. Boston: Little, Brown & Co., 1972.

Thomson, James C. *While China Faced West: American Reformers in Nationalist China, 1928–1937*. Cambridge: Harvard Univ. Press, 1970.

Thornton, Richard C. *China, The Struggle for Power, 1917–1972*. Bloomington: Indiana Univ. Press, 1974.

Tretiak, Daniel. *The Chinese Cultural Revolution and Foreign Policy*. Waltham, Mass.: Westinghouse Electric Corporation, 1970.

Truman, Harry S. *Memoirs*. 2 vols. New York: New American Library, 1965.

Tsou, Tang. *The Embroilment over Quemoy: Mao, Chiang, and Dulles*. Salt Lake City: Univ. of Utah Press, 1959.

————. *America's Failure in China, 1941–1950*. Chicago: Univ. of Chicago Press, 1963.

————. *China's Policies in Asia and America's Alternatives*. Chicago, Univ. of Chicago Press, 1968.

Tuchman, Barbara. *Stilwell and the American Experience in China, 1911–1945*. New York: Macmillian Pub. Co., 1970.

————. *Notes from China*. New York: Collier Books, 1972.

U.S. News and World Report, 1950–75.

U.S. Congress. Senate. Committee on Armed Services and Committee on Foreign Relations. *Military Situation in the Far East, Hearings*. 82d Cong., 1st sess. 5 parts. Washington, D.C.: Government Printing Office, 1949.

————. Committee on the Judiciary. Subcommittee to Investigate the

Administration of the Internal Security Act and Other Internal Security Laws. *Institute of Pacific Relations, Hearings.* 82d Cong., 1st and 2d sess. 15 parts. Washington, D.C.: Government Printing Office, 1951–52.

――――. Committee on the Judiciary. Subcommittee to Investigate the Administration of the Internal Security Act and Other Internal Security Laws. *The Amerasia Papers: A Clue to the Catastrophe of China.* Washington, D.C.: Government Printing Office, 1970.

――――. Subcommittee of the Committee on Foreign Relations. *State Department Employee Loyalty Investigation, Hearings.* 81st Cong., 2d sess. 3 parts. Washington, D.C.: Government Printing Office, 1950.

Van Ness, Feter. *Revolution and Chinese Foreign Policy: Peking's Support for Wars of National Liberation.* Berkeley: Univ. of California Press, 1970.

Van Slyke, Lyman P. *Enemies and Friends: The United Front in Chinese Communist History.* Stanford, Calif.: Stanford Univ. Press, 1967.

――――, ed. *The China White Paper.* Stanford, Calif.: Stanford Univ. Press, 1967.

――――, ed. *The Chinese Communist Movement: A Report of the United States War Department, July 1945.* Stanford, Calif.: Stanford Univ. Press, 1968.

Vincent, John C. *Extraterritorial System in China: Final Phase.* Cambridge: Harvard Univ. Press, 1969.

Vogel, Ezra F. *Canton under Communism.* Cambridge: Harvard Univ. Press, 1969.

Wales, Nym. See Snow, Helen Foster.

Washington, D.C. National Archives. Department of State files for 1930–50.

Washington Post, 1950–76.

White, Theodore H., and Annalee Jacoby. *Thunder out of China.* New York: William Sloane Associates, 1961.

Whiting, Allen S. *Soviet Policies in China, 1917–1924.* Stanford, Calif.: Stanford Univ. Press, 1954.

――――. *China Crosses the Yalu: The Decision to Enter the Korean War.* New York: Macmillian Pub Co., 1960.

――――. "Quemoy 1958: Mao's Miscalculations." *The China Quarterly* 62 (1975): 263–70.

Wich, Richard. "Chinese Allies and Adversaries." in *The Military and Political Power of China in the 1970s,* ed. William W. Whitson. New York: Praeger Pubs., 1972.

Wiens, Herold J. *China's March toward the Tropics.* Hamden, Conn.: Shoe String Press, 1954.

Williams, William A. *The Tragedy of American Diplomacy.* New York: World Pub. Co., 1962.

Wilson, Ian, ed. *China and the World Community.* Sydney: Australia Univ. Press, 1973.

Wint, Guy. "China and Asia." *The China Quarterly* 1 (1960): 61–71.

Young, Arthur N. *China and the Helping Hand, 1937–1945.* Cambridge: Harvard Univ. Press, 1963.

Young, Kenneth T. *Negotiating with the Chinese Communists: The United States Experience, 1953–1967.* New York: McGraw-Hill Book Co., 1968.

Young, Marilyn B. *The Rhetoric of Empire: American China Policy, 1895–1901.* Cambridge: Harvard Univ. Press, 1968.

———. *American Expansionism: The Critical Issues.* Boston: Little, Brown & Co., 1973.

Zagoria, Donald S. *The Sino-Soviet Conflict, 1956–1961.* Princeton: Princeton Univ. Press, 1962.

Index

Albania, relationship of, with PRC, 72, 85
Algeria, relationship of, with PRC, 65, 96
Ambassadorial talks. See U.S.–PRC ambassadorial talks
Anglo-Japanese alliance, 120–21
Anti-hegemony clause, 3, 103, 109–11, 113, 114
Asian Collective Security System, 103
Association of Southeast Asian Nations, 114

Balance of power in China, up to end of World War II, 15, 17, 18
Balance of power in East Asia, role of, in U.S.–China relations, 1–9, 28–29, 34, 44, 47, 64, 72–73, 94, 103–5, 118–22
Bandung Conference, 47, 54
Beleaguered City, 92
Brezhnev, Leonid, 1, 67, 87, 100, 103
Brezhnev doctrine of limited sovereignty, 1, 67
Bridgham, Philip, 67
Broz, Josip (Tito), 72
Bulganin, Nikolai A., 46; visit of, to China, 40–42
Burma, relationship of, with PRC, 65, 67–68
Burma Road, 23, 25

Cambodia: relationship of, with PRC, 65, 96; U.S. incursion into, 107
Canton uprising, 11
Ceylon, relationship of, with PRC, 65
Chang Chun-chiao, 117
Changsha uprising, 11

Chang Tsung-hsien, 38
Chen I, 65, 71
Chen Pao island, 89
Chiang Ching, 75, 78, 82, 91, 92, 117
Chiang Kai-shek, 4, 5, 7, 8, 13, 15, 16, 18, 19, 20, 21; disputes with General Stilwell, 23–24, 27; official post offered to, by Chou En-lai, 59–60; strategic power of, in China at end of World War II, 25–26
Chiao Kuan-hua, fetes Henry Kissinger, 115
Chinese civil war, 4, 6. See also Balance of power in China
Chinese Communist Party, 4, 5, 6. See also Chinese communists; People's Republic of China
Chinese communists: adherence of, to Soviet line in foreign affairs before World War II, 10–11; goals of, in policy toward the U.S. during World War II, 13–18, 23; initatives of, toward the U.S. in the 1950s, 8, 47–62; initiatives of, toward the U.S. during World War II, 5, 12–14, 21–23; negotiations of, with the Kuomintang, 20; negotiations of, with Patrick Hurley, 23, 30; policy of, toward the U.S. after World War II, 31–32; policy of, toward the U.S. prior to World War II, 10–11; split of, with the Kuomintang in 1927, 10; strategic weakness of, during World War II, 14, 15, 17, 26; united front of, with the Kuomintang, 12; vital interests of, during World War II, 5. See also People's Republic of China
Chinese nationalists, blockade of, against Chinese communists, 12–13, 14, 15, 23. See also Chiang Kai-shek

151

Chinese People's Political Consultative Conference, 42–43
Chinese People's Volunteers, 34–35, 41, 43
Chinese "puppet" forces during World War II, 13, 24
Chou En-lai, 1, 2, 19, 20, 21, 22, 75, 77, 81, 82, 93, 103; adopts more moderate line toward the U.S. in 1969, 98, 100, 101; appeals for CCP–KMT cooperation, 59–60; calls for U.S.–PRC talks, 47, 54; complains of no progress in U.S.–PRC ambassadorial talks, 61–62; death of, 116; disagrees with Khrushchev on Taiwan issue, 41–42; discusses U.S.–PRC relations prior to Geneva ambassadorial talks, 50, 54; hits U.S.–ROC treaty, 43; interacts with Americans during World War II, 13, 14; meets Cambodian delegation in 1969, 96; on PRC nuclear development in September 1969, 88; on Soviet aid to China, 42; on Soviet invasion of Czechoslovakia, 71; on Soviet pressure against China, 111–12; praises Romania, 71; refers to buildup of Soviet forces along Sino-Soviet border, 69; responds to U.S. ceasefire proposal on Taiwan, 44–45; sends message to Molotov, 39; sends message to Pakistan in 1969, 85; shows closer PRC relations with North Vietnam, 95; talks with Kosygin in 1969, 83, 88; talks with Nyerere, 66; travels to India and Burma in 1954, 36
Cockburn Sound, 114
Cold War, 8; impact of, on U.S.–China relations, 31–33
Comintern, 10, 11. See also Communist International
Communist International, 15; disbanded, 16. See also Comintern
Containment policy. See United States, containment policy of
Cuba, relations of, with PRC, 66
Cultural Revolution: impact of, on Chinese foreign policy, 2, 63, 64–67; impact of, on Chinese military preparedness, 1
Czechoslovakia: impact of Soviet invasion of, on PRC foreign policy, 67–72; relationship of, with PRC, 72, 85; Soviet invasion of, 1, 84, 88

Davies, John P.: discussions of, with Chinese communist leaders, 13–14; on U.S. China policy, 18–19, 27, 28

de Gaulle, Charles, 71
Diego Garcia, 114
Dulles, John Foster, 104; interview with, in *Life* in 1956, 58; report of, about secret note to ROC foreign minister, 43; strategy of, in the Geneva ambassadorial talks with the PRC, 48–50, 54–55, 57

East Germany, relationship of, with PRC, 96
Ekvall, Robert, 52–53
European Security Conference, 114

Fairbank, John K., 119
Fei I-min, 93–94
Ford, Gerald: firing of Defense Secretary Schlesinger by, 114–15; policy of, toward China, 112–16; travels to China, 115
Formosa Resolution, 44
France, relationship of, with PRC, 71

Geneva: big-power summit of 1955 in, 48; peace conference of 1954 in, 36, 48
Geneva ambassadorial talks. See U.S.–PRC ambassadorial talks
German-Japanese alliance, 120
German-Soviet Pact of 1939, 11
Gheorghe, Ion, 72
Great Britain, relationship of, with PRC, 36, 37, 43, 66
Great Leap Forward, 63
Grechko (Soviet defense minister), 87
Guinea, relationship of, with PRC, 66

Hai Jui Dismissed from Office (play), 78
Hawaii, 7
Heisha Tzu, 89
Hua Kuo-feng, 117
Huang Yung-sheng, 72; on anniversary of Korean War in 1970, 107–8; on Soviet pressure against China, 69–70
Hundred Flowers campaign, 62
Hurley, Patrick, 4; mission of, to China, 23, 26–30

Indochina, U.S. defeat of, in 1975, 112–14; implications of, for U.S.–PRC–Taiwan, 112. See also Cambodia; North Vietnam; Vietnam conflict
Indonesia, relationship of, with PRC, 36

Jackson, Henry M., 115
Japan, relationship of, with PRC, 36, 103
Johnson, Lyndon, 72; policy of, toward China, 64

Kennedy, John F., policy of, toward China, 64
Kenya, relationship of, with PRC, 65
Khabarovsk, 89
Khrushchev, Nikita S., comment of, on Taiwan during visit to China in 1954, 40–42
Kiangsi Soviet, 11
Kim Il-song, 65
Kissinger, Henry: travels to China in February 1973, 111; travels to China in July 1971, 105, 108; travels to China in October 1975, 115
Korean War, 4, 6, 8; anniversary of, in 1970, 107–8; impact of, on U.S. China policy, 32–33
Kosygin, Aleksei, 83, 88, 89
Kuomintang, 5. See also Chiang Kai-shek; Chinese nationalists
Kuo Mo-jo, 46

Leadership disputes. See People's Republic of China, leadership disputes in
Lenin's theory of imperialism, 11
Li Hsien-nien, 117
Lin Piao, 20; talks with Americans during World War II, 14
Liu Shao-chi: media attacks on the foreign policy line of, 75–82, 101–2; media attacks on the visit to Indonesia of, 76–77
Louis, Victor, 88

Malenkov, Georgi M.: on the balance of power in East Asia, 34–35; messages of, to Mao, 34, 35, 39
Mali, relationship of, with PRC, 66
Mao Tse-tung, 1, 17, 86; death of, 116; endorses German-Soviet Pact, 11; makes report to the 1949 plenum of the CCP Central Committee, 74–75; meets Edgar Snow in 1970, 108; "On Policy," 108–9; "On the Chungking Negotiations," 91, 108–9; sends messages to Malenkov, 34, 35, 39; talks with John Service, 22–23
May Day, anniversary of, in 1954, Sino-Soviet comment on, 35

Molotov, Vyacheslav M. (Soviet foreign minister), 39, 46
Mongolia, defense ties of, with U.S.S.R., 68
Munich agreement, 116

National Liberation Front-Provisional Revolutionary Government (NLF–PRG) of South Vietnam, relationship of, with PRC, 95
NATO, 116
Nepal, relationship of, with PRC, 65, 66
Netherlands, relationship of, with PRC, 36
New Fourth Army incident, 21
Nixon, Richard M., 108; economic report of, for 1970, 106; foreign policy report of, for 1970, 106; initiatives of, toward China, 97–98; policy of, in Asia, 2, 97–98; policy of, toward China, 9; State of the Union address of, in 1970, 106; treatment of, by Chinese media, 79–82; visit of, to China in 1972, 1, 4, 103, 109–11
Nixon Doctrine, 2, 98, 110
Nixon-Sato communiqué of November 1969, 96, 99
North Korea, relationship of, with PRC, 65, 71, 85, 95–96
North Vietnam, relationship of, with PRC, 65, 71, 85, 94–95, 111
Nyerere, Julius, 66

"On Policy" (report by Mao Tse-tung), 108–9
"On the Chungking Negotiations" (report by Mao Tse-tung), 91, 108–9
Open Door Notes, 7

Pakistan, relationship of, with PRC, 85
Paris peace talks on Vietnam, 70, 72, 75, 85, 95
Pearl Harbor, Japanese attack on, 15
People's Republic of China (PRC): concern of, over Soviet intentions toward China 1968–1969, 67–72; disagreement of, with Soviets over policy in East Asia in mid-1950s, 34–35; diplomatic initiatives of, against the U.S.S.R. in 1969, 93–97; foreign policy goals of, after the Korean War, 6; foreign policy initiatives of, against the U.S.S.R. 70–75; impact of ideol-

ogy of, on policy toward the United States, 82, 83, 85; increased polemics of, against the Nixon administration in 1968–1969, 79–82; initiatives of, toward the Nixon administration in 1968, 72–75; initiatives of, toward the U. S. in the 1950s, 8, 47–62; leadership disputes in, 1, 75–82, 90–93, 99–102, 105, 109; moderate stance of, on border dispute with U.S.S.R. in 1969, 86–90; objectives of, during the 1954–1955 Taiwan campaign, 36–37, 44; objectives of, in Geneva ambassadorial talks, 48, 50, 55–57, 58, 61–62; objectives of, of renewed moderation toward the Nixon administration in late 1969, 97–98; objectives of, in the Sino-Soviet border talks, 89–90; protest of, over defection of official to the United States in 1969, 78–82; protest of, to the United States in 1975, 115; reaction of, to U.S.–Soviet relations, 68, 70, 97, 107, 114–16; reduction of anti-U.S. polemics by, after 1970, 105–9; reduction of criticism of the Nixon administration by, 98–99; renewal of moderate approach by, toward the United States in late 1969, 96–102; stepping up polemics against the U.S.S.R. in March 1969 by, 85

Pham Van Don, visit of, to China in 1969, 95

Philippines, relationship of, with PRC, 113

Poland, relationship of, with PRC, 85

PRC. See People's Republic of China

Radford, Arthur William, 44

Red Guards, disrupt PRC foreign policy, 65–66

Renunciation of force. See Taiwan, renunciation of force over

Rhee, Syngman, 44

Rogers, William, 86, 98

Romania, relationship of, with PRC, 71, 72, 85

Roosevelt, Franklin D., 29

Schlesinger, James, 114–15

SEATO, 43

Service, John S.: talks with Mao, 22–23; on U.S.–China policy, 18–19, 27, 28

Shanghai communiqué, 109–16

Sian incident, 5, 15

Sinkiang, Soviet policy in, 16, 20

Sino-Japanese war, 15; annihilation campaigns in, 15; Japanese offensive of 1944 in, 23–24, 27

Sino-Soviet alliance, 6, 32, 33, 35, 40, 41, 120

Sino-Soviet border conflict: 1, 64, 103, 111–12; of 1969, 80, 83, 86, 93–94; PRC protests Soviet air intrusion in the, 69

Sino-Soviet border talks, 83, 88–89, 93

Sino-Soviet dispute, 64. See also Sino-Soviet border conflict; Sino-Soviet relations

Sino-Soviet relations, 3, 65, 103, 111–12

Snow, Edgar, 13, 21–22, 60; meets Mao in 1970, 107–8

Soviet Union: lack of full support of, for PRC during 1958 Taiwan crisis, 63; military pressure of, on China, 1, 2, 3, 68, 84–90, 93–94; policy of, in China after the Korean War, 6; policy of, in China after World War II, 6; policy of, in China during World War II, 5, 16, 21, 26; policy of, in Sinkiang, 16, 20; proposal of, for a negotiated settlement of Taiwan issue in 1955, 46; reaction of, to Sino-American relations, 2, 97; reduced support of, for PRC goals in Asia during the early 1950s, 33–46

Stalin, Joseph, 6; confirmation by, that U.S.S.R. will enter war against Japan, 19; impact of death of, on Soviet policy in Asia, 33

Stilwell, Joseph, 19; dispute of, with Chiang Kai-shek, 23–24, 27

Sun Yat-sen, 5

Su Yu, 38–39

Taiwan, 2, 6, 73, 74, 104, 107–8, 112, 115; absence of full Soviet support for PRC campaign against, 37–46; ceasefire proposal over, 44–45; crisis in 1958 over, 63; discussion of, during Geneva ambassadorial talks, 47–62; moderating PRC stance on, 47, 49–50; "peaceful liberation" of, 50, 59, 60; PRC campaign of 1954–1955 against, 33–34, 36–46; PRC military attacks against, 37, 44; renunciation of force over, 48, 54–57

Taiwan Straits, withdrawal of U.S. patrols from, 104

Taking the Bandits' Stronghold (play), 92
Tanaka, Kakuei, visit of, to China, 103
Tanzania, relationship of, with PRC, 66
Teng Hsiao-ping: demoted, 117; fetes Gerald Ford, 116
Thailand, relationship of, with PRC, 113
Tito. *See* Broz, Josip
Trans-Siberian Railway, 87
Truman Doctrine, 31
Tsou, Tang, 119
Tunisia, relationship of, with PRC, 65

United Arab Republic, relationship of, with PRC, 65
United Nations, PRC entry into, 103
United States: aid to Chiang Kai-shek from, 11, 25, 58–59; approach of, to Chinese communists during World War II, 20–21; change of policy in China at end of World War II by, 24–30; concern of, over Soviet policy in China, 19–21; containment policy of, against China, 8, 32–33, 58, 63, 64; deliberations of, over China policy during World War II, 18; demand of, that PRC renounce use of force against Taiwan, 48–49, 54–57; impact of ideology of, on policy toward China, 7–9, 28, 33, 64; impatience of, with Chiang Kai-shek, 27–28; involvement of, in Canton uprising, 11; involvement of, in Yochow and Chnagsha uprisings, 11; liaison work of, in CCP areas during World War II, 12, 13, 16, 17, 19, 21–23; policy of, in Asia during World War II, 7, 27–28; policy of, toward Asia after World War II, 31–33; policy of, toward China after World War II, 6; policy of, toward China during Hurley mission, 26–30; policy of, toward China following' Korean War, 32–33; policy of, toward Chinese communists prior to World War II, 10; PRC liaison offices of, 111; relations of, with U.S.S.R., 3, 7, 8, 28; security treaty of, with Republic of China, 42–43; trade embargo of, against PRC, 50, 54, 61; vital interests of, in East Asia, 7; *White Paper* by, on China, 32
United States–PRC ambassadorial talks, 6, 11, 47–62, 84, 97, 104, 108; discussion and agreement in, on mutual return of detained citizens, 51–54; discussion in, of higher level U.S.–PRC official meeting, 54–57, 61; discussion in, of renunciation of force, 54–57, 61; discussion in, of U.S.–PRC unofficial exchanges, 60; during 1958 Taiwan crisis, 63; Peking proposal in, to renew meetings in February 1969, 73–75; suspension of, in 1968, 65; suspension of, in 1969, 78–82, 107; suspension of, in 1970, 107; U.S. objectives during, 48–50, 54–55, 57

Van Fleet, James A., visit of, to Taiwan, 38
Vietnam. *See* Vietnam conflict; North Vietnam
Vietnam conflict, 3, 64, 98. *See also* Paris peace talks on Vietnam; North Vietnam
V-J Day, anniversary of, 34, 39, 40

Wallace, Henry A., 21
Wang Hung-wen, 117
Warsaw ambassadorial talks. *See* U.S.–PRC ambassadorial talks
Warsaw Pact, 88, 116
Watergate scandal, 112
World Communist Conference, 85

Yakubovsky (Soviet general), 87
Yalta conference, 7, 8, 28
Yao Wen-yuan, 117
Yeh Chien-ying, 117
Yen Hsi-shan, 21
Young, Kenneth, 51
Yudin (Soviet ambassador), 42
Yugoslavia, relationship of, with PRC, 72, 96

Library of Congress Cataloging in Publication Data

Sutter, Robert G
  China-watch.

  Bibliography: p. 137–49.
  Includes index.
  1. United States—Foreign relations—China.
2. China—Foreign relations—United States.
3. China—Foreign relations—Russia.   4. Russia
—Foreign relations—China. I. Title.
E183.8.C5S88   327.73'051   77–21486
ISBN 0–8018–2007–3